PRESIDENT FORD:
The Man and His Record

August 1974

CONGRESSIONAL QUARTERLY

1414 22ND ST. N.W., WASHINGTON, D.C. 20037

Congressional Quarterly Inc.

Congressional Quarterly Inc., an editorial research service and publishing company, serves clients in the fields of news, education, business and government. It combines specific coverage of Congress, government and politics by Congressional Quarterly with the more general subject range of an affiliated service, Editorial Research Reports.

Congressional Quarterly was founded in 1945 by Henrietta and Nelson Poynter. Its basic periodical publication was and still is the CQ *Weekly Report*, which is mailed to clients every Friday. The *Weekly Report* is cross-referenced quarterly in a cumulative *Index*.

The CQ *Almanac*, a compendium of legislation for one session of Congress, is published every spring. *Congress and the Nation* is published every four years as a record of government for one presidential term.

Congressional Quarterly also publishes paperback books on public affairs. These include the twice-yearly *Guide to Current American Government* and such recent titles as *Watergate: Chronology of a Crisis, Vols. I and II* and *Washington Lobby*.

CQ Direct Research is a consulting service which performs contract research and maintains a reference library and query desk for the convenience of clients.

Editorial Research Reports covers subjects beyond the specialized scope of Congressional Quarterly. It publishes reference material on foreign affairs, business, education, cultural affairs, national security, science and other topics of news interest. Service to clients includes a 300-word report five times a week and a 6,000-word report four times a month. Editorial Research Reports also publishes paperback books in its fields of coverage. Founded in 1923, the service was merged with Congressional Quarterly in 1956.

Book Service Editor: Robert A. Diamond.
Major Contributors: Mercer Cross, Donald Smith.
Other Contributors: Thomas J. Arrandale, Alan Ehrenhalt, Edna Frazier, Diantha Johnson, Mary Link, Warden Moxley, Joanna Shelton, Elizabeth Wehr, Elder Witt. **Editorial Assistant:** Robert Healy.

Cover Design: Howard Chapman. **Production Supervision:** Don Buck, Wayne Palmer. **Assistant Production Supervisor:** Richard Butler. **Cover Photo:** Wide World.

Library of Congress Catalog No. 74-17508
International Standard Book No. 0-87187-065-7

TABLE OF CONTENTS

Appendix

EMPHASIS ON CONCILIATION AS FORD TAKES OVER

Gerald Rudolph Ford took the oath of office as 38th President of the United States at 12:03 p.m. Friday, Aug. 9, 1974. His first act was to make a conciliatory speech directed at the American public, a speech whose purpose was to start repairing immediately the wide and deep damage of the scandals called Watergate. *(Ford's speech p. 2)*

The swearing in of the 61-year-old former Vice President and former House minority leader took place in the East Room of the White House. Many in the crowd were Ford's old friends from Congress, in which he had served for 25 years as the representative from Michigan's 5th District.

Only two hours earlier, Richard M. Nixon, the man Ford replaced as Chief Executive, had bade a tearful farewell to his staff in the same room. Then he and his wife had boarded the White House jet, the Spirit of '76, and departed for their home in San Clemente, Calif.

The actual transition of power had taken place a half hour before the swearing in. At 11:35 a.m. that day, Nixon's letter of resignation had been delivered to Secretary of State Henry A. Kissinger, in compliance with the constitutional requirement. The letter was brief. It said simply: "Dear Mr. Secretary: I hereby resign the office of President of the United States. Sincerely, Richard Nixon."

The moment the letter was delivered, Ford assumed the presidency.

No Fanfare

The swearing-in ceremony was unadorned by the trappings that customarily accompany momentous events. Chief Justice Warren E. Burger administered the oath. Ford's wife, Elizabeth, held the Bible on which her husband placed his left hand as he raised his right hand. Ford made his pledge in a strong, clear voice, nodding occasionally for emphasis.

Then, introduced by Burger as "the President of the United States," he stepped to a microphone and set the tone for his new administration. He began by making "an unprecedented compact with my countrymen. Not an inaugural address, not a fireside chat, not a campaign speech, just a little straight talk among friends."

He assured his listeners that "our long national nightmare is over. Our Constitution works. Our great republic is a government of laws and not of men. Here the people rule."

He emphasized some of the qualities that had characterized his performance as a congressional leader: "In all my public and private acts as your President, I expect to follow my instincts of openness and candor with full confidence that honesty is always the best policy in the end."

He made only one direct reference to Watergate: "As we bind up the internal wounds of Watergate, more painful and more poisonous than those of foreign wars, let us restore the golden rule to our political process. And let brotherly love purge our hearts of suspicion and of hate."

And he affirmed his desire to restore a friendly relationship between the White House and Capitol Hill by asking congressional leaders to meet with him after his speech.

The Vice Presidency

On Aug. 20, 11 days after he took office, Ford made his first important decision. He nominated Nelson A. Rockefeller, 66, former governor of New York (R 1959-73), as his Vice President.

Almost as soon as Ford had taken his hand off the Bible at his own swearing-in ceremony, speculation began concerning his vice presidential choice. The two names heard most often had been those of Rockefeller and Republican National Chairman George Bush.

Ford's brief announcement ceremony took place in the White House Oval Office. Present were members of the cabinet and leaders of Congress. The President's well-kept secret of the past few days was revealed when Rockefeller entered the room at his side.

Ford described Rockefeller, himself a long-time, unsuccessful seeker of the Republican presidential nomination, as "a good partner for me and I think a good partner for our country and the world." He said he had arrived at his decision after "a great deal of soul-searching" and added that it was "a tough call for a tough job." He had solicited advice from a broad spectrum of leaders and friends in both parties.

For the first time, the nation would have both a President and a Vice President who had not been elected to those positions. Rockefeller was expected to have little difficulty in being confirmed by the House and Senate. But he was assured of the same thorough investigation of his background to which Ford had been subjected after Nixon had named him to succeed the fallen Sprio T. Agnew. *(Ford confirmation, p. 39)*

Rockefeller, at a short news conference after Ford's Aug. 20 announcement, showed sensitivity to the investigation when he refused to answer reporters' questions about his wealth and how it would be handled during his tenure. He said only that he would "conform to the law" and answer all questions asked by the congressional committees investigating his nomination.

The New Yorker, a member of one of the country's wealthiest families, said he was "optimistic about the long-term future." Citing his past service to the country and his state, he said, "I'm in a position of relaxed desire to be helpful to this nation in any way I can."

Speech to Congress

On Aug. 12, three days after he took office, Ford delivered his first speech as President to a joint session of Congress. He started by expressing his love for the House and his respect for the traditions of the Senate.

"As President, within the limits of basic principles, my motto towards the Congress is communication, conciliation, compromise and cooperation," he said. "I do not want a honeymoon with you. I want a good marriage." *(Text, p. 75)*

Text of Ford's First Public Comments as President

Following is the text of President Ford's televised statement made immediately after he took the oath of office Aug. 9:

Mr. Chief Justice, my dear friends, my fellow Americans.

The oath I have taken is the same oath that was taken by George Washington and by every president under the Constitution. But I assume the presidency under extraordinary circumstances, never before experienced by Americans. This is an hour of history that troubles our minds and hurts our hearts.

Therefore, I feel it is my first duty to make an unprecedented compact with my countrymen. Not an inaugural speech, not a fireside chat, not a campaign speech, just a little straight talk among friends. And I intend it to be the first of many.

I am acutely aware that you have not elected me as your President by your ballots. So I ask you to confirm me as your President with your prayers. And I hope that such prayers will also be the first of many.

If you have not chosen me by secret ballot, neither have I gained office by any secret promises. I have not campaigned either for the presidency or the vice presidency. I have not subscribed to any partisan platform. I am indebted to no man and only to one woman—my dear wife—as I begin the most difficult job in the world.

I have not sought this enormous responsibility, but I will not shirk it. Those who nominated and confirmed me as Vice President were my friends and are my friends. They were of both parties, elected by all the people, and acting under the Constitution in their name. It is only fitting then, that I should pledge to them and to you that I will be the President of all the people.

Reliance on People

Thomas Jefferson said the people are the only sure reliance for the preservation of our liberty. And down the years Abraham Lincoln renewed this American article of faith, asking: "Is there any better way or equal hope in the world?"

I intend, on Monday next, to request of the speaker of the House of Representatives and the president pro tempore of the Senate the privilege of appearing before Congress to share with my former colleagues and with you, the American people, my views on the priority business of the nation, and to solicit your views and their views. And may I say to the speaker and the others if I could meet with you right after this, these remarks, I would appreciate it.

Even though this is late in an election year, there is no way we can go forward except together, and no way anybody can win except by serving the people's urgent needs. We cannot stand still or slip backwards. We must go forward, now, together.

Search for Peace

To the peoples and the governments of all friendly nations, and I hope that could encompass the whole world, I pledge an uninterrupted and sincere search for peace. America will remain strong and united, but its strength will remain dedicated to the safety and sanity of the entire family of man as well as to our own precious freedom.

I believe that truth is the glue that holds government together, not only our government, but civilization itself. That bond, though strained, is unbroken at home and abroad. In all my public and private acts as your President, I expect to follow my instincts of openness and candor with full confidence that honesty is always the best policy in the end.

My fellow Americans, our long national nightmare is over.

Our Constitution works; our great republic is a government of laws and not of men. Here the people rule. But there is a higher power, by whatever name we honor Him, who ordains not only righteousness but love, not only justice but mercy.

Purge Suspicion

As we bind up the internal wounds of Watergate, more painful and more poisonous than those of foreign wars, let us restore the golden rule to our political process, and let brotherly love purge our hearts of suspicion and of hate.

In the beginning I asked you to pray for me. Before closing I again ask your prayers for Richard Nixon and for his family.

May our former President, who brought peace to millions, find it for himself. May God bless and comfort his wonderful wife and daughters, whose love and loyalty will forever be a shining legacy to all who bear the lonely burdens of the White House.

I can only guess at those burdens, although I have witnessed at close hand the tragedies that befell three presidents and the lesser trials of others.

With all the strength and all the good sense I have gained from life, with all the confidence of my family and friends and dedicated staff impart to me, and with the goodwill of the countless Americans I have encountered in recent visits to 40 states, I now solemnly reaffirm my promise I made to you last December 6: to uphold the Constitution, to do what is right as God gives me to see the right, and to do the very best I can for America.

God helping me, I will not let you down.

Thank you.

The members of Congress responded in kind to their former colleague. There was almost constant applause for what he had to say. There was a wealth of good humor, with smiles, waves and first-name greetings for old friends, and jocular banter between Ford and Speaker Carl Albert, seated directly behind him on the dais. There was a stark contrast between the warm reception given Ford and the more partisan one given Nixon the last time he had come to the Hill to deliver the State of the Union address, Jan. 30, 1974.

Ford received his most prolonged applause when he made his one oblique reference to Watergate. "There will be no illegal tapings, eavesdropping, buggings or break-ins by my administration," he said.

He described himself as "the people's man," and he made this pledge: "To the limits of my strength and ability, I will be the President of the black, brown, red and white Americans, of old and young, of women's liberationists and male chauvinists and all the rest of us in between, of the poor and the rich, of native sons and new refugees, of those who work at lathes or at desks or in mines or in the fields, and of Christians, Jews, Moslems, Buddhists and atheists, if there really are any atheists after what we have all been through."

Ford said that his administration "starts off by seeking unity in diversity. My office door has always been open, and that is how it is going to be at the White House."

In discussing issues, the President placed special emphasis on inflation, which he described as "public enemy number one." He asked his audience to "join with me in getting this country revved up and moving." He urged reduced federal spending, volunteered to serve as chairman of an economic "summit meeting" and said he would reactivate the Nixon administration's Cost of Living Council.

Early Actions

Ford devoted the last part of his address to his foreign policy of continuing what he described as "a path of reason and fairness" established by the Nixon administration. This clearly was another priority item during the transition period. Two hours after he had been sworn in, Ford and Secretary of State Kissinger spent the afternoon and early evening with about 60 foreign ambassadors. He reassured them of continuity in existing policies.

He sent a personal message to Chinese and Soviet leaders, among others, on Aug. 10. The same day, Russian leaders sent Ford a congratulatory message. "We express confidence that relations between the USSR and the United States will receive further constructive development in the coming years for the benefit of our peoples, in the interest of strengthening universal peace and international security," it said.

Another of Ford's first acts as President was the appointment of a four-member committee to oversee the transition between administrations and to make recommendations for staff changes. All four were former elected officials and former associates in the House. They were:

● Donald M. Rumsfeld, ambassador to the North Atlantic Treaty Organization and a former Republican representative from Illinois (1963-69). Rumsfeld was designated coordinator of the four-man team.

● Secretary of the Interior Rogers C. B. Morton, a former Republican national chairman and a former representative from Maryland (1963-71).

● William W. Scranton, a former governor of Pennsylvania (1963-67) and a former Republican representative (1961-63).

● John O. Marsh Jr., a member of Ford's vice presidential staff and a former Democratic representative from Virginia (1963-71). Marsh also was named presidential counselor. *(Box, p. 4)*

Ford asked the members of the Nixon cabinet and heads of departments to remain in their jobs, at least temporarily. He dispensed with the traditional request for *pro forma* resignations and told the Cabinet members that he wanted to meet with them individually. The cabinet agreed to stay.

Even before he moved into the White House, the President appointed some of his chief advisers. Senior members of Nixon's White House staff were asked to remain during the transition period. Among the first members of the new White House staff, besides Marsh, were:

● Another counselor, Robert T. Hartmann, 57, Ford's chief of staff when he was Vice President. Hartmann, a former newspaperman, had joined Ford's House staff in 1966.

Jerald F. terHorst

● A press secretary, Jerald F. terHorst, 52, Washington bureau chief of *The Detroit News.* TerHorst had covered Ford's office for years and had written a book about him. He replaced Nixon's press secretary, Ronald L. Ziegler, who resigned and flew to San Clemente with the former president.

● Paul Miltich, Ford's vice presidential press secretary, and William Roberts, who had handled press and television for Ford previously. They became terHorst's assistants.

● Allan Greenspan, appointed by Nixon to be chairman of the Council of Economic Advisers in July. He was asked to stay.

● Nixon's chief congressional liaison men, William E. Timmons, Tom C. Korologos and Max L. Friedersdorf. They, too, were asked to remain.

A few days later, Ford made more appointments:

● Nixon's chief of staff, Alexander M. Haig Jr., was asked to keep his job "for the duration."

● John W. Hushen, director of information for the Justice Department, was named terHorst's chief aide in the press office.

● Philip W. Buchen, Ford's former law partner in Grand Rapids and director of the Domestic Council on the Rights of Privacy, which Ford headed as Vice President, was appointed White House counsel.

Presidential Prosecution

One question confronting Ford was what, if anything, to do about possible prosecution of Nixon for crimes committed while the former President was in the White House. Ford had the power, under the Constitution, to pardon Nixon, and an advance pardon would have the effect of granting Nixon immunity from prosecution. But, in testimony during his vice presidential confirmation hearings, Ford had said he did not think a president should do this. *(Box, p. 5)*

A federal grand jury, when it indicted seven men for their roles in the Watergate coverup, had named Nixon, among others, an unindicted co-conspirator. Whether an incumbent president could be indicted and tried in the same manner as an ordinary citizen remained an unresolved question.

With Nixon out of office, whatever protection he might have enjoyed as President had disappeared. Besides Ford's power to pardon, the Watergate special prosecutor, Leon Jaworski, had the authority to request a judge to grant immunity. But at the time of Nixon's resignation, Jaworski had issued a statement saying that his office had neither sought nor made any agreement or understanding with the former President in connection with the resignation. Nor did his office, said Jaworski, "participate in any way in the President's decision to resign."

Some sentiment was reported on Capitol Hill, particularly among Republicans, that Nixon had suffered enough already and should not be prosecuted. But the only power Congress had in such a case was to pass a "sense of Congress" resolution to that effect.

Nixon Resignation

Nixon's resignation came the day after Republican congressional leaders informed him that his only alternative was certain impeachment in the House and likely conviction in the Senate.

In a televised resignation speech at 9 p.m. Aug. 8, Nixon said that he was resigning because "It has become evident to me that I no longer have a strong enough political base in the Congress to justify continuing that effort" to stay in office. *(Text, p. 77)*

Nixon made no mention of impeachment in his speech, but the erosion of support for him—which eventually brought about his departure from office—was the direct

Biographies of the Ford Transition Team

Shortly after his inauguration, President Ford named four former representatives to help direct the White House transition and to make staff recommendations. While all four had served with Ford in the House during the 1960s, none held elective office at the time of their appointment. They were:

Donald M. Rumsfeld, 42, ambassador to the North Atlantic Treaty Organization. He was coordinator of the

transition staff. Born in Evanston, Ill., he was graduated from Princeton University in 1954. He served in Congress as a Republican representative from a suburban district north of Chicago from 1963 until May 1969, when he was appointed director of the Office of Economic Opportunity by President Nixon.

At the same time, he was made a presidential assistant with cabinet

Donald M. Rumsfeld

rank and a member of the Urban Affairs Council. Subsequently he was promoted to counselor to the President, and in October 1971, when Phase Two of the wage and price controls program was announced, Rumsfeld became director of the Cost of Living Council. Nixon named him to the NATO post on Dec. 4, 1972.

John O. Marsh Jr., 47, the only representative on the transition team from Ford's vice presidential staff. On Aug. 10, the new President appointed Marsh counselor to the President, with cabinet rank. Born in Winchester, Va., Marsh received a law degree from Washington and Lee University in 1951. While serving as a Democratic representative from Virginia from 1963 to 1971, he worked with Ford on the House Appropriations Committee. Marsh retired from Congress in 1971, and in 1973 he was appointed by Nixon to be assistant secretary of defense for legislative affairs. He joined the Vice President's staff on Jan. 29, 1974, as an assistant for defense and inter-

John O. Marsh Jr.

national affairs. A lifelong Democrat, Marsh later labeled himself an independent.

Rogers C. B. Morton, 59, secretary of the interior. He was Ford's transition aide in charge of federal agen-

cies and cabinet-level departments. A native of Louisville, Ky., Morton attended private school in Virginia and was graduated from Yale University in 1937. He was involved in a family milling concern in Kentucky until 1951, when he moved to the Eastern Shore of Maryland and began raising cattle. In 1962, he was elected to Congress from Maryland's first district.

Rogers C. B. Morton

Morton, Nixon's floor manager at the 1968 Republican national convention, was selected by the President in April 1969 to be chairman of the Republican National Committee, a position once held by his older brother, former Sen. Thruston B. Morton of Kentucky (1957-68). In January 1971, Nixon named him secretary of the interior, a post traditionally reserved for westerners.

William W. Scranton, 57, former governor of Pennsylvania (R 1963-67). He was in charge of shaping the new White House staff. Raised in Scranton, Pa., which took its name from his family, Scranton received both undergraduate and law degrees from Yale. He worked briefly as a special assistant to former Secretary of State Christian A. Herter. In 1960, he defeated a Democratic incumbent to win his only term in the House.

He was elected governor of Pennsylvania in

William W. Scranton

1962 and served the one four-year term allowed by state law. While governor, Scranton offered himself as an alternative to Sen. Barry Goldwater (R Ariz.) for the 1964 Republican presidential nomination. After reportedly turning down an offer to be Nixon's secretary of state, Scranton in 1970 chaired the President's Commission on Campus Unrest.

result of the charges lodged against him by the House Judiciary Committee. The committee late in July approved three articles of impeachment—obstruction of justice, abuse of his powers and contempt of Congress.

Debate in the House on impeachment was scheduled to begin Aug. 19. His supporters in the House were girding themselves to argue that the evidence was not sufficient to justify impeachment.

Final Blow

Their effort was shattered Aug. 5 by Nixon's release of three transcripts of conversations with former White House Chief of Staff H. R. Haldeman on July 23, 1972, six days after the Watergate break-in. Nixon acknowledged in an accompanying statement that he had withheld the contents of the tapes from his staff and his attorneys, despite the fact that they contradicted his previous declarations of non-involvement and lack of knowledge of the coverup.

The transcripts showed clearly Nixon's participation in the coverup, approving the invocation of CIA involvement as a means of obstructing the FBI investigation of the Watergate break-in.

With a few exceptions, members of Congress who had supported the President were left with no choice but to call for his departure from office, by resignation or by impeachment. Rep. Charles E. Wiggins (R Calif.), Nixon's most eloquent defender in the House, announced shortly after release of the transcripts that he would support impeachment. Within hours, every other member of the House Judiciary Committee who had opposed impeachment had shifted his vote to support the obstruction of justice charge.

Even before their release, Assistant Senate Minority Leader Robert P. Griffin (R Mich.) had called for Nixon's resignation. Afterward, Barber B. Conable Jr. (R N.Y.), chairman of the House Republican Policy Committee, commented, "It looks like a smoking gun to me." He said he would vote for impeachment. House Republican Leader John J. Rhodes (R Ariz.) also joined the pro-impeachment forces Aug. 6.

By Aug. 7, Rhodes and others of Nixon's own party leaders told Nixon he could muster no more than 10 or 15 votes in each chamber against impeachment.

The decision, made the evening of Aug. 7, was an agonizing one. The emotion which was controlled as Nixon gave his resignation speech broke forth as he met with 50 of his closest congressional friends an hour before.

One Republican representative present told Congressional Quarterly that after Nixon explained to them the reasons he would later relate to the nation for his decision, "he quit talking and was struggling against breaking down.... He finally choked...and said, 'I guess what I'm trying to say is that I hope I haven't let you down.' "

"There wasn't a dry eye in the house," commented the participant. "In fact, many of the members were crying openly...."

By choosing to become the first President in history to resign his office, Nixon avoided impeachment and conviction, also a historic first. The House Judiciary Committee report, in support of its recommendation of impeachment, was prepared and was filed with the House Aug. 20. Impeachment proceedings would go no further.

The question of the President's possible indictment on some of the charges lodged against him by the committee was left open. Members of Congress had discussed the possibility of passing a bill granting the President immunity from prosecution after his resignation, but the prospects for such a move were dimmed by a variety of questions about the propriety and the validity of such a measure.

Reaction of Relief

The reaction to the President's resignation and Ford's move to the Oval Office was one of overwhelming relief. Rhodes called it "an act of supreme statemanship."

Rep. Lawrence J. Hogan (R Md.), whose decision to support impeachment had been one of the elements in the momentum toward impeachment, described the President's action as "an admirable and patriotic act which merits the praise and respect of all Americans."

Congressional leaders hailed Ford, noting that he was "one of ours"—a man who had served in Congress for years

Ford on Presidential Prosecution

During his confirmation hearings for Vice President before the Senate Rules and Administration Committee, vice presidential nominee Gerald R. Ford was questioned by Committee Chairman Howard W. Cannon (D Nev.) on the related issues of presidential immunity and prosecution of a former president. The following excerpt comes from the record of the Nov. 5, 1973, hearing:

Cannon. ...do you believe that a President is immune from prosecution for a crime, so long as he holds office?

Ford. That is my understanding, under the Constitution, that before a President can be charged and convicted of a crime, he must be impeached and convicted under the impeachment clause....

Cannon. Do you believe that a President can legally prevent, or terminate any criminal investigation or prosecution involving the President?

Ford. I do not think he should, and as I think I said in response to Senator [Robert C.] Byrd's question, when we got into executive privilege, that where you are talking about documents and data involving criminality and executive privilege, certainly the strong, strong, strong, presumption is that those documents should be made available to the prosecution. And I cannot imagine a President—I hope that there will never be a President who will take such action.

Cannon. If a President resigned his office before his term expired, would his successor have the power to prevent or to terminate any investigation or criminal prosecution against the former President?

Ford. Would he have the authority?

Cannon. Yes, would he have the power?

Ford. I do not think the public would stand for it. I think—and whether he has the technical authority or not, I cannot give you a categorical answer.

The Attorney General, in my opinion, with the help and support of the American people, would be the controlling factor.

with many of them. Ford's move and Nixon's departure were also expected to alter drastically the political equation in the upcoming elections, removing the issue of Watergate, which had so unified Democrats and haunted Republicans.

The Final Week

Release of the damning transcripts and their accompanying statement came within a week after the House Judiciary Committee had recommended Nixon's impeachment.

During the week, the public optimism of the White House had been slowly deflated by the recognition that impeachment was likely—and conviction by the Senate was a possibility. "You would have to put the President in the role of the underdog," said Deputy White House Press Secretary Gerald L. Warren Aug. 2, describing the battle expected in the House as "an uphill struggle." The President did not plan to resign, he said.

"The situation has eroded," said Ford Aug. 3, maintaining his belief that the President had not committed any impeachable offenses.

Sparking rumors of an impending announcement, the President summoned Chief of Staff Haig, Press Secretary Ziegler, lawyer James D. St. Clair and two speechwriters to Camp David Aug. 4.

Sen. Barry Goldwater

Sen. Hugh Scott

Rep. John J. Rhodes

Their visit to Nixon was final sign of loss of support.

The following morning, Griffin stated to reporters: "I think we've arrived at the point where both the national interest and his own interests would be best served by his [Nixon's] resigning."

'Act of Omission'

Then, in late afternoon Aug. 5, the announcement came that the President was releasing the transcripts of three recorded conversations on June 23, 1972, with H. R. Haldeman, then his chief of staff. The tapes of these conversations had been turned over to U.S. District Judge John J. Sirica Aug. 2.

Accompanying the transcripts was the President's statement taking full responsibility and stating deep regret for "this...serious act of omission." He made plain that neither his staff nor St. Clair had known of the contents of the conversations, leading to reports that Nixon had released the transcripts and made his statement only after St. Clair learned of their contents and threatened to resign. St. Clair had not heard the tapes until directed by Sirica the previous week to do so.

Reaction to this disclosure was immediate. "The most devastating thing that can be said of it," said Speaker Carl Albert (D Okla.) "is that it speaks for itself."

Nixon should resign, said Robert McClory (R Ill.), the most senior Republican on the House Judiciary Committee to support impeachment. Any delay was then "only a question of his personal stubbornness, personal stonewalling," he said.

House Majority Leader Thomas P. O'Neill Jr. (D Mass.) said he felt no more than 75 members would oppose impeachment.

That evening, Ford announced that he would cease to repeat his still-held belief in the President's innocence. He had not been informed before the President's statement of its contents.

As statements from members of Congress in favor of Nixon's departure from office—by resignation or impeachment—flooded Capitol Hill Aug. 6, Nixon called a sudden cabinet meeting. Queried afterward, cabinet members insisted that Nixon said he would not resign but would "fight on" to stay in office. Treasury Secretary William E. Simon said, "The President sincerely believes he has not committed an impeachable offense."

Rhodes Statement

In mid-afternoon, Minority Leader Rhodes made his announcement: he would vote for impeachment based on Article I, obstruction of justice, and perhaps—based on the new evidence—for Article II, abuse of powers.

Conable and John B. Anderson (R Ill.), chairman of the House Republican Conference, also expressed their support for impeachment. All three expressed doubts about the suggestion that the President be granted immunity by Congress, from prosecution after he left office.

Sen. Robert Dole (R Kan.), national party chairman during the 1972 election, said Aug. 6 that if the President had 40 votes the previous week in the Senate against conviction, he had no more than 20 left, far short of the 34 needed to survive a trial.

But Sen. Carl T. Curtis (R Neb.) continued to defend the President, warning against panic. The United States would become like a "banana republic," he said, if it ousted Nixon, placing Ford and Ford's choice for vice president—neither of whom had been elected to their offices—in the nation's highest posts.

The Decision

Rumors that the President would resign reached a crescendo Wednesday, Aug. 7. *The Providence Journal-Bulletin*, which late in 1973 had broken the story of Nixon's minimal income tax payments during his first term in the White House, reported that Nixon had made an "irrevocable" decision to resign. No longer denying such reports, Warren simply stated, "I cannot confirm that."

Senate Minority Leader Hugh Scott (R Pa.) said that the President's Aug. 5 statement had removed any presumption that he was innocent of the charges against him.

Shortly after five o'clock, President Nixon met with Sen. Barry Goldwater (R Ariz.), Scott and Rhodes. Afterward, Goldwater said: "There has been no decision made. We made no suggestions. We were merely there to offer what we see as the condition on both floors."

Scott added: "We have told him that the situation is very gloomy on Capitol Hill." Just how gloomy was shown by later reports that the Republican leaders had told Nixon he could not expect more than 10 votes in the House and 15 in the Senate against his impeachment and conviction.

But there were still some vocal supporters in Congress. Sen. William Lloyd Scott (R Va.) said that he continued to support the President. "There's no doubt he won't resign," Scott added. And Rep. Earl F. Landgrebe (R Ind.) told reporters: "Don't confuse me with the facts. I've got a closed mind. I will not vote for impeachment."

Just after noon Aug. 8, Ziegler announced that the President would meet with congressional leaders in the early evening and would address the nation at 9 o'clock. Rhodes said then that the President would resign. "I feel relief...sorrow...gratitude, but also optimism," he said. ∎

SURVEY OF PROBLEMS AND ISSUES FORD INHERITED

Hitting the ground running was one way to put it.

Not long after Gerald Ford was installed in the Oval Office, an old and close friend of the President stretched back in a chair in his Washington, D.C. trade association office and put it another way. "He's on a bus full of people that's flying down the road pretty fast," he said. "It's got some mechanical problems, and all of a sudden the driver jumps out. Ford's got to get in the seat and keep driving."

The President was assured of having at least a brief respite while he began to shape the framework of his new administration, a "honeymoon" period with Congress and the public. But it was clear that he would have to begin almost immediately dealing with the national problems that had gone long unattended during what Ford had called the "long national nightmare" of Watergate.

Domestic Summit

In his first major move, Ford bought time in the critical area of foreign policy by announcing Aug. 8 that he would keep Henry A. Kissinger as secretary of state. Then, in his Aug. 12 message to Congress, the President assured the nation that he was acting to deal with urgent domestic issues by announcing that he would accept a Capitol Hill proposal for a "domestic summit meeting" and that he would preside over it personally.

The Senate July 23 had approved a resolution calling for the summit of top government, business and labor leaders on the economy. The following day, the House Democratic Caucus unanimously approved an eight-point economic package that included a recommendation for tax reform measures to help the "middle- and lower-income families who have suffered most from inflation."

Ford called for the summit to take place "at an early date and in full view of the American public. They are as anxious to get the right answers as we are."

Ironically, many of the domestic issues that had burned so angrily during one part or another of Richard Nixon's administration, such as civil rights, crime, welfare and the energy crisis, had largely faded from view. The overriding problem facing the Ford administration was the economy, an umbrella term that covered a family of troubles. *(Box, p. 10)*

In this chapter, Congressional Quarterly examines the economy and other major problems the new President faced as he entered office.

Labor

One of the most powerful interests Ford would have to deal with was labor. Major union leaders unanimously agreed that inflation was the most urgent single issue facing the administration.

While expressing support for the new President, union chiefs made it clear they would not wait long for some indication of how Ford would go about finding solutions to inflation.

"It's a tremendous problem, and we view it from the point of view of victims," said AFL-CIO spokesman Al Zack.

The unions also would be watching the way Ford handled a melange of other issues that affected their members. Principal areas of concern included housing, unemployment, social security, veterans, health insurance and pension reform. Unions also were taking positions on foreign policy, congressional reform and campaign financing reforms.

Officials said they would monitor Ford's reaction to efforts in Congress to help stimulate the housing market, one of labor's bread-and-butter areas, as an early signal of Ford's approach to labor.

Conservative Votes

The unions were well acquainted with Ford's congressional record as a conservative. During his 25 years as a member of Congress, Ford supported labor in only 19 votes, compared to 109 anti-labor votes, according to an AFL-CIO study. However, leaders pledged support for Ford in a mood of accommodation with hopes he would become more sympathetic in his new position.

Labor leaders strongly disliked the labor secretary Ford inherited from Nixon, Peter J. Brennan. Many felt Brennan had "double-crossed" labor in 1973, in AFL-CIO chief George Meany's phrase, by first pledging that he would oppose Nixon's proposed youth minimum wage standard and then announcing he had changed his mind under pressure from the administration.

The AFL-CIO released a series of 16 position papers on various issues during the summer meeting of its executive council in Chicago Aug. 5 and 6. The declaration were hostile toward the Nixon administration and most proposals were directed toward Congress.

"The facts haven't changed by Ford's becoming President," said a union official. "And the solutions we propose are the same."

Agriculture

U.S. agriculture was in trouble. Plagued by serious drought conditions and spiraling inflation, food costs were being driven up. Meat, eggs and dairy producers already were receiving less for their products than it cost to produce them, and a shortage of corn and other feed grains following a serious drought in the grain belt during the summer of 1974 likely would push production costs even higher.

"Serious shortfalls in corn and other feed grains could have a severe impact on the ability of meat, egg and dairy producers to stay in business and on food prices to the consumer," said Senate Agriculture Committee Chairman Herman E. Talmadge (D Ga.).

Feed Grains

Crop production figures released in August by the Agriculture Department showed corn production was predicted to be down 12 per cent from 1973, an indication that the inflationary production costs faced by the livestock industry in 1974 could be even worse in 1975.

One Senate Agriculture Committee expert said the predicted shortages of corn and other feed grains would force the Ford administration to reconsider the government's position on:

- Trade with other countries that can pay for U.S. grains;
- Willingness to give grains away to poor countries, and
- Price freezes.

Asked what key agricultural issue the Ford administration should deal with promptly, Talmadge declared: "Inflation, Inflation, inflation!" Only a strong executive could provide the leadership necessary to solve "this increasing problem, and I hope President Ford recognizes this, and means to face it," he added.

Despite Ford's record of often voting against farm bills, Talmadge said he expected President Ford would rely on the advice of Agriculture Secretary Earl L. Butz and the Agriculture Department staff.

Butz predicted that the farm policies of the Nixon administration would continue under the Ford administration.

In the face of a dwindling stockpile of grain and other foodstuffs, brought about by the drought and cost-profit crunches or livestock producers, Butz said he expected President Ford, like Nixon, to continue resisting attempts to impose strict export controls to conserve U.S. commodities.

Housing

One of Ford's major economic headaches as he came into office was the dwindling supply of mortgage money frustrating prospective homeowners across the country. The housing market had slumped badly, primarily because of high interest rates resulting from a tight monetary policy. Based on June figures, annual housing starts for 1974 were down almost 30 per cent below 1973 levels.

Ford could expand the mortgage money supply by using secondary mortgage market operations initiated by Nixon or stimulate housing production by releasing unused federal subsidized housing funds. The new President had indicated that the problems of the housing industry deserved special attention, but did not propose any specific policies.

Unused Funds

An aide to William Proxmire (D Wis.), ranking Democrat on the Senate Banking, Housing and Urban Affairs Committee, suggested that Ford might be reluctant to release the unused housing funds. But given Ford's conciliatory attitude toward Congress, the aide added, the new President might agree to some "token processing" of applications for the funds.

The credit crunch, caused by the tight monetary policy imposed by the Federal Reserve Board, was beyond Ford's direct control, however. If the budget were cut, Ford said he hoped the Fed would ease its anti-inflationary policy.

Congress also was considering a number of measures designed to boost housing production. Legislation (S 3066) approved Aug. 6 by House-Senate conferees would increase maximum Federal Housing Administration (FHA)

mortgage guarantees, lower required FHA cash down payments and authorize some new funding for subsidized housing programs. Other bills pending in Congress would stimulate mortgage lending through secondary market operations.

Defense Spending

The escalating defense budget posed a difficult problem for the new President, and one that would not wait long to be addressed.

The troubled state of the economy assured that Ford would be under strong pressures to use defense spending as the single most effective instrument at his disposal for controlling fiscal policy, as well as the means to shape and enforce U.S. national security policy.

As Congress was completing work on a record defense appropriation of more than $80-billion for fiscal 1975, Pentagon planners already were at work on the fiscal 1976 budget request—certain to be even higher—that they would submit to the President in the fall.

Ford was expected to require the Defense Department to do its share of belt tightening. But everything in his make-up and background indicated that he generally would side with those who argue that defense spending must rise, even in peacetime, and that the deepest cuts to balance the budget and fight inflation would have to come elsewhere.

As a House member, Ford had built a solid reputation as a believer in a strong military and as a consistent opponent of defense cutbacks. He gained this reputation as a member of the Defense Appropriations Subcommittee for 12 years (1953-65) and reinforced it with his actions and statements during his years as minority leader and his short stint as vice president. *(Ford chronology, p. 70)*

Cutback Proposals

Efforts to reduce defense spending focused in 1974 primarily on three areas: military aid to South Vietnam, U.S. troop strength in Europe and proposals for ceilings on Pentagon budgets. Ford, who was likely to confront the same three issues early in his presidency, had a record of opposing similar cutbacks.

Before becoming Vice President in December 1973, Ford voted against a ceiling amendment and unilateral troop cuts in Europe. Neither was enacted. Military aid to South Vietnam, following the ceasefire, did not emerge as an issue until 1974. But, as Vice President, Ford spoke out strongly against cutting Vietnam aid. *(Ford chronology, p. 70)*

"That's a toughie [the Vietnam aid issue]. He'll have a lot of trouble with that," said House Appropriations Chairman George Mahon (D Texas). "The mood of the House is that they just don't want to hear any more about Vietnam."

The issue of U.S. troop strength in Europe also was likely to be among the first defense problems to confront the new President, according to Michael Hemphill, defense specialist for John G. Tower (R Texas), a veteran member of the Senate Armed Services Committee.

Hemphill said that Tower, who was close to Ford politically, would not support efforts to reduce military manpower costs by demobilizing a substantial number of the 320,000 U.S. troops billeted in Europe.

"Since most of the Pentagon managers will be staying on, we don't expect any dramatic shifts in defense policy," Hemphill said.

But a former high official of Ford's vice presidential staff, who did not want to be identified, took a different view. "Ford has the responsibility now," he said. "It's a different thing from just sitting in on the briefings. We'll have to give him time, but I imagine the Pentagon will be getting its share of budget cuts."

Foreign Policy

Ford's retention of Kissinger assured Americans and U.S. allies that no jarring changes would be made in foreign policy.

Capitol Hill observers confirmed that they expected little change in position on key foreign issues. They were hopeful, however, for a shift in the White House toward more accommodation of congressional views.

A key issue confronting the new President, in which some accommodation was forecast, was the trade reform bill. The measure was stalled in the Senate because of opposition to granting favorable trade status to the Soviet Union while it restricted emigration of Jewish citizens. An aide to Rep. Charles A. Vanik (D Ohio), sponsor with Sen. Henry M. Jackson (D Wash.) of an amendment tying Soviet trade status to its emigration policies, said he was more optimistic about compromise on the issue because" Ford understands the depth of feeling in Congress about this, which Nixon didn't."

"I think there will be presidential attention and backing up of Kissinger's effort to find a compromise," said Mark E. Talisman, administrative assistant to Vanik. "That was missing before."

Ford had urged passage of the bill in speeches, but he also had said that the search for peace did not mean "approval" of the Soviet domestic system.

The general issue of detente was to be considered by the Senate Foreign Relations Committee, and would be a continuing legislative consideration. Ford had called it "helpful rather than harmful."

Also of concern to the new President was the foreign aid program, with bills about to go to the floor in both houses. He consistently supported foreign aid and military assistance to allies, including Vietnam, while in Congress. That continued aid was facing strong hostility in Congress in 1974, however.

Rep. William S. Broomfield, fellow Michigan Republican and a member of the House Foreign Affairs Committee, told Congressional Quarterly that foreign aid was "in considerable trouble as far as sharp cuts," and was an area that could use Ford's active support.

Sources suggested, however, that the initial honeymoon with Ford could help foreign aid in the Senate, with fewer amendments on the floor to cut the amount of aid than would have been expected under Nixon.

Health

Ironically, Ford's presidency cleared the way for serious congressional consideration in 1974 of health insurance legislation, which had been one of Nixon's top domestic priorities. Until Nixon's resignation, the prospect of time-consuming impeachment proceedings had made action unlikely in the 93rd Congress.

The change in administrations, however, was not expected to result in any major modifications of Nixon's health insurance proposal. Health, Education and Welfare (HEW) Secretary Caspar W. Weinberger quickly reaffirmed Ford's support for the Nixon plan.

Ford had been instrumental in developing the proposal, and its key features satisfied Ford's desire to avoid creation of a budget-busting program run by a huge federal bureaucracy, according to Weinberger.

"It is essential that any plan be based on our present delivery system of private health care," Ford said May 26. "To let a vast new federal bureaucracy take over our health care system would be a burden which would be unbearable in cost."

Weinberger also said that health insurance would remain a very high priority in the new administration. As vice president, Ford had stressed the need to achieve enactment of a health insurance bill in 1974, pledging to "do my utmost" to work out a compromise approach. Ford again asked for action in 1974 in his Aug. 12 address to Congress.

Other experts suggested that Ford's reputation as a man of compromise and his close congressional ties also brightened prospects for passage of health insurance legislation in 1974. Ford "would view with favor a workable, sound health insurance plan which I think we can forge this year," former HEW Secretary Wilbur J. Cohen predicted Aug. 11. Cohen, considered an architect of the 1965 Medicare bill, was seeking to develop a compromise which could win the support of those backing various plans.

Opposed Medicare

If past decisions were any guide, however, Ford was likely to oppose a health insurance program financed through new Social Security taxes. He opposed creation of Medicare in 1965, he said, because the program relied on compulsory payroll-tax financing.

During the Nixon years, Ford generally supported the administration's position on most health issues and particularly agreed with efforts to hold down federal health spending. As House minority leader, Ford led efforts against congressional attempts to override Nixon's vetoes of two popular health bills—a 1970 extension of the Hill-Burton hospital construction act and a 1973 emergency medical services bill.

Education

In his first major legislative statement, Ford Aug. 12 announced that he would sign HR 69, the omnibus elementary and secondary education bill. "Any reservations I might have about some of its provisions—and I do have—fade in comparison to the urgent needs of America for quality education," Ford said in his address to Congress. *(Text, p. 75)*

Congress, in approving HR 69, rejected most of Nixon's proposal for education revenue sharing, choosing instead to retain the categorical grant system for major education programs, including compensatory education, impact aid, vocational education and education for the handicapped. But the bill provided for the consolidation of several more narrowly focused programs.

Busing

Congressional action on HR 69 also may have temporarily diffused the volatile issue of using busing to desegregate public schools by limiting busing of students to the school closest or next closest to their homes unless the courts determined that more extensive busing was

(Continued on p. 12)

Ford's Economics and His Speech to Congress . . .

Taking care to cast the fight against inflation in bipartisan terms, President Ford nonetheless has pledged to carry on the Nixon administration's fundamentalist approach to economic policy.

As Ford made clear in his vice presidential statements and his initial economic pronouncements as President, he planned few basic changes in President Nixon's "old-time religion" policy based on budget cuts and tight monetary restraints.

In an Aug. 12 address to Congress—and in an unexpected jawboning effort against automobile price increases—Ford hinted that he would make flexible use of the powers of his office to combat rising prices and wages.

Yet Ford's first answer to inflation was to cut the federal budget. A consistent foe of rising federal spending during his years in Congress, he clearly viewed fiscal restraint as the most effective contribution the federal government could make to reduce the double digit inflation that threatened economic and social stability.

In deliberate contrast to the Nixon presidency's rancorous battles with Congress over impoundments and spending vetos, Ford in his initial message invited congressional cooperation in making budget reductions. He ruled out "unwarranted cuts in national defense," however, and urged voters to support congressional candidates "who consistently vote for tough decisions to cut the cost of government, restrain federal spending and bring inflation under control."

Some members of Congress were skeptical. "It's not reasonable to talk about a balanced budget in 1976 without cutting military spending," Sen. Jacob K. Javits (R N.Y.) commented. "It can't be done."

Ford made other conciliatory gestures, accepting Senate Majority Leader Mike Mansfield's (D Mont.) call for a "domestic summit meeting" to seek economic solutions and praising congressional initiatives to reform budget procedures and make a six-month study of inflation.

He renewed Nixon's request that Congress reestablish the Cost of Living Council with power to monitor but not control wage and price increases. Earlier on Aug. 12, Ford had put presidential prestige in line against automobile price increases by expressing disappointment in a 10 per cent price increase announced by General Motors.

Through such actions, the President was trying to make good use of a "honeymoon" period to marshall the government, business and labor against inflation.

Superb Position

"The President is in a superb position right now to put in an effective anti-inflationary program," Sen. William Proxmire (D Wis.), vice chairman of the Joint Economic Committee, told Congressional Quarterly.

"Ford does subscribe to the old-time religion...," Rep. Henry S. Reuss (D Wis.), a leading critic of Nixon's policies, said Aug. 9. "But so do I and everyone else who's got their head screwed on."

But by itself, fiscal and monetary restraint was not enough, in Reuss' view, without federal efforts to relieve unemployment and ease inflationary burdens on working Americans.

"The lump needs to be leavened" by spreading the burdens of economic stagnation and inflation more evenly among the population, Reuss suggested. "And it's in the lump-leavening that our Democratic policies" of public service jobs, tax reductions and other measures went beyond administration policies.

Ford's Fundamentalism

Ford's congressional voting record and vice presidential pronouncements suggested there would be little basic change from Nixon's economic policies.

As House minority leader, Ford "went right down the line with President Nixon on economic policy, following every twist and turn," Proxmire pointed out.

And in speeches and interviews given while he was vice president, Ford generally concurred in the Nixonian stress on federal budget restraint as the primary contribution that the government could make to fighting inflation.

"The importance of reduced expenditures cannot be overestimated," the then vice president told an agricultural conference in an Aug. 6 speech that was delivered by an aide. "Reduced expenditures mean reduced government borrowing, reduced interest rates, and help for the Federal Reserve in its efforts to slow the inflationary expansion of money and credit."

Calling for vetos of "budget-busting" legislation, Ford said the nation "will need political guts to defer programs that are marginally desirable but not really essential. We cannot afford optional luxuries while striving to beat inflation."

Warning that Congress was considering measures that could increase fiscal 1975 federal spending to $312-billion, Ford argued that spending instead should be cut below the $305-billion proposed by Nixon when he submitted the fiscal 1975 budget.

"If you can avoid the added expenditures over $305-billion and make some honest and realistic adjustments—a couple of billion dollars below that level—I believe that this is what will be construed among Americans as the kind of leadership that is necessary," Ford said in an interview published in the August issue of *Dun's* magazine.

In other statements that were consistent with the policies he inherited from Nixon, Ford during that interview:

● Opposed both a tax increase or tax reductions.

● Found no prospect that new wage and price controls would be requested by the administration or approved by Congress.

● Expressed the hope that monetary policy would ease and interest rates decline once the Federal Reserve Board was convinced that budgetary restraints were being applied.

● Urged restraint by both labor and management in wage negotiations and criticized price increases by some industries as "extremely shortsighted."

. . . Indicate More of That 'Old-Time Religion'

Involving Congress

Ford was expected to continue Nixon's basic policies, but also to make more vigorous efforts to persuade Congress and labor that those measures were necessary.

"Ford is in a position to go to the Congress and bring them aboard, make them feel they're part of the policy," said Richard J. Whalen, a conservative economic and defense consultant who was critical of Nixon's handling of the economy. "Nixon never did that."

In exploring ways to control inflation, "I prefer an open and objective spirit of inquiry in which all views are given consideration," Ford said in the Aug. 6 speech. "Congressional involvement is essential."

To bring Congress into the anti-inflationary effort, Ford was expected to start a process of consultation among administration economic officials and congressional leaders in a search for budget reductions to cut over-all federal spending.

In that, at least, Congress clearly would cooperate. Senate Majority Leader Mike Mansfield (D Mont.) Aug. 12 suggested that Ford cut spending by $5- to $6-billion.

What programs should be curtailed could become a matter of dispute, however. Mansfield called for cuts in defense and foreign aid spending, areas where Ford was likely to resist reductions.

Whatever Ford's proposals, "I don't think Congress is going to run counter to the President for the next couple of months," Proxmire predicted. With Ford armed with a presidential veto and supported wholeheartedly by relieved congressional Republicans, "there's no way Congress would be able to contradict the President for awhile," Proxmire said.

Democratic Pressure

While Congress was likely to go along with Ford's economic fundamentalism in monetary and fiscal policy, there could be pressures from Democrats to ease the burden of inflation on hard-pressed groups and to encourage economic competition that would increase supplies and bring down prices.

The "old-time religion" was a "necessary but not sufficient condition" for controling inflation, Proxmire contended. What really was needed, he said, were tougher anti-trust actions and presidential jawboning against price increases by uncompetitive industries.

"Sheer raw economic power has been responsible for the guts of inflation," Proxmire argued. "No reduction in federal spending is going to be effective" unless the government toughens anti-trust enforcement.

Democrats also could press for programs to assist lower- and middle-income Americans most burdened by inflation as a trade-off for labor restraint in wage negotiations.

'Credible Alternative'

In an Aug. 11 letter to the new President, Reuss urged Ford to open talks with labor leaders on proposals to give "workers the credible alternative to huge wage increases which is now so desperately lacking.

"We need a new social contract between the government and the average citizen," Reuss wrote, "in which the government pledges to concern itself with the economic problems of the majority—cost of living, jobs and taxes—and workers...will be inclined to moderate their wage increase demands."

Reuss recommended measures similar to an economic program endorsed by the House Democratic Caucus. They included efforts to monitor price increases, public service jobs to combat unemployment, credit allocation and tax relief for most wage earners.

While Ford probably was not receptive to such Democratic alternatives, he had expressed some sympathy for measures to help persons who had been hardest hit by inflation.

"If the combination of high inflation and sharply increasing unemployment continues, the honeymoon would be abbreviated."

—Sen. William Proxmire (D Wis.)

Acknowledging that "some people are suffering more than others," Ford in the Aug. 6 speech said that "certain groups—older Americans, persons on fixed incomes, the unemployed—may require special help within budgetary limitations."

"Certain industries such as the public utilities, housing financial institutions and others have been especially hard hit," he added. Without being specific, Ford said that "there are suggested solutions that have merit and deserve prompt consideration."

Outlook

While Ford was expected to enjoy initial congressional and labor cooperation, that spirit could be short-lived.

"If the combination of high inflation and sharply increasing unemployment continues, the honeymoon would be abbreviated," Proxmire declared.

The role of labor could be the key. Ford's success in controlling inflation could depend on when unions push for maximum wage increases.

Whalen suggested that much will depend on whether Ford can rally the Republicans in the November congressional elections. "If the Republicans lose 40 to 50 seats, then we can expect labor to begin a real push," he said.

"The election is critical, and Ford and his people realize that fact," Whalen added.

In the meantime, Whalen concluded, "the transfer of power [from Nixon to Ford] has bought time for the orthodox policy, but not beyond next spring."

necessary to guarantee the constitutional rights of school children.

Although the bill contained the strongest anti-busing language yet enacted by Congress, the language was probably weaker than Ford would have preferred. "Forced busing has caused more trouble and more tension than almost anything else in our society," he told the Senate Rules Committee Nov. 5, 1973, during his vice presidential confirmation hearings. He also warned that "If the federal courts persist in trying to have forced busing to achieve racial balance in the public schools and there is no other way we could remedy that," he would favor a constitutional amendment prohibiting busing. He did not use the word "busing" in his Aug. 12 address.

An early critic of federal aid to education—he voted against the Elementary and Secondary Education Act (ESEA) in 1965 and 1967—Ford told the Rules Committee that he now found such aid acceptable. Ford had voted for an ESEA extension in 1969. But, like his predecessor, he favored returning more control over education programs to the states and local governments. While still a member of the House, Ford introduced Nixon's original 1971 education revenue-sharing bill.

Supplemental Budget Requests

Although he promised to sign HR 69, Ford warned Congress that he would closely watch funding of the programs authorized by the bill. "I must be frank," he said Aug. 12. "In implementing [the bill's] provisions, I will oppose excessive funding during this inflationary crisis."

The House did not consider funding for most of the programs extended by HR 69 when it passed the fiscal 1975 Labor-Health, Education and Welfare appropriations bill June 27, and the Senate was not expected to either when its version of the bill came up for consideration in late August or early September. Thus the new administration would have an opportunity to submit amended budget requests to reflect its sense of how extended and new programs authorized under HR 69 should be funded.

An Office of Education official said the supplemental education budget requests were almost ready for submission and that he did not expect the new administration to make any major changes. The official said he expected the request for compensatory education funds to be close to the $1,885,000,000 Nixon originally proposed for fiscal 1975.

Charles Lee of the Committee for Full Funding of Education said he did not expect Ford to take a markedly different approach from Nixon on education appropriations.

Other Issues

Congress also was laying the groundwork for legislation in three other education areas—student assistance, vocational education and education for the handicapped.

Ford did not make any reference to those topics in his Aug. 12 address, but Albert H. Quie (R Minn.), a close Ford friend and ranking minority member on the House education committee, said Ford was "strongly in favor of vocational education" and probably would seek a consolidation of some of the programs, as Nixon promised to do.

An Office of Education official said he thought Ford would "maintain his interest" in ensuring that college students from middle class backgrounds would receive financial assistance. He predicted that Ford would "pretty much follow" the Nixon administration position of

restricting federal funding for education of the handicapped to building the capacity of state and local education agencies to educate handicapped children.

Consumers

The most crucial consumer issue on Capitol Hill when the new President took office was creation of an independent consumer protection agency. The House had approved the agency for a second time in April. Supporters of a Senate version already had lost two votes to cut off a filibuster by conservative Republicans and southern Democrats, and were regrouping for another attempt.

Opponents of the bill in the business community were counting on Ford to repeat Nixon's threat to veto the Senate bill unless specific changes were made.

Consumer advocates noted, however, that Ford voted for an earlier version of the bill as a House member in 1971 and that he opposed an amendment to seriously weaken the measure.

In his speeches around the country as Vice President, Ford had not addressed the issue in detail. But he reportedly told a Chicago Republican group in June that he would have voted for the 1974 House bill, which gave the proposed agency a number of important powers not included in the 1971 measure.

Another factor working in their favor, supporters thought, was the end of what they called "impeachment politics"—Nixon's backing of conservative positions to maintain his support among possible anti-impeachment voters in the Senate.

"You couldn't tell what Nixon would do to keep [Sen.] Carl Curtis' [R. Neb.] vote," said Carol T. Foreman, head of the Consumer Federation of America (CFA). "I'd rather fight the bill on the issues."

Advocates of the consumer bill were hoping that with the impeachment issue out of the way, press coverage would increase—and with it, public pressure on Ford and Senate opponents.

"It will be hard for Ford to veto a consumer bill in the first month or two in office, especially when people are so disaffected with government," said Nancy Chasen of Congress Watch, a lobbying group founded by consumer advocate Ralph Nader.

Auto Insurance

Among the other consumer issues Ford was expected to face early in his term was a Senate-passed measure requiring states to enact no-fault auto insurance laws that met minimum federal standards. Nixon adamantly opposed the bill on grounds that states should write their own laws, despite a Transportation Department recommendation that he endorse it. Ford "can't be any more intransigent on the legislation than Nixon," commented an aide on the House committee that completed hearings on the bill in July. "There's some hope that he might be flexible."

Record Mixed

On consumer issues in general, Ford's House record was mixed. He had voted in favor of some items consumer groups favored, such as a 1973 rider to the Alaska Pipeline Bill giving the Federal Trade Commission (FTC) new consumer protection powers.

But he rarely spoke out in favor of strong consumer legislation, and his conservative record reflected the philosophy that government should not interfere in the marketplace. Sometimes when Ford violated that principle it was for the benefit of business, as on a 1972 vote for federal compensation of companies hurt by a government ban on an artificial food sweetener thought to be a health hazard.

Transportation

President Ford's past record on mass transit legislation did not augur well for proponents of a $20-billion long-range subsidy bill the House was preparing to consider when he took office. In a rare departure from the administration line in 1972 and 1973, Ford opposed opening the highway trust fund for mass transit projects in urban areas.

In 1973, Ford voted against an $800-million emergency mass transit measure backed by big-city members but opposed by many from rural areas. After both houses passed the measure in late 1973, Nixon made it clear he would veto it. The threat helped stall House consideration of the conference report until July, when the House killed the bill by sending the conference report back to committee.

Ford's old fifth Congressional District in Michigan included General Motors and other auto plants, and he was a consistent supporter of federal highway programs. In 1964, he voted against the first major mass transit bill to clear Congress. But when the administration supported a bill strengthening the program in 1970, Ford backed it.

The bill before the House in 1974 was by far the most comprehensive and expensive yet proposed for government support of mass transit. For the first time it would allow funds to be used to defray operating expenses—which in most cases meant reduction of deficits. About half the money would go to nine big cities that already had or were building large transit systems.

The Nixon administration firmly opposed operating subsidies for mass transit until it unveiled its own bill incorporating a limited version of the concept in early 1974. The measure authorized $12-billion—a sum Nixon was not willing to exceed, White House officials warned House members.

"If anything, [Ford] will probably be more tightfisted," predicted Larry Snowhite of the U.S. Conference of Mayors. Still, he added, "one can hope that he'll be seeing things in a broader perspective."

Before Nixon's resignation, prospects for Senate action on the mass transit bill did not look good even if the House did pass it. Mass transit supporters were uncertain whether Ford's arrival would encourage Senate sponsors of similar legislation to expedite committee work to move a bill to the floor before the 1974 session ended.

Energy and Environment

Some of the issues facing the Ford administration had the ghostly quality of problems that once had bedeviled his predecessors but had receded, at least temporarily. One of these was an incorrigible set of twins, energy and environment.

Ford's first task in the energy area would have to be the development of a coherent national energy policy, according to most experts.

"First and foremost, he has to formulate an energy policy to decide where we're going," declared Robert

Williams, deputy director of the Ford Foundation's Energy Policy Project.

Representatives Craig Hosmer (R Calif.) and Mike McCormack (D Wash.) agreed. Hosmer, ranking Republican on the Interior and Insular Affairs Committee, asserted that Ford must "keep Project Independence alive." The project had been announced by former President Nixon to make the nation independent of foreign energy supplies.

Both members said the second area needing priority attention was the federal energy policy-making structure. Hosmer urged the appointment of "five wise men" to an energy advisory role to the President. McCormack, chairman of the Science and Astronautics Energy Subcommittee, advocated the creation of a broad cabinet department to coordinate and administer energy and science policies and programs.

Both members thought Ford would grasp the energy issue quickly. "I think he will take a leadership position," said Hosmer.

There was little in Ford's record or speeches to indicate what position he might take on energy issues. Most critical energy votes came after his appointment as vice president. He voted against the creation of a Select House Committee on Energy Resources in 1971, but so did 217 other members.

In a key vote in 1974, Ford opposed an amendment supported by environmentalists that would have struck language from the trans-Alaskan pipeline legislation declaring all actions taken on the pipeline by the secretary of interior to be in compliance with the National Environmental Policy Act of 1969.

Environment

In the environmental area, Ford voted to override Nixon's veto of the Water Pollution Control Act of 1972. In 1960, he voted to uphold a veto by President Eisenhower of another water pollution control bill.

He voted against the Clean Air Act of 1963, but had supported clean air legislation since. "We must establish stringent national air quality standards, particularly for pollutants that are hazardous to health," he said on May 6.

The first major decision Ford would face on energy-environmental legislation was the controversial strip mining legislation that had passed both houses of Congress. His position was unknown. He had not taken part in debate or voted on an even tougher bill which passed the House in 1972. He did respond to a Congressional Quarterly poll as favoring the bill.

Crime and Law Enforcement

In sharp contrast to the atmosphere when Richard Nixon took office in 1969, crime was not such an obvious issue when Ford became President.

Some controversy was expected to arise over a series of "privacy bills," most of them supported by Senate Democrats, which would restrict such activities as military surveillance of civilians, national security wiretaps and criminal record data banks. Key officials in law enforcement, the CIA and the armed forces opposed such restrictions.

Headed Committee

As a member of Congress, Ford generally had supported wiretapping, preventive detention, no-knock entry authority for police, capital punishment and strong drug laws. However, as Vice President he had headed a Domestic

Council committee on privacy and had spoken out frequently against unwarranted intrusion.

Ford pointedly pledged during his Aug. 12 address, "There will be no illegal tappings, eavesdropping, bugging or break-ins in my administration. There will be hot pursuit of tough laws to prevent illegal invasions of privacy in both government and private activities."

Civil Liberties

Ford criticized anti-war campus demonstrators in the 1960s and voted to cut off federal funds to any students participating in disorders. Civil liberatrians were upset with Ford for his 1970 attempt to impeach Supreme Court Associate Justice William O. Douglas. Ford's use of unevaluated information supplied to him by the Justice Department was politically motivated, critics charged.

As President, Ford would have the job of naming an 11-member board of directors of the new Legal Services Corporation, signed into law by Nixon only two weeks before his resignation. In Congress, Ford had opposed the Office of Economic Opportunity and its legal services program from the beginning.

Other pending business in the law enforcement field was mostly of interest to professionals: revisions of the federal criminal code, rules of evidence and rules of criminal procedure.

All had been worked out over many months and were expected to receive the President's approval.

Civil Rights

With the controversy over school busing momentarily defused by Congress and the Supreme Court, civil rights groups were looking ahead to 1975 for action by President Ford and Congress on poverty and voting legislation.

Some civil rights leaders were encouraged by Ford's Aug. 12 pledge to "be the President of the black, brown, red and white Americans...." and his plans to meet with black leaders and members of Congress. But they were more interested in concrete action.

In 1975, the 10-year-old Voting Rights Act, one of the most effective civil rights laws ever enacted, would be brought up in Congress for extension. Recalling that in 1967 Ford sponsored a Nixon administration extension substitute that would have "restricted the effectiveness of the law," Clarence Mitchell, director of the Washington bureau of the National Association of Colored People (NAACP), said Aug. 10 that "at this point it would be hard to predict a Ford position" on a new extension bill.

But "I wouldn't write him off," Mitchell said, "I hope that he would support an extension on his own instincts."

As for busing, Mitchell expressed concern that Ford would not "go out and make a big claim like Nixon did that the nation should stop busing." He must "get down to the issue of education itself," Mitchell added.

"I'm actually proud of my civil rights voting record, and I'm proud of my personal attitude vis-a-vis minority groups," President Ford told the House Judiciary Committee Nov. 15 during his vice presidential confirmation hearings.

Civil rights leaders, however, were far from pleased with the votes he cast in the House. They pointed out that Ford consistently supported weakening amendments to civil rights bills, but then voted for final passage of the measures after the amendments were defeated.

Welfare

There was not going to be any "immediate problem" for the new Ford administration in the welfare area, U.S. Commissioner of Welfare Robert Carleson predicted.

Carleson said that while the Ford administration devoted itself to more "immediate problems" the Department of Health, Education and Welfare (HEW) would continue to work to improve and coordinate various welfare programs.

He pointed out that a welfare reform program begun in late 1972 to force states to purge ineligible recipients from welfare roles was ongoing and that the number of families that received Aid to Families with Dependent Children (AFDC) decreased in 1973. Under the program, federal funds would be withheld from any state that had not reduced the rate of ineligible recipients to three per cent by June 1975.

The Family Assistance Plan, a Nixon welfare reform program that was strongly supported by Ford in a speech to the House in 1969, since had been abandoned. Ford especially recommended measures in the plan for expanded work opportunities for welfare recipients and incentives for maintaining the family unit intact.

On welfare issues, Ford usually voted against low rent housing, Medicare and funds for the federal antipoverty program.

Like labor leaders, welfare spokesmen hoped that Ford's broader constituency as President would lead to more liberal policies. ∎

FORD PRESIDENCY RAISED REPUBLICAN PROSPECTS

For many Republicans, the succession of Gerald R. Ford to the presidency brought with it the promise of an end to despair within the party—a despair which grew as the Watergate scandal unfolded and deepened into panic as the 1974 congressional elections approached.

It was agreed that Ford himself would have a honeymoon period during which his popularity would depend more on his presence than on any of his specific programs. But would that honeymoon help Republican candidates avert the disaster that was predicted for them in November? No one could be sure.

What was certain was that things had rarely looked worse for the Republican Party than they did at the close of Richard Nixon's presidency. Many Republicans were joining in predictions that Democrats would gain enough seats in November to impose congressional government upon the nation.

The year's primaries indicated that Republican voters were using a simple method to express their dissatisfaction with President Nixon. They were not voting.

Spring 1974 Election Losses

Throughout most of 1973, Republicans predicted bravely that Watergate would have no serious impact on voting habits the following year. That confidence was broken in the spring of 1974, by Democratic victories in five special elections to fill five Republican-held House seats.

Four of the five districts had gone Republican by wide margins in 1972, and one was considered such a Republican stronghold that its transfer brought fear to even the most solidly entrenched Republican members of the House.

That victory came in Michigan's 5th District, and was doubly insulting to Republicans because the seat had belonged to Ford himself and was left vacant only when Ford accepted Nixon's invitation to become vice president in 1973.

It was a deeply conservative district, Republican in every election since 1912, and Ford had never received less than 60 per cent of the vote there since his first campaign in 1948. Republican James Vander Laan was the overwhelming choice to succeed Ford.

The Democratic choice was Richard Vander Veen, a liberal lawyer from Grand Rapids. Sixteen years before, he had run against Ford in a heavily Democratic year, and Ford had won by nearly 40,000 votes. Vander Veen returned to his law practice.

But in 1974, with political consultant John Marttila running his campaign and organized labor helping to finance it, Vander Veen used every opportunity to tie his opponent to the Republican administration. "James Vander Laan is Richard Nixon's man," a Democratic advertisement proclaimed. "Dick Vander Veen is his own man."

In the end, Vander Veen took the district by almost 7,000 votes and left the Republicans with the uncomfortable thought that no one among them was safe.

Turning Point

In many ways, that election was a turning point. Democrats had won a special election in Pennsylvania's 12th District the month before, but that victory was easy to explain. The margin was only 230 votes, the district was Democratic by registration, and the energy crisis had prevented rural Republicans from making it to the polls. In Michigan's 5th, none of those excuses held.

The panic grew worse in the following two months, as Democrats won two victories that were not quite as stunning but almost as painful. Thomas A. Luken won a Democratic victory in Ohio's 8th District, where Republican Rep. William J. Keating got 70.3 per cent of the vote in 1972 before resigning from the House to become president of the *Cincinnati Enquirer.* Luken had the all-out support of labor in his contest against moderate Republican Willis D. Gradison Jr., a mild-mannered campaigner who had to overcome troublesome primary opposition himself. Strategists from the Republican National Committee hurried to Cincinnati to try to stave off a second Grand Rapids. But they were unable to do it. Luken won by 4,000 votes.

A month later in Michigan, Democrat J. Robert Traxler won the seat being vacated by Republican Rep. James Harvey (R 1961-74), who had become a federal judge. It was a personal defeat for Nixon as well as for Republican nominee James Sparling, because Sparling, against the advice of local party leaders, invited the President to come to the district to campaign for him.

Nixon agreed to come and spent most of April 10 campaigning for Sparling. He stayed in the rural, consistently Republican area, barely venturing into Bay City, the Democratic stronghold that six days later provided Traxler with much of his winning margin of about 3,000 votes. It was the first time the district had gone Democratic since 1932.

There were two more special elections, neither of which proved very much. In California's 13th District, where experts said the Republican candidate could not lose, he did not lose. Robert J. Lagomarsino easily disposed of seven opponents to win the seat vacated by the death of Republican Rep. Charles Teague (R 1955-73). The last special election, in California's 6th District, sent Democrat John Burton to the House to take a seat that had previously belonged to Republican William S. Mailliard (R 1953-74). But Burton's win was expected; he was well-known and popular in the district, Mailliard had barely won it in 1972, and the Republicans had been unable to come up with a strong candidate.

GOP Primary Problems

As the 1974 primary season started in March, experts were divided between two theories: voters would seize the opportunity for revenge against Republican incumbents, or they would seize the opportunity for revenge against all incumbents, regardless of party. But neither of those things happened.

At the time of Ford's inauguration, 27 of the 50 states had held primaries. Voters had renominated 261 members of the House and defeated three. They had renominated 11 senators, and defeated two, one of whom had been appointed after the campaign began. Despite frequent assertions to the contrary by candidates and political writers, incumbent defeat was running behind its pace in 1970, when nine House members lost in primaries, and 1972, when the figure was seven.

Nor did the meager evidence of incumbent problems indicate that voters were singling out Republicans over Democrats. Both incumbent senators who lost—J.W. Fulbright of Arkansas and Howard W. Metzenbaum of Ohio—were Democrats. Two of the three defeated House members were Republicans, but one—Lawrence G. Williams of Pennsylvania—was dumped by his own local machine. Watergate was not a major issue in any of the campaigns.

Ethics did become a major factor in some of the primary campaigns, but only when one candidate had a personal issue to raise against another. Metzenbaum lost his primary contest to former astronaut John H. Glenn after Glenn complained about the years in which Metzenbaum paid little or no taxes even though he was a wealthy man. Former California Lt. Gov. Ed Reinecke suffered a humiliating defeat in the state's Republican gubernatorial primary following his indictment on charges that he lied to a federal grand jury. But when the charges were more nebulous, the reaction was not apparent.

Low GOP Turnout

Nevertheless, there was one important factor in the primary voting that portended disaster for Republicans in November. It was a shockingly low turnout. In state after state, Republican turnout in 1974 fell below that of the last midterm primaries four years earlier.

In Iowa, for the first time in history, the Democratic primary vote surpassed the Republican vote. "It would appear that Iowa has become a Democratic state," said Melvin Synhorst, the Republican elections commissioner.

Elsewhere, the same thing happened. In Ohio, Republican turnout was down 34 per cent in the gubernatorial primary compared to four years earlier. In California, a spirited contest for the Republican gubernatorial nomination drew 7.8 per cent fewer voters than came out in 1970, when Ronald Reagan ran unopposed.

Republican experts began talking of low turnout as their 1974 curse. "The turnout problem for the Republicans is going to be vicious," said Kevin Phillips, author of *The Emerging Republican Majority.* "I can't see how the Republicans can possibly come out of this election well."

There were other warning signs for the Republicans. A June 1974 Gallup Poll on congressional voting intentions showed Republican strength to be at its lowest level in 38 years of Gallup measurements. The poll reported that 58 per cent of those questioned planned to vote Democratic and 30 per cent Republican.

While poll figures cannot be translated automatically into a certain number of seats, a 57 per cent share of the vote for any party in congressional elections has resulted in a landslide. In 1936, Democrats won 333 House seats with 56.1 per cent of the vote. In 1958, they took 283 seats with 56.1 per cent, and, in 1964, they won 295 seats with 57.3 per cent. (A majority is 218 seats.)

Independent Shift

Moreover, Gallup found that one of the most dramatic shifts to the Democrats in 1974 was among voters who classified themselves as independent.

In the 1972 presidential election, the vote of independents was closely divided between the two parties. In later surveys, however, this vote was going 2-1 for Democratic congressional candidates.

In mid-April, still another Gallup Poll found that only 24 per cent of all voters considered themselves Republicans, fewer than in any election since 1940. At the same time, the number of voters considering themselves conservatives rose to 38 per cent, higher than at any time since the question was first asked in 1936. The frustrating conclusion for Republicans was that they had an unparalleled chance to take advantage of growing conservative sentiment—and were wasting it because of Watergate.

Republican problems were made worse by an unusual number of retirements from the House in 1974, which forced them to defend a large number of marginal districts without the incumbents who had been accustomed to winning in them.

At the time Ford took office, 44 members of the House, 21 of them Republicans, had announced that they would not be seeking re-election to the 94th Congress. Most of the Democratic seats were expected to remain Democratic by comfortable margins, but most of the Republican ones were thought likely to generate close races. In several cases, Republican incumbents who had managed only narrow victories in 1972 chose to retire rather than face an uphill contest in 1974.

Retirements were not so numerous in the Senate, but by Aug. 1 it was clear that there would be at least nine new senators in the coming Congress. Democrats Harold E. Hughes (Iowa), Alan Bible (Nev.) and Sam J. Ervin Jr. (N.C.), all announced their retirements, as did Republicans Norris Cotton (N.H.), Wallace F. Bennett (Utah), George D. Aiken (Vt.), and Edward J. Gurney (Fla.). Fulbright and Metzenbaum were beaten for renomination.

Watergate Strategies

When it still looked as if Richard Nixon would be president in November, Republican candidates were busy devising strategy for dealing with the problem of his presence.

The nation's leading consultants advised Republicans to stress their sincerity and commitment to reform, and contrast themselves with the more venal politicians holding office at the moment. "Everyone is trying to put out the facade of honesty and holiness," commented Sanford Weiner, a California consultant who has done much business advising moderate Republicans.

For many Republicans, running a campaign on the integrity issue meant running away from President Nixon. Many of the most vulnerable Republican incumbents advertised their independent voting records, if they had such records, made their finances public and called for strict regulations on campaign spending. Others took the further step of placing a limit on the size of the contributions they would accept for their own campaigns.

"I think it would be easier for me if Gerald Ford were President," agreed Sen. Peter Dominick (R Colo.). "But I don't think the President is going to turn over control that way."

(Continued on p. 18)

Ford's Poll Standings: The Steady GOP Favorite

Gerald R. Ford became the top choice of Republicans and independents for the 1976 presidential nomination after President Nixon had nominated him to the vice presidency, according to both the Harris Survey and the Gallup Poll. He steadily maintained his lead throughout his vice presidency.

In the Harris Survey, California Gov. Ronald Reagan had led the Republican field in October 1973, before Vice President Spiro T. Agnew resigned. The switch occurred in November interviewing, a month after Ford had been nominated Oct. 12.

The table below compares Ford's popularity in Harris polls published in December 1973 and March and July 1974. The question: "If you had to choose right now, who would be your first choice for the Republican nomination for president in 1976?"

	July 1974	March 1974	December 1973
Ford	23%	21%	21%
Reagan	15	17	16
Nelson A. Rockefeller	10	13	6
Sen. Charles H. Percy (Ill.)	9	10	11
John B. Connally	8	9	9
Sen. Howard H. Baker Jr. (Tenn.)	6	7	10
Elliot L. Richardson	4	3	4
Sen. James L. Buckley (N.Y.)	3	3	2
Sen. Robert Taft Jr. (Ohio)	2	1	—
Sen. Lowell P. Weicker Jr. (Conn.)	2	2	1
None or not sure	18	14	18

Ford led nine other prospective candidates for the 1976 Republican nomination in a Gallup Poll published Jan. 27, 1974. The question, in polling of 377 Republican voters Jan. 4-7, was: "Which one would you like to see nominated as the Republican candidate for president in 1976?"

Ford	24%
Reagan	20
Rockefeller	18
Connally	9
Percy	8
Baker	5
Richardson	3
Sen. Mark O. Hatfield (R Ore.)	2
Buckley	2
Sen. Edward M. Brooke (R Mass.)	1
Others, no preference	8

County Chairmen

Despite Ford's high standing with rank-and-file Republicans, a Gallup Poll published March 24, 1974, found that Reagan was the presidential choice of a large plurality of Republican county chairmen. The poll results were based on the return of 2,384 questionnaires, 64 per cent of the total mailed in January and February. The chairmen's choices:

Reagan	39%
Ford	24
Rockefeller	12
Connally	7
Sen. Barry Goldwater (Ariz.)	6
Richardson	4
Percy	3
Baker	2
Buckley	1
Hatfield	1
Brooke	*
No preference	1

*Less than one-half of 1 per cent

The chairmen whose first choice for the nomination was Ford were asked to indicate their second choice. These were the results with Ford's support divided among other prospects:

Reagan	55%
Rockefeller	15
Connally	12
Others/no preference	18

Ford vs. Kennedy

Trial heats by the pollsters, running Ford against Sen. Edward M. Kennedy of Massachusetts, the early Democratic front-runner for the presidency in 1976, came up with mixed results.

For a Harris Survey published Dec. 27, 1973, 1,103 likely voters were asked: "If the 1976 elections were being held today, and you had to choose, would you vote for Gerald Ford on the Republican ticket for president or for Sen. Edward Kennedy on the Democratic ticket?"

Ford	48%
Kennedy	44
Not sure	8

Ford did less well in a trial heat against another Democratic possibility, Sen. Henry M. Jackson of Washington, in the same poll:

Ford	43%
Jackson	41
Not sure	16

Kennedy had a wide lead in a trial heat published by Gallup June 2, 1974, nearly six months after Ford had become Vice President. Gallup interviewers asked 1,543 adults May 10-13: "Suppose the presidential election were being held today. If Vice President Gerald Ford were the Republican candidate and Sen. Edward Kennedy were the Democratic candidate, which would you like to see win?"

Kennedy	50%
Ford	39
Undecided	11

(Continued from p. 16)

On Aug. 9, the President did turn over control that way, and it brought many Republicans like Dominick new hope that the rules of 1974 politics would suddenly change. But with the election three months away, and Democrats running well throughout the country, it was still sensible to temper the new mood of hope with a reminder that Watergate was not like to vanish quickly from the electorate's mind.

Both national political parties looked for delicate ways to deal with the Nixon scandals. Republicans looked for a credible way to escape the fallout from Watergate without disowning the administration in which it occurred. Democrats struggled to keep the issue in the public mind without appearing to use it for partisan advantage.

A walk through Republican headquarters in mid-1974 showed that pictures of Nixon were in nearly every office in the building. "You don't see pictures of Gordon Liddy," commented George Bush, the Republican chairman. "You see them of Nixon. I don't feel inhibited from criticizing Watergate. I do believe in supporting the President. I don't think that's contradictory." *First Monday*, the monthly publication of the Republican National Committee, continued to express its support for Nixon well into the 1974 political year.

And even when the President's Republican support began to crumble on Capitol Hill, Bush was reluctant to join in. The day after Nixon released the transcript of his incriminating June 23, 1972, conversation with H. R. Haldeman, Bush issued only a mild statement of reaction.

Bush expressed his "deep feeling for those who supported the President on the basis of the facts...which they believed to be true," and said he was confident that "the President will do what is right—what is best for the country." Bush said only Nixon should decide whether or not resignation was a good idea.

Bush was among the first to admit that Watergate had caused the party serious financial problems for 1974. Between January and November 1973, the party took in $5.2-million, a full million less than had been projected. Small gifts held up well, with the party having set out to get $4-million in contributions of less than $100 and actually getting $4.4-million. But instead of having 1,500 people give gifts of $1,000 or more, as was expected, there were only 500 gifts of that size—hence, a shortage of $1-million.

The Democratic problem was less painful, but equally complex. Robert S. Strauss, chairman of the Democratic National Committee, said often in the closing days of the Nixon administration that the party could not win by running solely against Watergate.

"While Watergate is a factor, it's only one of many," Strauss said early in the year.... "We have to deal with the economy, the human needs of people.... If we go to the public and yell 'Watergate,' then we don't deserve to win."

By the spring of 1974, some Democrats were using the

The Prescient Ford

At the end of his remarks at the annual dinner of the Gridiron Club in Washington, D.C., on March 9, 1968, House Minority Leader Ford, after disavowing any intention of seeking higher office, confided to his audience that it would be nice to have a home in town.

"Let me assure the distinguished Vice President of the United States, before all of you, that I have absolutely no designs on his job.

"How many others in this room can make that statment?

"I'm serious. I'm not at all interested in the vice presidency.

"I love the House of Representatives, despite the long irregular hours.

"Sometimes, though, when it's late and I'm tired and hungry—on that long drive home to Alexandria—as I go past 1600 Pennsylvania Avenue, I do seem to hear a little voice saying:

"If you lived here, you'd be home now.'"

---

term "veto-proof" Congress, originally invoked by labor unions to express their desire for Democratic majorities sufficient to legislate in spite of President Nixon.

But even before Nixon left office, there were signs that this strategy was beginning to backfire. Republicans began using the counter claim that the country did not need a liberal majority so big it would ram its priorities through without objection. By mid-summer, some Republicans were claiming that the arrogance of the "veto-proof" idea was the best issue available to them for the fall campaign.

Democrats began to retrench. Sen. Lloyd Bentsen (D Texas), chairman of the Senate Democratic Campaign Committee, warned the party's candidates against trying to ask voters to bring about a veto-proof Congress. As the prospect of a Ford presidency moved closer and closer, other Democrats noted that the "veto-proof" issue could backfire on the party if Nixon were out and a less veto-minded President were in as his replacement.

In many campaigns, the idea of a veto-proof Congress was replaced as the leading issue by Democratic complaints about inflation and Nixon's handling of the economy. There were few specific solutions to the problem from candidates of either party, but there was no shortage of rhetoric.

New social issues—abortion and capital punishment—attracted attention in congressional campaigns, apparently replacing busing and street crime—the leading social issues of 1970 and 1972. But in general, the early months of the 1974 political year produced an unusually small amount of serious talk about the important domestic problems of the day—housing, health care, transportation and welfare, among others. ∎

TIRELESS GOP CAMPAIGNER AND FUNDRAISER

"I know something about power," Vice President Gerald R. Ford joked during a June 17 appearance at a Montgomery County, Maryland, high school graduation. "At least I did before I became Vice President."

Ford's quip referred to the miniscule authority vested in the Vice President by the U.S. Constitution, and the considerable power he had given up when he left his post as House minority leader. But as Ford completed eight months in office on Aug. 6 and was already considered an imminent successor to the presidency, he had assumed a niche doublessly undreamed of by the authors of the Constitution, and one that was particularly appropriate to the Watergate era of American government: that of chief fundraiser and guidon for the Republican Party in its year of distress.

As of the end of June 1974, Ford had traveled an estimated 100,000 miles throughout the country, visited 33 states and made some 400 public appearances. He had appeared as the principal speaker at approximately 75 Republican fundraising events—most of them small, county-level affairs—and campaigned for Republican congressional candidates in three special elections. And his schedule of political appearances was steadily increasing as the heavy fundraising season of early fall approached.

Ford's political activities were giving him considerable leverage in Congress as a lobbyist for administration policies, according to Capitol Hill sources. These sources pointed to Ford's successful efforts, along with those of Secretary of State Henry A. Kissinger and Defense Secretary James R. Schlesinger, to prevent reductions in the administration's $95-billion defense budget.

"Ford is dynamite," said Rep. Les Aspin (D Wis.). "Few Republicans can turn him down because he's the only one who can raise funds for them in November."

The actual amounts Ford was raising were not great compared to top Republican fundraisers in past years. Unofficial estimates by Republican National Committee sources put the amount raised by Ford at somewhere between $500,000 and $1-million as of late June. These sources acknowledged that Ford had not been raising as much money for the party as had his predecessor, former Vice President Spiro T. Agnew, during the off-year buildup of 1970. During that year, Agnew brought in between $5- and $6-million.

"It's hard to judge exactly how much he (Ford) has helped raise," one committee official told Congressional Quarterly. "He's done so many of these small receptions and in some cases the money wasn't raised until after the event."

Committee aides give two reasons for the lag in actual dollars raised by Ford. First, 1974 was shaping up as a bad year for all political fundraisers because of suspicion of politics in general on the part of would-be donors and because of tighter campaign financing and disclosure laws. Second, Ford had a late start on the 1974 fundraising trail. By the time he was confirmed as vice president on Dec. 6, 1973, sponsors of most of the large, state-wide functions scheduled for the spring already had chosen speakers.

(Continued on p. 21)

High school children cluster around Vice President Gerald R. Ford during a February 1974 appearance at Tinley Park, Ill.
[Wide World Photo]

Ford, the Fundraiser: 'I Really Enjoy It'

Following is the text of a June 15, 1974, interview with Vice President Ford, who was returning to Washington aboard Air Force Two from a Republican furndraising swing through three New York congressional districts:

CQ: You frequently refer to a projection that Republicans stand to lose from 50 to 100 seats in Congress this fall because of Watergate. Do you agree with that projection?

Ford: No. I normally qualify that by saying I don't agree with it. But I like to present the problem as some people are forecasting.

CQ: You don't make any predictions at all?

Ford: No. I simply use what these people are saying, 50 or 100, and say, 'This is what will be the fact if these predictions are forthcoming.' *(i.e. a veto-proof Congress—ed.)*

CQ: You did say at one time you disagreed with Sen. Barry Goldwater's (R Ariz.) warning *(that polls showed Watergate would cost every Republican candidate for office 10 per cent of the vote in 1974—ed.).* Is that still your position?

Ford: Oh, yes. But I have not gotten into a numbers game.

CQ: Many of these fundraisers you've attended recently have been comparatively small, and the Republican National Committee estimates you've raised only somewhere between $500,000 and $1-million to date....

Ford: I think that's better than anybody else has.

CQ: In general, how would you assess Republican fundraising to date?

Ford: All I know, and this is from personal experience, any place I've been it's been a sell-out. Whatever they set as their objective, they've sold out.

CQ: Do you think Republicans will have a lot of trouble raising money this year?

Ford: All I can judge is where I've been, and as I said a moment ago, they've all been sell-outs. Tonight they told me they could have sold twice as many as they sold, if they'd had a place that could have handled it.

CQ: Everybody seems to be having trouble raising money. How do you think the Republicans will fare this year?

Ford: Well, I think it is a hard year for everybody. But as the issues get refined, and as the situation develops, I think you may see a better response.

CQ: And what do you see as the essential issues?

Ford: The issues I talked about tonight. The issue I use, one of them, I like to present the dire side of a veto-proof Congress, which I think is a very serious one, as I think you can detect. But I also use the affirmative approach, that people ought to be responsive to an administration that has done so much to achieve peace. One is an approach of concern and one is an approach of satisfaction.

CQ: Do you plan to continue campaigning for candidates wherever you're asked?

Ford: Not wherever I'm asked; wherever I think I can help, wherever my time permits, wherever I can work it into the schedule.

CQ: Could a Republican member of Congress campaigning for re-election expect to see you in his district at some point during the campaign, if he requested you?

Ford: I would say, any that come from a marginal area that have been pretty good team players.

CQ: You have said on a number of occasions that you plan to be your own man, to follow your own lights. But on the other hand you are the Vice President and you have some loyalty to the President. How do you see your role in that regard? What are the limits of being your own man?

Ford: One, I have a loyalty to the man who appointed me, but on the other hand I have a loyalty to the people I served for 25 years (in Congress). The net result is, where you have a mixture of loyalties, you have to be perfectly candid or you lose the respect of both. The net result is, I call them as I see them. That doesn't mean I'm zig-zagging. It's just that I zig when people on one side want me only to zag. When I zag, people on the zig side only want me to zig. So I end up, I speak my mind, and sometimes one group likes it and sometimes another group likes it. That isn't zigzagging. It's being candid. The zaggers always want me to zag. The ziggers always want me to zig. They're the inflexible ones.

CQ: You were one of the architects of revenue sharing. Do you see eye-to-eye with the President on most other domestic issues?

Ford: Yes, I believe strongly in general revenue sharing. I believe our local programs will work a lot better if we have special revenue sharing or block grants. I think the Better Communities Act, the Better Education Act, are all far more effective than the categorical grant programs you had, which were too inflexible, too bureaucratically controlled, too non-responsive to the needs of the teachers and the school system, the cities and communities. In this area I strongly agree with his positions. On the other hand, as a matter of record, I think the programs to divert from the highway trust fund, to institute even on an optional basis operational subsidies, are fundamentally bottomless pits, and are non-productive, irresponsible government. I think you only have to look at the failure of mass transit systems to see why I feel that way.

CQ: Are there other domestic policies that you differ with the President on?

Ford: No significant differences. Differences of emphasis or differences of minor specifics, but no broad differences.

CQ: You've said you have no intention of running for president in 1976. But the kind of grassroots campaigning you've been doing would be bound to help you if you were to become a candidate. Has that entered your mind?

Ford: Not consciously. I enjoy it. I really enjoy people. I enjoy crowds, like we saw today. They were all friendly. It's like campaigning at home, only on a broader scale. I really enjoy it.

(Continued from p. 19)

"Many of the things he did early in the year were things he'd previously committed himself to doing when he was minority leader," said a Republican National Committee executive. "That prevented him from doing some of the other things that might have been larger events. And the invitation and acceptance process can take anywhere from six to seven months to get on-stream. He lost six months of invitation time after he was sworn in."

Probably more important than the money Ford helped raise as vice president during the first seven months of 1974 was the enthusiasm he generated among local state Republican leaders and workers as he moved through their communities at a time when many of them regarded Watergate and President Nixon as an obvious burden to the party with frightening potential for damage at the polls at virtually all levels in November.

Ford's succession to the presidency enhanced the value he could have as a fundraiser and campaigner for Republican candidates in the fall of 1974.

Feedback

"He certainly isn't the most colorful fundraiser, but he's always been fairly successful at it," an official of the New York State Republican Committee told Congressional Quarterly. He recalled the work Ford had done in the state as minority leader in 1972: "He drew good audiences at that time, and he's attracting larger audiences now, mostly because of his considerably more exalted position, and his reputation as well. I think the reputation factor is much greater today than it was in 1972."

"He's the most sought-after Republican in the country at the present time in terms of fundraising and speaking appearances," said Gordon Luce, chairman of the California Republican Committee. "He does an excellent job when he appears. We're all proud that he's our Vice President and that he's doing so much to help build the party and to help candidates throughout the country. To have the Vice President of the United States helping you is a very important edge, and if you're very effective at it, as I think Jerry Ford is, it's a double edge."

State and local party officials interviewed agreed that Ford also would be of great value campaigning for most House and some Senate candidates, though he probably would not add to many gubernatorial races, where candidates as a rule rarely invite outside national figures in to help them.

However, "If what I've seen to date is any indication, Ford will be invited to virtually every congressional district where there's a Republican chance," said a national party official. "Too many of these congressmen want him so badly. They want to associate with him, and because of that he'll be visiting many areas where it's unusual to have a vice president or a president visit."

Zigging and Zagging

As of late June, Ford was receiving most audience response at political meetings for his warnings of the effects of a Democratic landslide in Congress in November. He also was touting President Nixon's foreign policy achievements and the administration's revenue-sharing proposals. *(Box, next page)*

At various times, Ford also commented on the progress of the House Judiciary Committee's impeachment proceedings and Special Watergate Prosecutor Leon Jaworski's criminal investigation. While many local Republicans seemed to take delight in Ford's apparent determination to remain independent of official White House positions on Watergate-related matters, there seemed to be a growing concern on the part of some officials that Ford might damage his effectiveness by apparent shifts in his support of Nixon.

"There have been some critics who've claimed that he has zigged and zagged in his support for the President," noted a New York party official. "But I don't think this is a general criticism among people outside of Washington, at least not yet. I think he's still regarded as a man of basic integrity in the political field, and as an individual who's honest and trying to do his best in a very difficult job. His position is something the Vice President himself has to determine, and it's hard to offer any kind of advice to him when you have a situation that is so fluid as this seems to be with a new rash of headlines every day, many of them in conflict with themselves, and when you have members of the Judiciary Committee saying the Watergate tapes indicate one thing and some of them who say they indicate another."

Press Coverage

One obvious result of Ford's insistence on speaking out about the Watergate proceedings was that it had assured him of continued press coverage.

At one point in mid-May, only three or four national reporters had signed up to accompany Ford on a May 24 appearance in Lansing, Mich. But on May 21, Judge John J. Sirica ordered Nixon to turn over tapes to him that had been requested by Special Watergate Prosecutor Leon Jaworski. Ford stated that he hoped "there will be some compromise, so as to avoid further litigation." The following day Ford said he hoped Nixon would give additional material to the House Judiciary Committee, "the sooner the better." And the next day, Ford and Nixon had a meeting at the White House that apparently ended in disagreement over turning over tapes and documents.

By the time Ford took off from Washington to Lansing on the 24th, the front compartment of Air Force Two was packed with reporters.

Ford was criticized for speaking out on White House Watergate strategy, but refused to desist. "I have a loyalty to the man who appointed me, but on the other hand I have a loyalty to the people I served for 25 years [in Congress]," Ford told Congressional Quarterly during a June 15 interview. "The net result is, where you have a mixture of loyalties, you have to be perfectly candid or you lose the respect of both. The net result is, I call them as I see them. That doesn't mean I'm zig-zagging." *(Text of interview, p. 20)*

Independence

Ford began staking out his independence from White House Watergate positions even before his confirmation as Vice President. On Oct. 17, 1973, only five days after Nixon announced his nomination as Agnew's successor, Ford was quoted as saying Nixon ought to release tapes requested by then Watergate Special Prosecutor Archibald Cox—who was fired three days later for refusing to accept a White House offer of a compromise on turning over the tapes. While supporting the President, Ford then obliquely criticized Nixon's angry reaction to press coverage of the firing and its aftermath, and continued to speak out in support of turning over tapes and documents.

(Continued on p. 23)

Ford On A Typical Campaign Day

Mary Ellen Smith was speechless: it was the first time she had ever shaken hands with a vice president of the United States. As Gerald R. Ford swept past her into a small auditorium at Harriman College, a small Catholic school near Newburgh, N.Y., to speak at a local Republican fundraising event, Miss Smith stared for a moment at her hand and then fell back into the arms of two other hostesses in a mock swoon. "I think he's a really good-looking guy," the 19-year-old murmured.

Ford, trailed by Secret Service agents and more than a dozen national reporters, generated excitement everywhere he stopped during the June 15 fundraising swing through three New York congressional districts: Rep. Benjamin A. Gilman's 26th District, Rep. Donald J. Mitchell's 31st and Rep. Hamilton Fish Jr.'s 25th. The eight-hour tour was part of a rigorous schedule of fundraising and campaigning that Ford had kept up since his confirmation as vice president Dec. 6, 1973, and it was typical of the kind of reaction he received from local Republicans and of the message he beamed to them.

"I think he's a great person," said another fan, Mary Cardillo, a 59-year-old party worker in Mitchell's district, the first leg of Ford's trip. "He's an honest and sincere man," she said, gazing admiringly at Ford, who was standing a few feet away in a reception room in the Oneida County airport near Utica, N.Y., signing autographs.

Ford left the reception and walked to a nearby hangar where about 400 party faithful had gathered for the main rally in a carnival atmosphere, complete with a band, multicolor balloons, straw campaign hats and hand-lettered posters with such messages as "Mohawk Valley Welcomes Our VP" and "We're 4 You."

Fine, Powerful, Popular

The crowd roared as Ford emerged on a portable bandshell and Mitchell introduced him as "one of the finest, most powerful, most popular men on this earth." Ford in turn praised Mitchell as "a person who has broad experience as a state legislator" and as an effective member of the House Armed Services Committee.

Then Ford began what had become a standard three-part speech, delivered without notes at each stop and varied to suit his allotted time and audience. The standard talk included a warning of the effects of a Democratic sweep on Congress in the November elections, praise for President Nixon's foreign policy achievements coupled with criticsm of news leaks concerning Secretary of State Henry A. Kissinger's role in national security wiretapping, and advocacy of the Nixon administration's "New Federalism" program to allow local jurisdictions more control over federal spending. Ford tied each point to the importance of working for the re-election of the representative in whose district he appeared.

"Now let me expand from very specific remarks about Don to some general observations which I think have to be told in Utica, have to be repeated in every one of the other congressional districts throughout our country," Ford told the airport crowd. "Some of our good Democratic friends, and some of the so-called wise people in the political atmosphere in Washington are forecasting and predicting, and in some cases they are demanding, that the voters in November of this year elect what they call a veto-proof Congress. If that should happen, it means probably that good members of the House like Don Mitchell will be defeated. I don't think that's going to happen, but that's what they are projecting. This is what they're working for, this is what they're demanding."

Ford warned that a "veto-proof Congress" would upset the "very delicate balance that we have in the federal government between the legislative, executive and judicial branches" and would mean that "the most

A Democratic sweep "means that the doors to the federal treasury will be wide open,...that deficit will be piled on deficit...."

liberal elements of the Democratic party will be in control not only of the legislative branch of the Congress but will also be in a position to dominate the executive branch of the President."

The "pragmatic side" of such a sweep, Ford said, "means that the American people better tighten up their seatbelts because they're going on the greatest inflationary ride we've ever had in America. It means that the doors to the federal treasury will be open wide. It means that deficit will be piled on deficit and getting bigger every year. It means that there will be no effort to control expenditures, inflation will get worse, and inevitably we will turn to a prohibitive tax raise.... Now, the American people don't like dictatorships. The American people don't want their tax money squandered.... So I don't think this is going to happen. But it depends on you. It could happen if you don't go out and work as hard as you possibly can for guys like Don Mitchell." The crowd burst into applause at mention of the representative's name.

"That was the great conciliator," a reporter who regularly traveled with Ford quipped sardonically while waiting for the Vice President to return to Air Force Two for the short flight to the next stop. After his confirmation Ford had pledged to work as a mediator between the White House and the Democratic-controlled Congress. But Ford had good rapport with his traveling press.

By the time Ford reached his last stop, a $75-a-plate dinner at a Westchester County country club for Rep. Fish, attended by about 450, he was visibly tiring. At one point in his speech he repeated a line about Kissinger which usually drew applause, but there was no reaction. Still, the enthusiasm for Ford among the Fish audience, which included some Democrats, was palpable.

All three representatives on whose behalf Ford appeared were favored to win re-election in November.

(Continued from p. 21)

At the same time, Ford consistently said information he had seen indicated to him that Nixon was innocent of the planning or cover-up of Watergate.

With a speech before the American Farm Bureau Federation in Atlantic City Jan. 15, 1974, Ford began attacking those he said were exploiting Watergate to bring about a defeat of Nixon administration policies. And, beginning with a Jan. 26 B'nai B'rith Anti-Defamation League appearance, Ford added strong praise of Nixon's foreign policy to his personal equation of independence from Nixon vs. vice presidential loyalty.

The record of Ford's public statements on the possible damage of Watergate to the Republican Party indicated a sharp turnaround in Ford's thinking, dating from two special elections in February 1974, both of them won by Democrats. One of them was an election to pick a successor for his own congressional seat in the 5th District of Michigan.

In his first news conference after being confirmed as Vice President, Ford Dec. 7 declared that President Nixon was "not a political liability to any candidate" and that campaign appearances by Nixon "ought to be an asset." On Jan. 25, 1974, Ford disagreed with Sen. Barry Goldwater's (R Ariz.) forecast that Watergate would cost every Republican candidate 10 per cent of the vote in 1974. "I don't think Republicans are going to have that kind of drop-off in their vote," Ford said, expressing optimism that Republican candidate Harry Fox could win the Feb. 5 special election in Pennsylvania's 12th District.

As it turned out, the election was won by a Democrat, John P. Murtha, who had campaigned heavily on the Watergate theme. When Richard Vander Veen Feb. 18 won the first Democratic victory in Ford's home district since 1910, Ford reacted with disbelief.

"You can't mean that," he said when notified of the results. "Well, it's a beating, I'm very upset," he told newsmen the next day, adding that he was rather "frightened" by it.

Later that week, while campaigning in Cincinnati, Ohio, for a March 5 special election, Ford went on the offensive with a "give 'em hell" approach, blaming "labor outsiders" for the Michigan loss. "You have to be on the offensive," Ford said later, explaining his new campaign style.

Again, the Republican candidate lost, and Ford's speaking style became progressively scrappier—and his appearances more frequent.

To meet his heavy travel schedule and still spend two or three days in Washington each week at his quarters in the Executive Office Building and his offices on Capitol Hill, Ford normally slept only six hours a night, according to spokesman Paul Miltich.

"You have to bear in mind that he's an iron man," said Miltich.

Ford was receiving "several hundred" invitations for appearances every week, many of them from local Republican organizations throughout the country, according to Miltich. At one point in mid-spring, 1974, the invitations were running at a peak of about 900 a week. Often the political invitations were reinforced by endorsements by the Republican National Committee and the Republican Congressional Committee.

Ford's political consultant, Gwen Anderson, a former national committeewoman from Washington, and other members of Ford's staff sifted through the invitations each week and decided which ones to accept. Ford in many cases made personal commitments to friends and former colleagues on Capitol Hill.

"I would say, any (Republican members of Congress) that come from a marginal area that have been pretty good team players" could expect him to accept an invitation to appear in their behalf, the Vice President told Congressional Quarterly.

Historical Parallels

Raising money for Republican congressional candidates and appearing in their campaigns promised great rewards in future White House-congressional relations when Ford assumed the Oval Office Aug. 9, and Richard Nixon's term ended abruptly with resignation. Ford's campaigning and fundraising also placed him in a strong position to meet any challenge to his nomination as presidential candidate at the 1976 Republican national convention—a position Ford consistently denied he was seeking when he was vice president.

At his appearances, Ford rarely failed to explain his motives for such extensive travel.

"You know, I get a lot of advice these days from people who tell me I ought to stay on the banks of the Potomac and be barricaded and listen only to the strident voices that dominate the atmosphere in Washington," Ford said during his June 15 appearance in New York's 26th District. "Well, I'm not going to take that advice. I want to come out and share your problems with you. I want to come out and listen to you, and I want to come out and meet you."

But local party officials who looked for further motives generally winked at Ford's frequent assertions that he had no presidential ambitions. Some recalled another prominent Republican who had courted delegate support the same way—on the fundraising trail—during another dry spell for the Republican party. At that time, from 1964 to 1968, the then-current administration, headed by Lyndon B. Johnson, seemed to be self-destructing over another obsessive issue—the war in Vietnam.

For those who appreciated irony, the parallels were rich. The sought-after Republican during those years was Richard Nixon. ∎

VP FORD KEPT A LOW PROFILE ON CAPITOL HILL

Gerald R. Ford kept a low profile on Capitol Hill during his short tenure as vice president—so low that his impact as a lobbyist for the Nixon administration appeared to have been minimal.

Soon after he was confirmed by the Senate, Ford was touted as the administration's future super-lobbyist. But some Republicans were disappointed.

"I'm not degrading any of his abilities, but I had hoped he would become more active than he has been," said Rep. James T. Broyhill, a veteran North Carolina Republican.

"I think his reported role in legislation is inflated," an influential House Republican leader told Congressional Quarterly. "How can he be lobbying for legislation when he's running from Maine to California on speaking trips?"

"He does help [the White House]," said a source familiar with the administration's legislative liaison office. "But there's a lot of smoke there, too, as opposed to fire."

A high-ranking Senate Republican staff aide said, "My guess is he's had a moderate but not very great impact."

Ford aides, however, cited the Vice President's work on legislation dealing with defense matters and with the energy crisis as evidence of his effectiveness as an administration lobbyist. They noted that Ford's background as a former member gave him an extra edge in dealing with legislators, and that Ford's fundraising activities for members who were up for re-election in 1974 helped him round up votes on some bills. (See chapter on campaigning, p. 19)

'Muscling Around'

Ford received credit from many, including some resentful Democrats, for helping turn back cuts in the 1975 defense budget. President Nixon had assigned special responsibilities in the defense area to Ford, who once was the ranking Republican on the House Defense Appropriations Subcommittee. "We kept hearing he was muscling around," said one Democrat.

One of the members Ford lobbied was Broyhill, who supported a move led by Rep. Les Aspin (D Wis.) to cut a defense procurement authorization (HR 14592) by setting a ceiling on spending equivalent to the 1974 appropriation plus an adjustment for inflation. The White House lobbied vigorously against the ceiling.

As Broyhill recalled it, the meeting was not very dramatic. "We happened to see each other in the House chamber and we talked," he said. "It was more or less a friendly jibe at my position. That was all. I didn't take it as arm-twisting. He just came up with a grin and said, 'I'm surprised to see you taking that position.' I said, 'This is is a position I've taken before, as you know, and it's not inconsistent.' That's about all there was to it."

Broyhill was unmoved. On May 22, he was one of 52 Republicans who voted for the reduction—which was rejected anyway, 185-209.

Administration supporters were able to turn back several other challenges to the budget. But most supporters gave credit for the decisive lobbying effort, not to Ford, but to the White House's regular congressional liaison staff, headed by presidential assistant William E. Timmons.

Subtlety

Ford aides claimed the Vice President's methods of lobbying members were purposely subtle, thus making his actual effectiveness difficult to gauge.

Ford was not an "active lobbyist," acknowledged Walter L. Mote, who ran Ford's Senate office. "He's not out twisting arms or beating people. But he commands a lot of respect in both chambers and he's able to state with a certain degree of knowledge the administration's position. And he has a good memory for the background of issues that were coming up when he was serving in the House."

As a former member, respected by virtually all sides in Congress, Ford had an obvious advantage in dealing with members. Soon after he was sworn in, House Speaker Carl Albert (D Okla.) gave Ford use of a small office on the House side to use for conferences with members. The House office was unprecedented for a vice president, whose duties as president of the Senate entitled him to quarters in the Senate wing only.

Other evidence of Ford's good relations with members was easy to find. The Vice President had a standing invitation to attend the Senate Republican Policy Committee's weekly luncheon meetings. He went often, and, according to other participants, he was treated as an insider.

Spiro T. Agnew, Ford's predecessor, attended only when a special invitation was issued, and then he was treated with cool correctness. His visits usually included a speech, which he delivered from a special podium, and a question-and-answer session.

Agnew "always looked a little uncomfortable," said a regular observer. "He was never a participant. Everybody said and did the right thing, but they were cautious in expressing opinions because they didn't know where he stood on some of the things. In Ford's case that's just not part of the equation."

The meeting took place every Tuesday. It was an important focal point since it was usually the only chance all Republican senators had to meet and discuss the timing of legislation for that week and to discuss strategy and trade opinions. Ford routinely sat at the head table in the large reception room just off the Senate floor. John G. Tower (R Texas), who chaired the group, would go through an agenda and senior senators such as Minority Leader Hugh Scott (R Pa.) and ranking committee members commented on bills. The format was informal and gave everyone who wished to speak a chance to do so. Ford reportedly spoke a little more than the average time taken by senators not at the head table and rarely engaged in long colloquies. His contribution was usually an opinion on a bill or information about House activities.

"My guess is that he takes a supportive role of the administration or says nothing," said a participant. "He always asks for permission to speak and he's recognized in order like the senators. He puts on no airs of any sort. They interrupt him, too."

Ford occasionally did have differences with the administration, generally minor and expressed privately.

Refreshing Change

Many senators found Ford's presence a refreshing change from that of Agnew when he was in office. Agnew acquired a reputation during his first two years in office as

Profiles of the Vice President's Key Staff Members

Vice President Ford's staff as of the end of July 1974 included:

Robert T. Hartmann, 57, chief of staff. A native of Rapid City, S.D., and a 1938 graduate of Stanford University, Hartmann was chief of the *Los Angeles Times* Washington bureau from 1954 to 1963. Associated with Ford since 1966, he became his legislative assistant in 1969.

L. William Seidman, 53, management and budget consultant. Seidman was born in Grand Rapids, Mich., and is a graduate of Dartmouth College, Harvard Law School and the University of Michigan Graduate Business School. He took a leave of absence from Seidman and Seidman, an international accounting firm in which he was managing partner, to join the Ford staff Feb. 1, 1974.

John O. Marsh Jr., 47, assistant for defense and international affairs. Born in Winchester, Va., Marsh is a graduate of Washington and Lee University Law School. He served in the House as a Democrat from 1962 to 1970 and in 1973 was named by Nixon to be assistant secretary of defense for legislative affairs. He joined Ford on Jan. 29, 1974.

Richard T. Burress, 52, assistant for legislation and domestic affairs. Born in Omaha, Neb., Burress is a graduate of the University of Omaha, the University of Iowa Law School and the New York University Graduate Law School. A Marine veteran and once an FBI agent, Burress served as minority counsel for the House Education and Labor Committee from 1961 to 1963, and had the combined jobs of director of the House Republican Policy Committee, counsel to the House Republican Leadership and House minority sergeant at arms from 1965 to 1969. He was deputy counsel and deputy assistant to Nixon from 1969 to 1971 and served as chairman of the Renegotiation Board from 1971 to 1973.

Walter L. Mote, 50, chief of Ford's Senate office. Born in Plainview, Neb., Mote began his Hill career in 1946 as a Capitol elevator operator while attending George Washington and American Universities. He clerked in the U.S. Tax Court for a brief period before joining the 1952 presidential campaign of Robert A. Taft as director of Taft's Washington headquarters. He became chief clerk and then postmaster of the Senate until 1958, when he became the minority staff member of the Senate Rules Committee. He was appointed to the Senate staff job by Agnew in January 1969, and stayed on with Ford.

Paul A. Miltich, 54, press secretary. Miltich was born in Virginia, Minn. He is a graduate of the University of Minnesota School of Education. After briefly teaching school in St. Paul, Miltich spent 12 years as a reporter and editor for the *Saginaw News*. He became Washington correspondent for the Booth newspapers in 1957 and joined the Ford congressional staff as press secretary in 1966.

William E. Casselman II, 32, legal counsel. A native of Washington, Pa., brought up in Deerfield, Ill., Casselman was graduated from Claremont (Calif.) Men's College and George Washington University Law School. He was a legislative assistant to Rep. Robert McClory (R Ill.) from 1965 to 1969 and was an advance man in Nixon's 1968 campaign. He then served on the White House legislative staff during the first part of the first Nixon administration. He was named the youngest general counsel of the General Services Administration in June 1971, and joined the Ford staff directly from that job.

Gwen Anderson, 44, political counsultant. Mrs. Anderson was born in Kennewick, Wash., and was a former Republican Natiional Committeewoman from the state. She is Ford's official liaison with the Republican Party and other non-governmental groups.

Warren Rustand, 31, scheduling officer. Rustand, a native of Fergus Falls, Minn., is a graduate of the University of Arizona, where he also received a master's degree in education. He was a faculty member at the university from 1965 to 1968 and played professional basketball. From 1969 until 1973 he was president and board chairman of a Tuscon, Ariz., investment analysis firm. He came to Washington in the fall of 1973 as a White House fellow and was assigned to the Commerce Department until joining the Ford staff Dec. 18, 1973.

Milton Friedman, 50, principal speechwriter. Born in Portsmouth, Va., Friedman attended the College of William and Mary and George Washington University. He was a reporter for the Norfolk *Virginian-Pilot* and the Wisconsin *State Journal* before joining the Jewish Telegraphic Agency. He was Washington bureau chief and a traveling correspondent before being named in 1970 as director of special projects for the National Republican Congressional Committee, where he wrote speeches and developed issues for Republicans. He served as press secretary for Sen. Jacob K. Javits (R N.Y.) during 1972 and joined the Ford staff Feb. 1, 1974.

Philip W. Buchen, 58, executive director of the Domestic Council Committee on the Right of Privacy. Buchen, a resident of Grand Rapids, Mich., is a graduate of the University of Michigan and the University of Michigan Law School. He is a former law partner of the Vice President. Buchen, who served on the board of directors of the COMSAT Corporation since 1969, joined the staff March 15, 1974.

John W. (Bill) Roberts, 55, deputy press secretary. Born in Ft. Atkinson, Wis., Roberts is a graduate of Ripon College. He was a radio and television newsman in Cedar Rapids, and Davenport, Iowa, from 1948 to 1958, when he became Washington bureau chief of radio and television stations owned by Time, Inc. He became bureau chief for McGraw-Hill television stations in 1972 and joined Ford's staff Dec. 11, 1973.

a heavy-handed lobbyist who lacked appreciation for congressional traditions.

This reputation—which may have been overblown—grew principally from a 1970 incident on the Senate floor during debate over the administration's Safeguard (ABM) missile system proposal. A few minutes before debate ended, Agnew walked over to Sen. Len B. Jordan (R Idaho) and asked how he planned to vote. Jordan, then 71 years old, became irate and told Agnew, according to one version, "Don't twist my arm."

"I'm not trying to," Agnew said, startled. "I'm just curious as to how you're going to vote on this."

"Well, you'll find out when I vote," Jordan replied angrily.

Agnew's interest in Congress dropped off sharply thereafter. "He was not a legislative creature to begin with, and Ford is," said Mote, who served Agnew in the Senate at the time of the incident and who was retained by Ford. "That just frightened him and he ran the other way."

"That is something Jerry would never get himself into," a veteran Republican congressional aide said of the Jordan story. "One of the first things you learn when you come here is that there is indeed a certain amount of nose-counting, but don't ever get caught doing it unless some senator told you to, and don't ever be caught trying to tell a senator how he ought to be voting."

Another possible explanation for Ford's low Capitol Hill profile was the tightrope he walked in trying not to offend the White House's normal channels to Republican legislators: the Republican leadership. If Ford had been more aggressive in trying to push legislation, according to this view, he risked collision with the leadership structure, headed by Scott in the Senate and John J. Rhodes (R Ariz.) in the House. Ford avoided this pitfall successfully, although some observers detected traces of resentment below the Scott-Rhodes level.

Routine

Ford spent about a third of his week on Capitol Hill, according to Paul Miltich, his press secretary. Another third was spent at the White House and his Executive Office Building suite, and another on speaking tours.

On the day he was in Washington, he arrived at his office about 7:45 a.m. and normally did not leave until 7 p.m. He had no typical day, varying his schedule to fit the day's events. Ford regularly attended meetings of the Cabinet. He received the same daily intelligence briefing as Nixon and periodically Secretary of State Henry A. Kissinger briefed him on foreign affairs. Every Wednesday afternoon Timmons and Kenneth R. Cole Jr., director of the Domestic Council, briefed Ford in his EOB office on legislation.

Ford said he was satisfied with his access to Nixon while he was vice president and that he had met with the President whenever Ford felt the need.

Ford's access to Nixon and to White House officials added to his prestige in Congress. Many members believed Ford offered a pipeline to the top echelon of the administration, including the powerful Office of Management and Budget. They often asked him to convey messages when they felt they were not being heard through normal liaison channels.

The Vice President went to great lengths to remain available to members. Mote and others on Ford's staff were

under standing instructions to usher in any member who wanted to see Ford, regardless of his schedule.

Staff

The Ford staff took a beating in the press over its age and quality. One Republican leader described Ford's senior staff—whose average age was 52—as a "geriatrics ward."

"The honeymoon is over," Miltich sighed to a reporter after reading a July 10, 1974, story in the *Wall Street Journal* describing Ford's staff as "not especially noted for brilliance." The story also depicted Ford's chief of staff, Robert T. Hartmann, as "so abrasive that colleagues find it takes considerable skill just to get along with him," and Miltich himself as "pleasant but inept."

"The Vice President's feeling is that his is an operational staff, not a policy formulation staff," said Miltich. "He's not running for President and he's not running the White House, and he thinks it's an excellent staff as far as an operational staff is concerned."

"I think the staff would hold up against anybody's professional staff on Capitol Hill rather well," said Mote. "We have no self-starters, people out to make ripples for themselves. It's a legislatively oriented staff and it's quite politically oriented. I think that was done in part deliberately."

Ford's defenders noted that the Vice President had access to White House policy-makers for advice, and that if he became president he could quickly assemble his own brain trust. "Traditionally the Vice President has never had a large staff and it has never had much of a chance to show a lot of glitter and brilliance," said a source close to the staff. "What they are doing involves mostly scheduling and speechifying."

Mote attended George Washington and American Universities while working on Capitol Hill, but did not graduate from either. "I went to school to get an education, not a degree," he said. Milton Friedman, 50, Ford's principal speechwriter, attended the College of William and Mary and George Washington University.

Friction

Ford's two administrative chiefs were Hartmann, 57, who had been with Ford since 1965, when he became the House minority leader, and L. William Seidman, 53, a millionaire accountant and lawyer from Ford's home town of Grand Rapids.

Aides denied recurring reports of rifts on the staff, particularly between Seidman and Hartmann, other than what one called "the normal frictions of an expanding office, which are all minor." However, other sources said that soon after his arrival Seidman was assigned the job of examining the management structure of the Ford office. He drew up a plan for streamlining the staff and delegating some of Hartmann's responsibilities to others. Hartmann "was probably rather brutal in saying no" to the plan, said one knowledgeable observer. "It takes a little practice to find out that trees don't always bend in government the way they do outside."

After a period of about a month, during which time tensions rose within the staff, Ford decided on a compromise. On June 1, he issued a new organizational chart and a six-page memo explaining the new order, which left Hartmann in firm control of the office but widened staff access to Ford—one of Seidman's main objectives. ∎

FORD'S POLITICAL RECORD: CONSISTENT CONSERVATISM

President Gerald R. Ford's record during 25 years in the House made it unlikely that he would strike out in major new directions from Nixon administration policies.

Ford favored a strong defense establishment and advocated limiting federal involvement to solve social issues. He was among the first to propose revenue sharing with the states, a key element of Nixon's "new federalism."

Ford's voting record in Congress was one of close agreement with Nixon. In 1973, for example, Ford supported the President on 80 per cent of the House votes on which Nixon had taken a position. That put Ford ahead of all but one of his colleagues. *(Box, p. 30)*

He voted to sustain every Nixon veto the House considered in 1973. About the only serious difference came on mass transit legislation. Ford, a native of automobile-dependent Michigan, opposed diverting highway trust fund money for mass transit use, a proposal supported by Nixon. *(Key votes, p. 33)*

Ford's ties to Nixon did not simply reflect personal loyalty. They bespoke a conservative kinship that had existed for nearly 30 years, from the one term they served together in the House in the 1940s, through Nixon's vice presidency and Ford's elevation as House minority leader in 1965, and into Ford's last months as faithful Vice President under a chief executive discredited by scandal.

Ford sought to discourage any efforts to label him as a conservative ideologue. "I am a moderate on domestic issues," he told a congressional committee looking into his confirmation, "a conservative in fiscal affairs and a dyed-in-the-wool internationalist."

Many liberals, however, insisted he was no moderate at all.

"They'll rue the day," complained Rep. Don Edwards (D Calif.) after the choice was made. "He's more conservative than Nixon, and his judgment's not as good." *(Confirmation, p. 39)*

Government's Role. Ford's judgment was not a matter of public record. But his conservatism was, and it showed up in the thousands of votes he had taken since he arrived in the House in 1949. The new President shared his predecessor's skepticism about expanding the role of the federal government, his reluctance to make substantial reductions in the defense budget and his hostility toward militant expressions of social protest.

In 1967, Ford attacked the philosophy of "everything can be cured through federal dictation and federal funds, doled out through grants-in-aid which keep Washington as the manipulator of all the strings."

During the 1950s and 1960s, Ford voted against most legislation expanding the federal role in solving modern social welfare programs. He opposed federal aid to education in the early 1960s, voted against creation of the Office of Economic Opportunity and against Medicare and opposed federal help for state water pollution programs in 1956 and 1960.

Tax Sharing. By the last years of the Johnson administration, Ford was publicly advocating revenue sharing as an alternative to continued federal government expansion. "Tax sharing," he said in 1967, "would restore the needed vitality and diversity to our federal system... Republicans have faith in the constitutional concept of federalism, which requires strong and vigorous state as well as federal action on a variety of national problems."

Ford sought to limit the federal government in the protection of civil rights. He voted for some civil rights bills, such as the Civil Rights Act of 1964 and the Voting Rights Act of 1965. But he backed weaker substitutes for these bills before their passage, and he endorsed the Nixon administration's efforts to water down the Voting Rights Act in 1969. He opposed federal open housing legislation in 1966 but supported it in 1968, when it passed Congress and became law.

Ford's suspicious attitude toward federal spending did not extend to spending for national defense. A member of the Defense Appropriations Subcommittee for many years before his election as Republican leader, Ford consistently fought in favor of giving the Defense Department the resources it wanted.

In 1952, Ford was one of only 11 Republicans to vote against an amendment limiting defense spending to $46-billion; he was still voting against similar amendments during his last days in the House in 1973.

Hawk on Vietnam. Another point consistently at issue between Ford and liberals was the Vietnam war. He was critical of President Johnson for not pursuing the war more vigorously, and in 1967 he gave a speech on the House floor entitled, "Why are we pulling our best punches in Vietnam?"

Ford supported Nixon's policy of gradual Vietnamization and endorsed the 1973 peace treaty. Through the end of his House career, he continued to oppose any legislation to end the war faster than Nixon wanted to move. This included amendments Ford voted against to end U.S. bombing of Cambodia in the summer of 1973.

On matters of social protest, Ford took a consistently conservative position. Even while criticizing the Johnson Vietnam policy, he lashed out at those who opposed the war from the left. "Today," he said in 1965, "our so-called 'teach-ins' and 'peace' demonstrations call for 'peace at any price'—while the seeds of Communist atrocity take root. And yet the appeasers speak of morality."

Amnesty Opposition. He took a hard line on the question of amnesty. "Unconditional blanket amnesty to anyone who illegally evaded or fled military service is wrong," Ford insisted in a speech Aug. 5, 1974.

Ford supported a 1968 amendment that would have required colleges to cut off federal aid to students who participated in campus disruptions. He endorsed the Nixon administration's handling of the 1971 "May

Day" war protest, in which police used mass arrests to clear 12,000 persons off the street on the scheduled day of demonstrations.

Douglas Impeachment. Ford quickly gained a reputation among liberals as being a hard-liner on civil liberties because of his 1970 attack on Supreme Court Justice William O. Douglas. Shortly after Douglas wrote a book, *Points of Rebellion,* which defended civil disobedience, Ford called the book "a fuzzy harangue evidently intended to give historic legitimacy to the militant-hippie-yippie movement."

Combining his complaints against the book with charges that Douglas maintained improper financial connections with a private foundation, Ford urged that Douglas be impeached. Ford denied that a crime was required for impeachment. "An impeachable offense," he said, "is whatever the House of Representatives considers it to be at a given moment in history."

Ford's House Reputation

To his colleagues in Congress, Ford built a reputation for being solid, dependable and loyal—a man more comfortable carrying out the programs of others than in initiating things on his own.

Rugged, even tough-looking in appearance, Ford's performance as House minority leader revealed a much more gentle nature than his background as a college football lineman would suggest. "He doesn't twist arms," Rep. Edward J. Derwinski (R Ill.) told Congressional Quarterly at the time of Ford's vice presidential nomination in October 1973. "He looks at you with a sad look in his eye, as if to say, 'Pal, I need you.' Sometimes you go along just because it's to help an old pal.

"He's an open tactician," Derwinski added. "He doesn't look for clever ways to sneak in behind you. He does the obvious, which is usually common sense. He doesn't try to be gimmicky."

A Democratic assessment of Ford came from Sen. William Proxmire of Wisconsin, who was on the freshman boxing and football teams at Yale while Ford, a law student, was a part-time boxing and football coach in the 1930s. "In many ways (Ford) is the same kind of man now that he was then...solid and square," Proxmire told the Senate Oct. 13, the day after Nixon's announcement. "He is not a man of imagination and humor."

Presidential Promise. Speculation about Ford's political future began as soon as he was nominated. He met it with an immediate disclaimer. "I have no intention of being a candidate for any political office, president or vice president," he told reporters Oct. 13, 1973. But he declined to say that he would not change his mind under any conditions whatsoever. Not being clairvoyant, he had no way of knowing that Richard Nixon would not serve out his second term.

When their long-time colleague ascended to the number two job, predictions among members of Congress about his eventual rise to the White House were plentiful. His Republican friends were generally effusive, and even left-handed compliments such as those of Proxmire predicted successes for the man from Michigan.

Ford's Background

Profession: Attorney.
Born: July 14, 1913, Omaha, Neb.
Home: Grand Rapids, Mich.
Religion: Episcopal.
Education: University of Michigan, B. A., 1935; Yale University Law School, LL. B, 1941.
Offices: House of Representatives since 1949.
Military: U.S. Navy in World War II.
Memberships: Interparliamentary Union, U.S.-Canadian Interparliamentary Group, American Legion, VFW, AMVETS, Masons, Elks, Rotary.
Family: Wife, Elizabeth; four children.

Committees: House minority leader, 1965-73; Appropriations Committee, 1951-65; Public Works Committee, 1949-50.

Career Highlights: Ford was a star of the University of Michigan's undefeated, national championship football teams of 1932 and 1933. In 1934, he was voted the Michigan Wolverines' most valuable player. As a law student at Yale, he served as assistant varsity football coach.

In 1949, the year he entered the House, he was selected by the U.S. Junior Chamber of Commerce as one of the country's 10 outstanding young men.

The American Political Science Association gave Ford its distinguished congressional service award in 1961.

In 1963, he was chosen chairman of the House Republican Conference. In 1965, he was elected minority leader, defeating the incumbent, former Rep. Charles A. Halleck (R Ind.). He was permanent chairman of the 1968 and 1972 Republican national conventions.

Ford was appointed by President Johnson in November 1963 to serve on the Warren Commission to investigate the assassination of President Kennedy. Ford collaborated with John R. Stiles in 1965 to write a book, *Portrait of an Assassin,* about his findings while on the commission.

"He is a man that the country may be looking for," said Proxmire. "As I have known him, he has always appeared to be a man of integrity and character. In spite of his present disclaimers, he may be the most likely Republican nominee for President in 1976. He could be a tough, strong candidate...because he has the kind of wholesome sincerity, the kind of loyal consistency that many voters may be looking for. Of course, I think he has been consistently wrong on almost every issue...(but)...he may come on like a tiger because of what the public perceives of his straightforward, reliable, direct character."

There was relatively little announced opposition to Ford's confirmation, although many members remained uncommitted just after his nomination. Some Democrats argued that Ford should disavow Nixon's refusal to release Watergate tapes.

Sen. Edward M. Kennedy (D Mass.) said Oct. 18 that if Ford did not acknowledge the President's obligation to comply with a future Supreme Court decision on the tapes, "then Congress has the right and duty to refuse his confirmation."

Interest Group Ratings of Ford

Americans for Democratic Action (ADA)— ADA ratings are based on the number of times a representative voted, was paired for or announced for the ADA position on selected issues.

National Farmers Union (NFU)—NFU ratings are based on the number of times a representative voted, was paired for or announced for the NFU position.

AFL-CIO Committee on Political Education (COPE)—COPE ratings reflect the percentage of the times a representative voted in accordance with or was paired in favor of the COPE position.

Americans for Constitutional Action (ACA)— ACA ratings record the percentage of the times a representative voted in accordance with the ACA position.

Following are Ford's ratings since Congressional Quarterly began publishing them in 1960:

	ADA[1]	ACA	COPE[3]	NFU[3]
1973	0	83	22	15
1972	6	68	11	20
1971	8	79	25	27
1970	12[4]	68	0	54
1969	7	53	33	40
1968	17	74	50	56
1967	13	85	8	11
1966	0	74	0[2]	22
1965	11	81	0[2]	19
1964	15	79	9[2]	21[2]
1963	0	89	9[2]	21[2]
1962	13	82[2]	0[2]	10[2]
1961	10	82[2]	0[2]	10[2]
1960	33	60	10[2]	20[2]
1959	22	88[5]	10[2]	20[2]

1 Failure to vote lowers score.
2 Scores listed twice indicate rating compiled for entire Congress.
3 Percentages compiled by CQ from information provided by groups.
4 ADA score includes some votes from December 1969.
5 ACA score covers years 1957, 1958, 1959.

Mediocrity Issue. Democratic opposition to Ford during his consideration for the vice presidency generally focused on assessment—sometimes echoed anonymously by Republicans—that he was a man of limited depth and mediocre capability.

Rep. Michael J. Harrington (D Mass.), first member of Congress to announce opposition to the Ford nomination, said he based his stand on "my observation of Mr. Ford's limited intellectual qualities, his total and active support of the Nixon foreign policy on the Vietnam war; his staunch defense of the President's domestic program ...and his blanket defense—regardless of merit—of administration officials involved in the Watergate inquiry.

"In all of these areas, Mr. Ford has shown that he is not the kind of person who should serve as vice president," Harrington said in an Oct. 15, 1973, statement. He said Nixon "has preferred to surround himself with a collection of people best noted for their mediocrity."

This assessment of Ford was sharply disputed by former Rep. James Harvey (R Mich. 1961-74), who said anybody who underestimated Ford's intelligence was making a mistake. "Jerry Ford is a workhorse," Harvey told Congressional Quarterly in an interview Oct. 17, 1973. "There are better innovators in the House; he's not an innovator in the sense that Bradford Morse (R Mass. 1961-72) or Barber Conable (R N.Y.) or John Erlenborn (R Ill.) have been. But anybody who underestimates Jerry Ford's thinking power is making a grave error.

"I grant that he's not as articulate as John Anderson (R Ill.) or the late Hale Boggs (D La.)," Harvey continued. "But he gets out there on the floor and projects a sincerity those others don't have. He projects an awful lot of common sense."

Rep. John J. Rhodes (R Ariz.), who replaced Ford as minority leader, said Ford, who won the post in 1965, gradually developed into an excellent leader, able through his likable personality and close relations with all Republicans to establish a working party unity.

"He's become an effective speaker," said Derwinski. "The first term he left something to be desired as a debater and tactician."

Praise of Ford. Senate Minority Leader Hugh Scott (Pa.) called Ford's selection "a happy appointment" which met with widespread approval in Congress. "It is a very fortuitous selection, because...it would help toward the healing process and the recognition of the necessity for continued and constructive legislative progress."

Sen. Robert P. Griffin (Mich.), assistant minority leader, said Ford's nomination would "help greatly to heal some of the divisions that have developed and grown too wide as between the executive and legislative branches" and "do much to restore confidence in government at this time in our history when that is sorely needed." He said Ford's record was an "open book" and predicted quick confirmation.

Sen. Charles McC. Mathias Jr. (R Md.) said Ford "has a positive record on legislative experience and political success."

On the Democratic side of the Senate aisle, Claiborne Pell (R.I.) said he was disappointed that Nixon had omitted character, honesty and integrity from his criteria for vice president, but added: "I believe that Mr. Ford has these qualities, and that he will be approved."

Senate Majority Leader Mike Mansfield (D Mont.) said, "Gerald Ford is the kind of man whom one would expect the President to nominate—an activist, not a caretaker; a loyal Republican; a man loyal to the President, but a man who is understanding of the attitude and the factors which motivate the other side as well."

Political Career

Elected to Congress in 1949, Ford first won national attention in 1963, when he was elected chairman of the House Republican Conference. That election was a victory for "young Turks" of Republican ranks in the House, who ousted 67-year-old Charles B. Hoeven (R Iowa 1943-65) from the post.

Ford's Ratings in Congressional Quarterly Vote Studies

Listed below are the results of Congressional Quarterly voting studies on the record of Gerald R. Ford during his years in the House. The studies are defined as follows:

Voting participation—Percentage of recorded votes on which Ford voted "yea" or "nay."

Presidential support—Percentage of presidential-issue recorded votes on which Ford voted "yea" or "nay" in agreement with the President's position. These votes are on specific legislative requests or stands by the President. Failures to vote lower both support and opposition scores.

Presidential opposition—Percentage of presidential-issue votes on which Ford voted "yea" or "nay" in disagreement with the President's position. Failures to vote lower both support and opposition scores.

Conservative coalition support—Percentage of conservative coalition recorded votes on which Ford voted "yea" or "nay" in agreement with the position of the conservative coalition. (The conservative coalition occurs when a majority of voting southern Democrats and a majority of voting Republicans oppose the position of the majority of voting nothern Democrats.)

Conservative coalition opposition—Percentage of conservative coalition votes on which Ford voted "yea" or "nay" in disagreement with the position of the conservative coalition.

Party unity—Percentage of recorded votes on which Ford voted "yea" or "nay" in agreement with a majority of his party. (Party unity votes are those on which a majority of voting Democrats opposed a majority of voting Republicans.) Failures to vote lower both party unity and party opposition scores.

Party opposition—Percentage of party unity votes on which Ford voted "yea" or "nay" in disagreement with a majority of his party.

Bipartisan support—Percentage of bipartisan recorded votes on which Ford voted "yea" or "nay" in agreement with majorities of voting Democrats and voting Republicans. Failures to vote lower both support and opposition scores.

Bipartisan opposition—Percentage of bipartisan votes on which Ford voted "yea" or "nay" in disagreement with majorities of voting Democrats and voting Republicans.

Year	Voting Participation[1]	Presidential		Conservative Coalition[3]		Party Voting[1]		Bipartisan Voting[1]	
		Support	Opposition[2]	Support	Opposition	Party Unity	Party Opposition	Bipartisan Support	Bipartisan Opposition
1973	89%	80%	16%	75%	13%	75%	17%	77%	9%
1972	84	70	8	73	17	73	16	75	7
1971	87	89	7	87	8	81	12	83	2
1970	90	89	8	64	18	69	26	85	3
1969	92	76	18	61	34	57	35	85	7
1968	90	63	28	63	25	66	24	82	7
1967	85	50	41	70	17	74	18	74	7
1966	81	40	46	70	16	69	10	74	9
1965	86	46	46	73	18	70	16	78	7
1964	88	38	56	67	33	84	10	71	12
1963	84	35	54	67	20	69	17	72	10
1962	90	52	40	37	44	72	21	78	8
1961	82	42	51	83	4	76	9	71	8
1960	97	84	12	84	16	84	14	84	11
1959	75	63	13	100	0	77	0	64	8
1958	99	76	24			70	27	91	9
1957	98	73	23			83	17	83	12
1956	100	94	6			84	16	90	10
1955	97	88	12			68	32	82	13
1954	96	89	11						
1953	99	94	6						

1 Study began earlier but was compiled on a different basis.
2 Study began in 1953.
3 Study began in 1959.

Ford's election was engineered by three representatives who later went widely separate ways: Melvin R. Laird (Wis. 1953-69), who became secretary of defense and, later, a counselor to Nixon; Charles E. Goodell (N.Y. 1959-68), named a senator in 1968 but defeated in an election bid in 1970, partly because of White House opposition, and Sen. Griffin of Michigan.

In 1965, in another revolt against established House leadership, Ford was elected House minority leader, ousting Charles A. Halleck (Ind. 1935-69). Again, Ford's election was engineered by Laird, Goodell and Griffin. The secret ballot vote was close: 73 to 67.

"The southerners really loved Charlie Halleck," Rep. Rhodes recalled. "When Jerry came in, there was

Ford's 1972 Contributions

According to an analysis by Common Cause, committees backing Rep. Gerald R. Ford's re-election in 1972 raised a total of $98,576 in contributions of more than $100 and spent $87,345 from April 25, 1972, through Jan. 22, 1973. The committee reported receiving no loans of more than $100.

Over $24,000 of the total amount raised for the Michigan Republican came from individuals, with political party and special-interest groups contributing about $59,000. Donations from Republican campaign committees totaled $3,350.

The largest contribution from a special-interest organization was $5,000 from a group representing the Marine Engineers' Beneficial Association, AFL-CIO. Another campaign committee associated with the Marine Engineers donated $2,500.

Other contributions from special-interest groups listed by Common Cause included $2,500 from the National Bankers' Group, $2,000 from the International Brotherhood of Teamsters and $1,000 from the National Restaurant Association.

Contributions from individuals included $2,500 from Richard Scaife, heir to the Mellon oil and banking fortune. Twenty-two employees of General Dynamics outside Michigan made small donations totaling $1,130.

The Ford committees gave to other congressional candidates $9,450 of the $87,345 they reported spending, according to the analysis. The largest amount—$3,000—went to Sen. Robert P. Griffin (R Mich.), who won re-election by a small margin.

a kind of stand-offish attitude. For the first few years, he (Ford) didn't have too kindly an attitude toward them. But in recent years, there have been closer relations on some issues."

"I had many sharp differences of opinion with him when he first became minority leader," Harvey said. "In recent years, he has shown more of a mellowness in accepting differences of opinion within the party. Now he knows some people have to vote differently."

The growth of Ford's tolerance for differing opinions also was reflected by the comment of Speaker Carl Albert (D Okla.) who had enjoyed a close personal relationship with Ford. "I think I was the first in Congress to tell the President that Jerry would be the easiest candidate (for vice president) to sell to the House," he said. "He's a very fine man to work with. I think he earned this."

Albert held the job to which, according to many accounts, Ford had long aspired. But Ford had been mentioned in years past as a possible vice presidential candidate. His name was suggested in 1960, for example, when Nixon ran the first time and settled on Henry Cabot Lodge as his running mate.

Ford remained an administration loyalist throughout his House service. In July 1971, when Rep. William (Bill) Clay (D Mo.) bitterly attacked Spiro T. Agnew for remarks the then Vice President had made in Africa, Ford rose to Agnew's defense. Clay said Agnew was "seriously ill" and an "intellectual misfit" whose "tirade against black leadership is just part of a game played by him—called mental masturbation. Apparently Mr. Agnew is an intellectual sadist who experiences intellectual orgasms by attacking, humiliating and kicking the oppressed."

Ford responded by charging that Clay "used language in reference to a high official in the U.S. government that I have never seen used or heard used in this chamber." He called Clay's speech "most shocking" and "degrading to the House." And he said, "It seems to me that we in this body, regardless of our political affiliation, should conduct ourselves with a certain degree of common decency."

During a controversy over presidential impoundment of appropriated funds, Ford emerged from a White House meeting in March 1973 and charged the Democrats with a "lust for spending."

Nixon made a television speech April 30, 1973, in which he announced the resignation of four key men in his administration and pledged that "justice will be pursued fairly, fully and impartially." He gave Elliot L. Richardson, attorney general-designate in the wake of Attorney General Richard G. Kleindienst's resignation, authority to appoint an outside investigator of Watergate.

Ford responded enthusiastically to Nixon's speech. He said the President "fully deserves the trust and confidence of the American people.... I have the greatest confidence in the President and am absolutely positive he had nothing to do with this mess."

Ford was permanent chairman of the Republican national conventions of both 1968 and 1972.

Campaign Contributions

After his nomination as Vice President, Ford was quizzed by reporters about the way campaign contributions were handled in his 1970 and 1972 House re-election campaigns.

Ford told reporters he had nothing to hide and said he hoped congressional hearings on his confirmation would be "the most open and in depth" ever held by Congress.

1970 Campaign. In his 1970 race, Ford filed what could be interpreted to be an inaccurate sworn statement failing to list $11,500 in campaign contributions by Wall Street money men, bankers, an oil man, physicians and a labor union.

Ford told newsmen that although checks from these sources were made out to him, he had endorsed them over to the Republican Congressional Campaign Committee for use by other candidates. However, another Republican fund sent $12,233 into Ford's district to pay some of his campaign advertising and printing bills.

The Michigan representative denied that this exchange of funds was planned or that the actions had been used to "launder" the contributions. "There was absolutely no connection between the two," he told *The Washington Post.*

Since Ford had served as his own treasurer during the campaign and had filed sworn statements with the House that failed to list the contributions, the issue could have been important during his confirmation hearings. But the question was passed over.

Ford's Election Results: Big Victories Since 1948

The table below shows the results of Ford's 13 general election races for the House and the results of the 1948 Republican primary, the only one in which he was opposed and in which he defeated incumbent Bartel J. Jonkman (1940-49). In all the contests, the votes of minor-party candidates have been omitted.

1972

Ford (R)	118,027	61.1%
Jean McKee (D)	72,782	37.7%
	Plurality: 45,245	

1970

Ford (R)	88,208	61.4%
Jean McKee (D)	55,337	38.5%
	Plurality: 32,871	

1968

Ford (R)	105,085	62.7%
Laurence E. Howard (D)	62,219	37.2%
	Plurality: 42,866	

1966

Ford (R)	88,108	68.5%
James M. Catchick (D)	40,435	31.5%
	Plurality: 47,673	

1964

Ford (R)	101,810	61.2%
William G. Reamon (D)	64,488	38.8%
	Plurality: 37,322	

1962

Ford (R)	110,043	67.0%
William G. Reamon (D)	54,112	33.0%
	Plurality: 55,931	

1960

Ford (R)	131,461	66.8%
William G. Reamon (D)	65,064	33.1%
	Plurality: 66,397	

1958

Ford (R)	88,156	63.6%
R. F. Vander Veen (D)	50,203	36.2%
	Plurality: 37,953	

1956

Ford (R)	120,349	67.1%
George E. Clay (D)	58,899	32.9%
	Plurality: 61,450	

1954

Ford (R)	81,702	63.3%
R. S. McAllister (D)	47,453	36.7%
	Plurality: 34,249	

1952

Ford (R)	109,807	66.3%
Vincent E. O'Neill (D)	55,147	33.3%
	Plurality: 54,660	

1950

Ford (R)	72,829	66.7%
J. H. McLaughlin (D)	35,927	32.9%
	Plurality: 36,902	

1948

Primary		
Ford	23,632	62.2%
Bartel J. Jonkman	14,341	37.8%
	Plurality: 9,291	
General		
Ford (R)	74,191	60.5%
Fred J. Barr (D)	46,972	38.3%
	Plurality: 27,219	

Contributions received by Ford and endorsed over to the congressional campaign committee included these: from the Securities Industry Campaign Committee, $5,000; oil tycoon John M. Shaheen, $3,000; the Bankers Political Action Committee, $2,000; the Boilermakers-Blacksmiths union of Kansas City, Kan., $1,000, and a Michigan physicians' fund, $500.

1972 Campaign. Ford's 1972 campaign was financed in large part by a secret fund-raising setup which concealed the names of the donors. The arrangement was legal. The money was funneled through a loophole—since plugged—in federal campaign financing laws which did not require full public reports by fundraising groups in the District of Columbia.

A total of $38,216—more than one-third of what Ford spent in the 1972 campaign—was handled through such a committee: the Committee to Re-elect Jerry Ford, in Washington. "I don't know who contributed to the committee, and I think it's better that I don't know," Ford told *The Washington Star-News.*

Ford's Record on Key Issues Votes in The House, 1949-1973

Agriculture

1953. Soil Conservation (HR 5227). Amendment to fiscal 1954 agriculture appropriations bill reducing funds for the soil conservation program from $195-million to $140-million. Rejected 196-201 (R 152-54; D 44-146), May 20. Ford VOTED FOR.

1955. Price Supports (HR 12). Bill replacing flexible price supports of 75 to 90 per cent of parity with rigid supports at 90 per cent of parity for five basic farm crops. Passed 206-201 (R 21-172; D 185-29), May 5. Ford VOTED AGAINST.

1958. Price Supports (S J Res 162). Bill preventing reductions in price supports and acreage allotments for all farm commodities below 1957 levels. Passed 211-172 (R 44-41; D 167-31), March 20. Ford VOTED AGAINST.

1959. REA Loans (S 144). Bill transferring from the secretary of agriculture to the administrator of the Rural Electrification Administration (REA) authority to approve or disapprove REA loans. Failed to pass over veto 280-146 (R 6-142; D 274-4), April 30. Ford VOTED AGAINST.

1962. Farm Bill (HR 12391). Conference report on bill authorizing one-year programs to reduce corn, other feed grain and wheat surpluses and to establish a supply management program for wheat. Adopted 202-197 (R 2-160; D 200-37), Sept. 20. Ford VOTED AGAINST.

1963. Cotton Subsidy (HR 6196). Bill authorizing subsidy program for domestic cotton mills in order to eliminate the competitive inequity between raw cotton prices on the world market and those on the domestic market. Passed 216-182 (R 34-134; D 182-48), Dec. 4. Ford VOTED AGAINST.

1970. Farm Bill (HR 18546). Bill providing three-year price support program for wool, wheat, feed grains and cotton. Bill also provided for a dairy program and limited subsidy payments to $55,000 per crop. Passed 212-171: R 86-88; D 126-85), Aug. 5. Ford VOTED FOR.

1973. Emergency Loans (HR 1975). Amendment to emergency farm loan bill allowing eligible farmers in 555 counties designated by the secretary of agriculture to apply for emergency disaster loans. Adopted 196-190 (R 19-139; D 177-21), Feb. 22. Ford VOTED AGAINST.

1973. Price Supports (HR 8619). Amendment to fiscal 1974 agricultural appropriations bill reducing 1974 price support ceilings from $55,000 per crop to $20,000 per person. Adopted 195-157 (R 109-50; D 86-107), June 15. Ford VOTED AGAINST.

Civil Rights, States' Rights

1949. Poll Tax (HR 3199). Bill outlawing payment of a poll tax as a prerequisite for voting in federal elections. Passed 273-116 (R 121-24; D 151-92), July 26. Ford VOTED FOR.

1956. School Desegregation (HR 7535). Amendment to a school construction aid bill prohibiting allotment of funds to states failing to comply with the 1954 Supreme Court decision on school desegregation. Adopted 225-192 (R 148-46; D 77-146), July 5. Ford VOTED FOR.

1957. Civil Rights Act (HR 6127). Amendment providing for jury trials in any criminal contempt action arising under the legislation. Rejected 158-251 (R 45-139; D 113-112), June 18. Ford VOTED AGAINST.

1959. Pre-emption Doctrine (HR 3). Bill permitting federal courts to strike down state laws under the federal pre-emption doctrine only if Congress specified its intention to pre-empt the field of legislation involved or if a state and a federal law were in irreconcilable conflict, and permitting state enforcement of laws barring subversive activities against the federal government. Passed 225-192 (R 114-30; D 111-162), June 24. Ford VOTED FOR.

1960. Civil Rights Act (HR 8601). Amendment authorizing court-appointed referees to help Negroes register and vote where a "pattern or practice" of discrimination existed. Adopted 295-124 (R 123-24; D 172-100), March 23. Ford VOTED FOR.

1964. Civil Rights Act (HR 7152). Bill enforcing the right to vote; preventing discrimination in access to public accommodations and facilities; expediting school desegregation. Passed 290-130 (R 138-34; D 152-96), Feb. 10. Ford VOTED FOR.

1965. Voting Rights (HR 6400). Bill suspending the use of literacy tests in certain states and areas; authorizing appointment of federal voting examiners to order the registration of Negroes in states and voting districts whose voter activity had fallen below certain specified levels, and imposing a ban on the use of poll taxes in any election. Passed 333-85 (R 112-24; D 221-61), July 9. Ford VOTED FOR.

1966. Civil Rights Act (HR 14765). Amendment deleting the open housing sections of the bill. Rejected 190-222 (R 86-50; D 104-172), Aug. 9. Ford VOTED FOR.

1968. Open Housing (H Res 1100, HR 2516). Resolution agreeing to Senate version of the bill which prohibited discrimination in the sale or rental of housing. Adopted 250-172 (R 100-84; D 150-88), April 10. Ford VOTED FOR.

1969. Voting Rights (HR 4249). Amendment extending nationwide the provisions of the 1965 Voting Rights Act in place of the committee bill extending the law as enacted, which covered certain states and voting districts. Adopted 208-204 (R 129-49; D 79-155), Dec. 11. Ford VOTED FOR.

1970. School Desegregation (HR 16916). Vote on motion designed to retain provisions of the Office of Education appropriations bill prohibiting use of funds to force busing or closing of schools, and providing for freedom of choice plans. Motion agreed to 191-157 (R 107-35; D 84-122), June 30. Ford VOTED FOR.

1971. EEOC Enforcement (HR 1746). Amendment allowing the Equal Employment Opportunity Commission (EEOC) to bring suit against recalcitrant discriminatory employers in federal court, rather than allowing the EEOC to issue cease and desist orders to such employers. Adopted 200-195 (R 131-29; D 69-166), Sept. 16. Ford VOTED FOR.

1971. Busing (HR 7248). Amendment to the Higher Education Act of 1971 postponing effectiveness of any federal court order requiring busing for racial, sexual, religious or socio-economic balance until all appeals—or the time for all appeals—had been exhausted. Adopted 235-125 (R 129-17; D 106-108), Nov. 4. Ford VOTED FOR.

1972. Busing (HR 13915). Amendment—to a bill prohibiting busing of school children and allowing the reopening of past school desegregation court cases—providing that nothing in the act was intended to be inconsistent with or violate any provision of the Constitution. Rejected 178-197 (R 55-98; D 123-99), Aug. 18. Ford VOTED AGAINST.

Defense

1952. Defense Spending (HR 7391). Amendment to the fiscal 1953 Defense Department appropriations bill limiting military spending to $46-billion. Adopted 220-131 (R 160-11; D 60-120), April 9. Ford VOTED AGAINST.

1969. Draft (HR 14001). Bill amending the Selective Service Act by removing a provision prohibiting the President from instituting a lottery system for induction into the armed forces. Passed 383-12 (R 175-1; D 208-11), Oct. 30. Ford VOTED FOR.

1971. Draft (HR 6531). Amendment providing a one-year extension of the military draft instead of two. Rejected 198-200 (R 65-105; D 133-95), March 31. Ford VOTED AGAINST.

1973. War Powers (H J Res 542). Bill requiring the president to report to Congress within 72 hours any commitment or increasing commitment of U.S. combat troops abroad; requiring the president to terminate any such action within 120 days of his report unless Congress authorized continuation, and allowing Congress to direct the termination of U.S. commitment at any time. Passed 244-170 (R 72-109; D 172-61), July 18. Ford VOTED AGAINST.

1973. War Powers (H J Res 542). Motion override President Nixon's veto of a bill to establish a 60-day limit on a president's power to commit U.S. troops abroad, unless Congress declared war or specifically authorized the action or was unable to meet because of an armed attack on the United States; and to permit Congress to end such a commitment at any time by passing a concurrent resolution not requiring the president's signature. Overridden 284-135 (R 86-103; D 198-32), Nov. 7. Ford VOTED AGAINST.

Education

1956. School Construction (HR 7535). Bill authorizing $1.6-billion over four years to state educational agencies for school construction. Rejected 194-224 (R 75-119; D 119-105), July 5. Ford VOTED AGAINST.

1961. Emergency School Aid (HR 8890). Motion to consider the emergency education act, authorizing $325-million for school construction assistance, continuation of National Defense Education Act loan authorizations and impacted areas school aid. Rejected 170-242 (R 6-160; D 164-82), Aug. 30. Ford VOTED AGAINST.

1962. College Aid (HR 8900). Amendment deleting section of bill authorizing loans and grants to students.

Adopted 214-186 (R 130-30; D 84-156), Sept. 20. Ford VOTED FOR.

1963. Vocational Education (HR 4955). Passage of the bill authorizing a new matching grant program with the states to improve state vocational education programs. Passed 378-21 (R 154-9; D 224-12), Aug. 6. Ford VOTED FOR.

1965. School Aid (HR 2362). Bill providing a three-year program of grants to states for allocation to school districts with large numbers of poor children and providing grants for purchase of library materials. Passed 263-153 (R 35-96; D 228-57), March 26. Ford VOTED AGAINST.

1968. Campus Disorders. (HR 15067). Amendment to a higher education aid bill requiring colleges to deny federal funds to students who participated in serious campus disorders. Adopted 260-146 (R 134-43; D 126-103), July 25. Ford VOTED FOR.

1969. Education Funds (HR 13111). Amendment to appropriations bill for the Departments of Labor and Health, Education and Welfare adding $894.5-million for elementary and secondary education, aid to impacted areas, higher education and vocational education. Adopted 294-119 (R 99-81; D 195-38), July 31. Ford VOTED AGAINST.

1969. School Aid (HR 514). Amendment to the elementary and secondary education act extension bill extending aid for two years and consolidating several programs. Adopted 235-184 (R 175-9; D 60-175), April 23. Ford VOTED FOR.

1971. Higher Education Amendments (HR 7248). Amendment to the bill to strike out a section authorizing general federal aid for institutions of higher education. Rejected 84-310 (R 72-92; D 12-218), Nov. 3. Ford VOTED AGAINST.

1972. Funding (HR 15417). Motion to override a veto of the bill appropriating $4,125,962,000 for education in fiscal 1973. Veto override rejected 203-171 (R 22-129; D 181-42), Aug. 16. Ford VOTED AGAINST.

Foreign Policy

1950. Korean Aid (HR 5330). Bill authorizing $60-million in aid to South Korea. Rejected 191-192 (R 21-130; D 170-61), Jan. 19. Ford VOTED AGAINST.

1951. Trade Act Extension (HR 1612). Amendment directing the Tariff Commission to determine points below which tariffs could not be cut without "peril" to U.S. industries, and to recommend minimum rates to which tarrifs should be raised to protect domestic industry. Adopted 225-168 (R 183-4; D 42-163), Feb. 7. Ford VOTED FOR.

1954. Trade Act Extension (HR 9474). Bill extending for one year the Prsident's authority to enter into reciprocal trade agreements. Passed 281-53 (R 126-39; D 154-14), June 11. Ford VOTED FOR.

1951. Foreign Aid (HR 5113). Amendment cutting $350-million from the fiscal 1952 foreign aid bill. Adopted

186-177 (R 149-14; D 37-162), Aug. 17. Ford VOTED FOR.

1956. Foreign Aid. (HR 12130). Bill appropriating $3.4-billion for foreign aid in fiscal 1957. Passed 284-120 (R 124-70; D 160-50), July 11. Ford VOTED FOR.

1957. Foreign Aid (HR 9302). Amendment restoring $715-million in foreign aid appropriations which had been cut from the bill by the House Appropriations Committee. Rejected 129-254 (R 86-83; D 43-171), Aug. 15. Ford VOTED FOR.

1961. Peace Corps (HR 7500). Bill giving the Peace Corps permanent status and authorizing $40-million for it in fiscal 1962. Passed 288-97 (R 82-68; D 206-29), Sept. 14. Ford PAIRED FOR.

1962. Trade Expansion Act. (HR 11970). Bill authorizing the president to negotiate new tariff cuts and compensate injured industries and workers through financial aid or by raising tariffs. Passed 298-125 (R 80-90; D 218-35), June 28. Ford VOTED FOR.

1962. UN Bonds. (S 2768). Bill authorizing the president to match up to $100-million in purchases of United Nations bonds by other UN members. Passed 257-134 (R 66-88; D 191-46), Sept. 14. Ford VOTED FOR.

1964. Foreign Aid (HR 11812). Amendment cutting funds in the fiscal 1965 foreign aid appropriations bill by $247.8-million. Rejected 198-208 (R 143-23; D 55-185), July 1. Ford VOTED FOR.

1965. Foreign Aid (HR 7750). Amendment to the fiscal 1966 foreign aid authorization reducing funds for development loans by $130,958,000 and stipulating that labor unions participating in Latin American housing projects be "non-Communist-dominated" as well as "free." Rejected 178-219 (R 116-14; D 62-205), May 25. Ford VOTED FOR.

1965. Immigration (HR 2580). Bill amending the immigration laws to eliminate the national origins quota system and to set general priorities for the admission of immigrants to the United States. Passed 318-95 (R 109-25; D 209-70), Aug. 25. Ford VOTED FOR.

1970. Cambodia (HR 15628). Motion designed to prevent inclusion in the Foreign Military Sales Act language which would curb U.S. military operations in Cambodia (Cooper-Church amendment). Agreed to 237-153 (R 138-33; D 99-120), July 9. Ford VOTED FOR.

1972. UN Funds (HR 14989). Amendment restoring $25,103,500 in funds for the United Nations, which was deleted from the fiscal 1973 Department of State appropriations bill by the House Appropriations Committee, and removing a committee provision limiting U.S. contributions to the UN to 25 per cent of their total annual assessment. Rejected 156-202 (R 56-99; D 100-103), May 18. Ford VOTED FOR.

1972. Southeast Asia (HR 16029). Amendment to foreign military aid authorization deleting provision terminating U.S. involvement in the Indochina war by Oct. 1, 1972, subject to release of U.S. prisoners of war, an accounting of men missing in action and a cease-fire to the extent required to protect U.S. withdrawal. Adopted 229-177 (R 149-23; D 80-154), Aug. 10. Ford VOTED FOR.

1973. Cambodia (HR 7447). Amendment to fiscal 1973 supplemental appropriations bill deleting language authorizing the Defense Department to transfer funds from other defense programs for use in Southeast Asia, including the bombing of Cambodia. Adopted 219-188 (R 35-143; D 184-45), May 10. Ford VOTED AGAINST.

1973. Cambodia (HR 7447). Amendment postponing until after Sept. 1, 1973, the prohibition against using any funds in the bill (second supplemental appropriations) or funds in any other previously enacted appropriations bill from being used to carry on military activities in or over Cambodia or Laos. Rejected 204-204 (R 147-37; D 57-167), June 25. Ford VOTED FOR.

1973. Foreign Aid (HR 9360). Bill authorizing $978.9-million in fiscal 1974 for foreign economic assistance, $632-million for Indochina postwar reconstruction, $1.15-billion for foreign military assistance and credit sales, and authorizing $821-million for foreign economic assistance in fiscal 1975. Passed 188-183 (R 69-89; D 119-94), July 26. Ford PAIRED FOR.

Labor, Economic Policy

1952. Steel Strike (HR 8210). Amendment to the Defense Production Act amendments bill requesting the President to invoke the Taft-Hartley Act to enjoin steel workers from striking. Adopted 228-164 (R 146-47; D 82-117), June 26. Ford VOTED FOR.

1959. Labor Regulation (HR 8342). Amendment substituting the Landrum-Griffin bill for the text of an Education and Labor Committee bill. The Landrum-Griffin bill contained curbs on secondary boycotts and organizational and recognition picketing and gave the states power to handle "no man's land" labor disputes. Adopted 229-201 (R 134-17; D 95-184), Aug. 13. Ford VOTED FOR.

1961. Minimum Wage (HR 3935). Amendment to Education and Labor Committee bill reducing from $1.25 to $1.15 an hour the increase in the minimum wage for workers covered by the Fair Labor Standards Act and extending coverage under the act to an additional 1,300,000 workers. Adopted 216-203 (R 142-26; D 74-177), March 24. Ford VOTED FOR.

1962. Manpower Development and Training (HR 8399). Bill authorizing a two-year, $262-million program to train unemployed workers. Passed 354-62 (R 145-22; D 209-40), Feb. 28. Ford VOTED FOR.

1963. Tax Cut (HR 8363). Revenue Act of 1963, lowering personal and corporate income taxes by $11.5-billion. Passed 271-155 (R 48-126; D 223-29), Sept. 25. Ford VOTED AGAINST.

1965. Right-to-Work (HR 77). Bill repealing Section 14 (b) of the Taft-Hartley Act, permitting state right-to-work laws under which the union shop is prohibited. Passed 221-203 (R 21-117; D 200-86), July 28. Ford VOTED AGAINST.

1966. Minimum Wage (HR 13712). Motion designed to delay for one year—until Feb. 1, 1969—the final step of an increase in the minimum wage from $1.25 to $1.60 an hour. Rejected 163-183 (R 101-18; D 62-165), Sept. 7. Ford VOTED FOR.

1968. Tax Surcharge (HR 15414). Conference report on a bill imposing a 10 per cent surcharge on personal and corporate income taxes and imposing a limit on federal spending in fiscal 1969. Adopted 268-150 (R 114-73; D 154-77), June 20. Ford VOTED FOR.

1969. Tax Reform (HR 13270). Bill reducing individual income taxes by an average of 5 per cent, extending the income surtax at 5 per cent through June 30, 1970, repealing the investment tax credit and reducing mineral and oil depletion allowances. Passed 395-30 (R 176-10; D 219-20), Aug. 7. Ford VOTED FOR.

1971. Lockheed Loan (HR 8432). Bill authorizing a federal guarantee of bank loans for failing major businesses (Lockheed Aircraft Corporation). Passed 192-189 (R 90-60; D 102-129), July 30. Ford VOTED FOR.

1972. Revenue Sharing (HR 14370). Bill providing assistance payments totaling $29.6-billion over five years to states and local governments for high-priority expenditures, encouraging states to broaden their tax systems and authorizing federal collection of state personal income taxes. Passed 275-122 (R 122-42; D 153-80), June 22. Ford VOTED FOR.

1973. Wage-Price Controls (HR 6168). Bill extending the president's authority to control wages and prices for one year, to April 30, 1974. Passed 293-114 (R 152-31; D 141-83), April 16. Ford VOTED FOR.

1973. Impoundment Control (HR 8480). Bill setting a $267.1-billion ceiling on federal spending in fiscal 1974, providing procedures for either the House or Senate to force the president to release impounded funds and directing the president to impound funds proportionately from controllable federal spending programs to meet the spending ceiling. Passed 254-164 (R 36-150; D 218-14), July 25. Ford VOTED AGAINST.

Transportation

1956. Highways (HR 10660). Bill authorizing a $30-billion, 13-year highway construction program and raising taxes on highway user items such as gasoline and tires over a 16-year period to finance the project. Passed 388-19 (R 188-4; D 200-15), April 27. Ford VOTED FOR.

1970. SST Development (HR 17755). Motion designed to retain in the Department of Transportation appropriations bill for fiscal 1971, funding of $289.9-million for development of the supersonic transport (SST). Agreed to 213-175 (R 105-62; D 108-113), Dec. 8. Ford VOTED FOR.

1973. Mass Transit. (S 502). Amendment to the Federal-Aid Highway Act permitting urban areas to use up to $700-million in each of fiscal years 1974-76 from the Highway Trust Fund for mass transit projects or for roads. Rejected 190-215 (R 70-114; D 120-101), April 19. Ford VOTED AGAINST.

1973. Mass Transit. (HR 6452). Bill authorizing $800-million for fiscal 1974-75 grants to state and local agencies for urban mass transit operating subsidies and increasing the federal share of assistance for mass transit capital grant programs. Passed 219-195 (R 41-142; D 178-53), Oct. 3. Ford VOTED AGAINST.

Welfare, Housing

1949. Low-Rent Housing (HR 4009). Amendment to Housing Act of 1949 deleting section providing low-rent public housing. Rejected 204-209 (R 140-24; D 64-184), June 29. Ford VOTED FOR.

1961. Housing (HR 6028). Bill authorizing a $4.9-billion housing program over four years. Passed 235-178 (R 25-140; D 210-38), June 22. Ford VOTED AGAINST.

1965. Medicare (HR 6675). Bill providing a basic compulsory health insurance program for the aged, financed primarily by a payroll tax; a supplementary voluntary health insurance program financed by general revenue and contributions from participants; increases in Social Security cash benefits, and expansion of the Kerr-Mills health program, child health-care programs and other federal-state public assistance programs. Passed 313-115 (R 65-73; D 248-42), April 8. Ford VOTED AGAINST.

1965. Rent Supplements (HR 7984). Amendment to the Housing and Urban Development Act, deleting rent supplement payments to low-income families and home improvement grants to homeowners in urban renewal areas. Rejected 202-208 (R 130-4; D 72-204), June 30. Ford VOTED FOR.

1966. War on Poverty (HR 15111). Motion to kill the bill providing $1.75-billion for antipoverty programs in fiscal 1967. Rejected 156-208 (R 107-15; D 49-193), Sept. 29. Ford VOTED FOR.

1966. Urban Renewal (S 3708). Bill providing demonstration city grants for community renewal and other housing programs. Passed 178-141 (R 16-81; D 162-60), Oct. 14. Ford VOTED AGAINST.

1967. Model Cities (HR 9960). Amendment to an appropriations bill for the Department of Housing and Urban Development deleting $225-million in model cities funds, leaving the program with only $12-million in planning funds. Rejected 193-213 (R 141-35; D 52-178), May 17. Ford VOTED FOR.

1967. Antipoverty (S 2388). Amendment reducing funds in the bill authorizing antipoverty funds for fiscal 1968 from $2.1-billion to $1.6-billion. Adopted 221-190 (R 148-28; D 73-162), Nov. 15. Ford VOTED FOR.

1968. Housing Programs (S 3497). Conference report on the bill providing new programs of federal assistance for home ownership and rental housing for low-income families, federal reinsurance for insurance industry riot losses, flood insurance for homeowners, federal assistance for developers of entire new towns and new communities, and extending a number of existing housing and urban development programs. Adopted 228-135 (R 72-92; D 156-43), July 26. Ford VOTED FOR.

1969. Antipoverty (HR 12321). Amendment to the Office of Economic Opportunity authorization bill for fiscal 1970, turning control of the antipoverty program over to the states. Rejected 163-231 (R 103-63; D 60-168), Dec. 12. Ford VOTED FOR.

1970. Family Assistance (HR 16311). Bill replacing the Aid to Families with Dependent Children program with a family assistance plan providing guaranteed federal payments to poor families. Passed 243-155 (R 102-72; D 141-83), April 16. Ford VOTED FOR.

1973. Antipoverty (HR 8877). Amendment to the bill appropriating funds for the Departments of Labor and Health, Education and Welfare reducing the appropriation for the Office of Economic Opportunity from $333.8-million to $141.3-million. Rejected 110-288 (R 90-90; D 20-198), June 26. Ford VOTED FOR.

THE FORDS AT HOME: 'AN EXTREMELY CLOSE FAMILY'

In a capital notorious for its broken homes and its gossip of extramarital affairs, Jerry and Betty Ford were models of happiness and serenity. The parents of four healthy children, they lived lives of comparative normalcy in their four-bedroom brick and frame house on Crown View Drive in suburban Alexandria, Va.

They were robbed of much of that normalcy on Dec. 6, 1973, when Ford was sworn in as the nation's 40th Vice President. Substantial remodeling was necessary to accommodate the contingent of Secret Service men who became regular occupants of their home.

When Ford became Vice President, the family voted to stay in the house, which they had built to their plans in 1955 for $34,000. But by July 1974, they had decided the house was inadequate for their growing needs, and they were preparing to move into Admiral's House, the former home of the chief of naval operations, on Massachusetts Ave. in Washington, D.C. Congress had made the house the official home of vice presidents.

The reluctant move was made unnecessary Aug. 9, when Gerald R. Ford, 61, took the oath as 38th President of the United States. For at least the next 2½ years, the Fords would be residents of a much larger and more splendid house at 1600 Pennsylvania Ave.

The new President would miss the early-morning and evening swims he had enjoyed so much in the 20-by-40-foot pool the Fords had built in their back yard in 1961. In his first informal meeting with reporters after the swearing in, he joked about restoring the former White House swimming pool that had been covered by a refurbished press room during the Nixon administration.

A Close Family

The athletic activities of the Ford family, long the nucleus of many of their gatherings, were threatened with at least some curtailment by the inevitable demands of the presidency. In doubt, for example, was the annual family visit to their condominium at Vail, Colo., for a week's skiing at Christmastime. And Ford probably could expect to spend far less time than before on the golf course.

But it was a safe bet among all who knew the Fords that they would manage, despite all the demands and restrictions placed on them by the nation's highest office, to get together for some wholesome exercise now and then. This had always been their way of life. They described themselves, and their neighbors described them, as "an extremely close family." Before the cataclysmic events of 1973 and 1974, Ford had, at his wife's urging, planned to seek one more House term and then return to a more leisurely life.

Ford made repeated references to his wife and children in his public statements. One such reference was in his brief speech to a joint session of Congress after he had been sworn in as Vice President. Using the kind of snyntax that lent itself to comparisons with the Eisenhower years, Ford said with feeling: "For standing by my side, as she always has, there are no words to tell you, my dear wife and mother

of our four wonderful children, how much their being here means to me."

In his brief remarks after being sworn in as President, Ford said in the East Room of the White House: "I have not subscribed to any partisan platform. I am indebted to no man and only one woman—my dear wife—as I begin the most difficult job in the world."

Betty Ford

The woman who held the Bible at her husband's swearing in had been born Elizabeth Bloomer 56 years earlier (on April 8, 1918) in Chicago. She was a slender, attractive woman with chestnut hair. She still carried herself with the lithe grace she had acquired years before in New York City, where she had been a dancing student of the famous Martha Graham and had been a professional fashion model.

Betty and Jerry had known each other in Grand Rapids, Mich., and Betty was working as fashion coordinator at a local department store when she and Jerry became engaged in May 1948. Jerry was establishing himself as a lawyer. He also was running for Congress. He and Betty were married Oct. 15, 1948, three weeks before Jerry, then 35, was elected to the House after defeating isolationist Rep. Bartel J. Jonkman (R 1940-49) in the Republican primary.

For six years before her marriage to Ford, Betty had been married to William C. Warren, a traveling salesman from Grand Rapids. The marriage ended in divorce in September 1947.

As Ford's responsibilities in the House increased and he became one of the chief Republican speechmakers, his absences took their toll on Mrs. Ford. She developed a pinched nerve in her neck, a problem that continued over the years but reportedly was lessening somewhat during Ford's months as Vice President.

The pinched nerve caused her, on doctors' advice, to see a psychiatrist for a few years during the 1960s. The sessions helped her work out "tensions and resentments" brought on by the burden of child-raising while her husband was often absent, she told one interviewer. "The psychiatrist persuaded me that I shouldn't give up everything for my husband and children, but had to think about what mattered to me," she said.

Among her interests were PTA and church work. She taught Sunday school at Alexandria's Episcopal Immanuel Church-on-the-Hill. When Ford became Vice President, a family friend, Nancy Howe, became Mrs. Ford's secretary. When Mrs. Ford became first lady, she indicated an interest in dong some work with the arts.

The Children

Only two of the four Ford children were living with their parents when their father became President. Only the youngest was expected to be a resident of the White House by fall of 1974. They were:

● Michael Gerald, born March 15, 1950. Michael, a 1972 graduate of Wake Forest University, was a ministerial student at Gordon Conwell, a non-denominational seminary near Boston. In July 1974, he married Gayle Brumbaugh of Catonsville, Md.

• John Gardner, born March 16, 1952. Jack was a forestry student at Utah State University. He spent the summer of 1974 as a ranger at Yellowstone National Park in Wyoming, a job his father had held as a young man.

• Steven Meigs, born May 19, 1956. Steven, who graduated in June 1974 from T. C. Williams High School in Alexandria, was weighing two possibilities for the fall: studying oceanography at Duke University or spending a year on a Utah cattle ranch. After his father became President, Steven opted to postpone entering Duke.

• Susan Elizabeth, born July 6, 1957. Susan was a senior at Holton Arms, a girls' preparatory school in Bethesda, Md., a Washington suburb.

The family owned a Siamese cat named Shan.

Ford's Early Years

The man who was to become the 38th President started life with a different name. He was born Leslie Lynch King Jr. on July 14, 1913, in Omaha, Neb. His parents were Dorothy Gardner King and Leslie King, a Montana wool trader.

When young Leslie was less than 2, his parents were divorced. His mother moved to Grand Rapids, where she had friends. There she met and married Gerald Rudolph Ford, who was in the paint and varnish business. Ford adopted little Leslie and gave him his name.

Gerald Sr. was the principal influence on Jerry Jr. and Jerry's three younger stepbrothers, Thomas, James and Richard. Thomas and Richard went into the family paint business. James became an optometrist. The senior Fords died in the 1960s.

By the time Jerry Jr. was in his teens and working part-time in a restaurant across the street from South High School in Grand Rapids, he had developed great skill as a football player. He was all-city and all-state center on the South team. When he was a senior, he won a local movie theater promotion as "most popular high school senior."

College, then Navy

Ford took his football prowess with him to the University of Michigan. He earned his football letter three years and played on the national championship teams of 1932 and 1933. In 1934, he was named the university's most valuable player. His ability earned him the nickname of "Junie," because he scooted around the field like a June bug.

At Michigan, Ford helped put himself through by waiting tables at the fraternity of which he was a member, Delta Kappa Upsilon. He graduated with a B.A. degree in liberal arts in 1935; he had a B grade average.

Money was short in the Depression year of 1935, and Ford had two choices: he could either play professional football or take a job as assistant football coach and freshman boxing coach at Yale,, where he could study law at the same time. He went to Yale, graduating from law school in 1941 in the top third of his class.

Having passed the Michigan bar examination in June 1941, Ford returned to Grand Rapids and started a law practice with Philip Bucher. It was his intention to specialize in labor law.

World War II interrupted his career, and in April 1942 he entered the Navy as an ensign. He was part of a program to recruit athletes to help give physical training to recruits. A year later, bored with this assignment, he was trained in

gunnery and shipped out to the South Pacific. He fought in major battles as an officer on the aircraft carrier *USS Monterey*, with the 3rd and 5th Fleets. Discharged in 1945 at age 32, Ford was a lieutenant commander with 10 battle stars.

The Rising Politician

Back he went to his law practice in Grand Rapids. He became active in civic affairs, including the Red Cross and Boy Scouts (he had been an Eagle Scout).

And he became active in Republican politics, partly because of his activist father, who was party chairman for Kent County. Jerry Jr. attended the county and state Republican conventions in 1946 and 1948. At the urging of his father and the late Sen. Arthur H. Vandenberg (R Mich. 1928-51), he took on Jonken and went on to win the 1948 general election with 60.5 per cent. It was his smallest margin in 13 elections to the House.

Ford's rise to prominence, once he arrived at the Capitol, was quite swift when measured against the frequently glacial progress of seniority-bound representatives. He became a member of the organization of young, ambitious and conservative House Republicans known as the Chowder and Marching Society.

With the society's backing, Ford challenged—and defeated—the older, more traditional Rep. Charles B. Hoeven (Iowa 1943-65) for chairmanship for the Republican Conference in 1963. And two years later, again with the help of society members, he toppled Rep. Charles A. Halleck (R Ind. 1935-69) for the job of minority leader.

'No Enemies'

Characteristically, the pipe-puffing Ford staged his coups in the House without bringing personal wrath from his opponents ringing around his ears. The night President Nixon stepped down, Ford said on his front lawn in Alexandria: "I've been very fortunate in my lifetime in public office to have a good many adversaries in the political arena in Congress. But I don't think I have a single enemy in the Congress."

That was not to say Ford did not come under harsh attack, and frequently. He was always a strong defender of the Republican position in the House and of the Republican presidents under whom he served. His attitude inspired President Johnson to make the cutting but quotable comments that Ford had played too much football without a helmet and that he was unable to walk and chew gum at the same time.

Columnists Rowland Evans Jr. and Robert D. Novak, in the August 1974 *Atlantic*, defended the then Vice President. "Ford's ponderous way with words, his inability to turn a nice phrase, and the slow pace with which he receives and tries to answer questions cloak a respectable intellect," they wrote.

Along with Ford's capacity to operate without personal vindictiveness was a quality described by some as a genuine liking for people in general, including those with whom he disagreed on the issues. Rep. Donald W. Riegle Jr., a Republican-turned-Democrat from Ford's home state of Michigan, told an interviewer in November 1973, when Ford was going through confirmation proceedings for the vice presidency:

"He has the kind of sensitivity that gives him a potential for growth. He can grow in terms of national leadership because he's a human being. That's very important at this particular time." ∎

HUGE MARGINS IN BOTH HOUSES FOR VICE PRESIDENCY

With a pledge to do "the very best that I can for America," Gerald R. Ford of Michigan became the 40th vice president of the United States Dec. 6, an hour after the House of Representatives voted 387-5 to confirm him. The Senate had approved the nomination Nov. 27 by a 92-3 vote.

Ford was the first vice president to be selected under the 25th Amendment to the Constitution, which governs presidential and vice presidential succession. Ratified in 1967, the amendment required confirmation of the nominee by a majority of both houses of Congress.

The country had been without a vice president for eight weeks, since Spiro T. Agnew resigned Oct. 10. He was sentenced on a charge of federal income tax evasion. *(Box p. 44)*

Ford, the 60-year-old Republican minority leader of the House, took the oath of office before a joint session of Congress, as President Nixon, his cabinet, the entire Supreme Court, members of the diplomatic corps and galleries packed with friends and visitors looked on. It was the first time a vice president was sworn in separately from a president.

Ford's wife held the Bible as Chief Justice Warren E. Burger administered the oath in the chamber of the House, which Ford called his home for 25 years. A "man of Congress," like 30 of his 39 predecessors, Ford was first elected in 1948. He frequently said his life's ambition was to be speaker of the House. Since his nomination by Nixon Oct. 12, he had said repeatedly he did not seek the presidency and did not intend to run in 1976. However, his confirmation heightened speculation that he would become president—if Nixon were to resign or be impeached.

Nixon accompanied Ford to the swearing in but did not speak. In his speech, Ford pledged "dedication to the rule of law and equal justice for all Americans."

After the swearing-in ceremony, Ford led senators back to the Senate chamber and addressed them briefly.

Confirmation Procedure

In considering the nomination of Gerald Ford, Congress was establishing precedent as it went along.

In 1965, in approving the measure which became the 25th Amendment, Congress staked out a role for itself in filling a vacant vice presidency. Both chambers approved language stating that "whenever there is a vacancy in the office of the Vice President, the President shall nominate a Vice President who shall take office *upon con-*

firmation by a majority vote of both Houses of Congress." (Italics added) However that amendment failed to specify a procedure to follow in confirming a vice presidential nominee. Discussion of the legislation that became the 25th Amendment focused almost exclusively on presiden-

tial disability; little thought was given to the details of vice-presidential replacement.

The major procedural question to be worked out was what committee would handle the nomination in each chamber. In the House it was quickly decided that the Judiciary Committee would have jurisdiction. In the Senate there was vigorous debate between members who wanted to set up a special committee to consider the nomination and those who wanted to refer it to the Rules Committee. The conflict was resolved when Senate Republicans joined with the Democratic leadership and gave the Rules Committee jurisdiction.

Each committee held separate hearings, rather than holding one set of hearings under a special joint committee, as had been suggested by some, including former Vice President Hubert H. Humphrey (D Minn.).

The nine member Senate Rules Committee, chaired by Howard W. Cannon (D Nev.), opened hearings Nov. 1. Chairman Peter W. Rodino Jr. (D N.J.) opened House Judiciary Committee hearings Nov. 15.

CLOSE SCRUTINY

Because of the cloud of scandal under which former Vice President Agnew resigned, and the growing specula-

A White House Extravaganza for Ford's Nomination

President Nixon made a gala state ceremony of his nationally televised announcement Oct. 12, 1973, that Rep. Gerald R. Ford (R Mich.) was his vice presidential nominee. Cabinet officers, congressional leaders and members of the diplomatic corps filed into the East Room of the White House promptly at 9 p.m., as did the President's family—Patricia Nixon, Tricia Cox and Julie and David Eisenhower. "Hail to the Chief" was played as the President entered.

Nixon, smiling and jovial, appeared to relish the suspense he had created about the selection. Making no mention of former Vice President Agnew, he said, "...it is vital that we turn away from the obsessions of the past.... This is a time for a new beginning for America."

A few minutes into his speech, Nixon let out his carefully guarded secret when he revealed that the nominee was "a man who has served for 25 years in the House of Representatives with great distinction." The audience then knew that Ford was the President's choice, and it burst into enthusiastic applause. Nixon, laughing, cautioned, "...there's several here who have served 25 years in the House of Representatives." Four sentences later he mentioned Ford by name.

Ford, who had been sitting between House Speaker Carl Albert (D Okla.) and Majority Leader Thomas P. O'Neill Jr. (D Mass.), joined the President at the podium. The two placed their arms around each other's shoulders in the manner of nominees at a national political convention. The microphone picked up some off-stage whispers. Nixon: "They like you." Ford: "I have a couple of friends out there."

Bipartisan Cooperation. Nixon had emphasized that his new vice president should be able to work with members of both parties in Congress "at this particular time when we have the executive in the hands of one party and the Congress controlled by another party ...." Speaker Albert had advised Nixon that Ford would have little difficulty in being confirmed by Congress.

In accepting the nomination, Ford promised to "do my utmost to the best of my ability to serve this country well and to perform those duties that will be my new assignment as effectively and efficiently and with as much accomplishment as possible."

Absentees. The justices of the Supreme Court had been invited to the ceremony, but none came. A court spokesman declined comment when asked why by Congressional Quarterly. Just three hours before the ceremony, the U.S. Court of Appeals had announced a ruling that Nixon must turn over disputed White House tape recordings related to the Watergate scandal to U.S. District Judge John J. Sirica. An appeal by the White House would take the case to the Supreme Court.

Senate Majority Leader Mike Mansfield (D Mont.) told the Senate Oct. 13 that he was perhaps the only member of Congress who did not know whom the President had nominated until 5:30 that morning, when he turned on the radio. Mansfield, who had been invited to the ceremony, explained, "It had been a pretty tough week, so far as I was concerned personally. I went to bed rather early, took the phone off the hook and had a good night's sleep." Senate Assistant Majority Leader Robert C. Byrd (D W.Va.) attended the ceremony.

Nixon's Decision-Making. Nixon reportedly had narrowed his list of possible vice presidential nominees to five when he went to Camp David, Md., late Oct. 11 to ponder his decision. Besides Ford, the list was said to include Gov. Nelson A. Rockefeller (R N.Y.); Gov. Ronald Reagan (R Calif.); former Texas Gov. John B. Connally, and Attorney General Elliot L. Richardson.

The President returned to the White House at 8:30 a.m. Oct. 12 and told his staff he had arrived at a decision. Afterward, he met with Ford and Senate Minority Leader Hugh Scott (R Pa.) to talk about procedural matters related to the nomination but not about his selection. Ford was said not to have been told that he was the man until 90 minutes before the East Room ceremony. However, one report indicated he had been informed before noon Oct. 12.

Not even Mrs. Nixon knew about the choice until the ceremony, according to reports from the White House. Secret Service agents were told to stand by but were not given the identity of the nominee.

tion that Ford might succeed to the presidency, members of both houses and both parties asked for a thorough investigation of his background.

Indicating the sweeping nature of the investigation, William M. Cochrane, Senate Rules Committee staff director, said that in addition to a full FBI check, the committee had:

• Asked Nixon to order the Internal Revenue Service to turn over Ford's federal income tax returns filed since 1965 and to conduct detailed audits of his returns for the past five years.

• Asked the Library of Congress to compile a complete record of Ford's positions on issues during his 25 years in the House.

In the House the Judiciary Committee voted to give Rodino power to issue subpoenas for witnesses and documents.

The hearings moved along quickly in both houses. The Senate committee in its questioning of Ford dealt mainly with how he would act if he were President. Other questions dealt with charges of influence-peddling and his record on civil rights, which some members considered poor. In the House Judiciary Committee there were several members who objected to confirming Ford on the grounds that Nixon should not be allowed to pick his own successor. However, a motion by Elizabeth Holtzman (D N.Y.) to table the nomination was defeated.

After the committee hearings were completed in each chamber the nomination was brought to the floor for consideration by the full House and Senate where a simple majority was needed to confirm.

Senate Committee Action

Hearings

The Senate Rules and Administration Committee held hearings Nov. 1-14 on the nomination of Rep. Gerald R. Ford (R Mich.) to be vice president of the United States.

NOV. 1, 1973

Ford walked a tightrope in his nationally-televised opening appearance before the committee—supporting the views and policies of President Nixon, who nominated him, without alienating the Democratic-controlled Congress, which confirmed him.

Committee members probed repeatedly into Ford's views on executive privilege, presidential obedience of the law, separation of powers, impoundment of funds appropriated by Congress, the independence of a new special Watergate prosecutor and the President's right to withhold information which could conceal criminal activity in the executive branch.

They also questioned Ford about allegations of irregularities in his personal and campaign finances and reports that he had been treated by a psychiatrist.

Ford denied all the allegations in vigorous terms—"total fabrications," "way out," "asinine," "unreliable" and "lies." He came prepared to answer all charges; there were no surprises. Ford already had undergone the most thorough investigation of any candidate for any office in the nation's history, and the press had reported old and new allegations widely.

Committee chairman Howard W. Cannon (D Nev.) and ranking Republican member Marlow W. Cook (Ky.) had been given a 1,400-page "raw file" of data compiled by the FBI, and summarized it for the other committee members. Ford also gave the committee copies of his income tax returns for the past seven years and a statement of his financial holdings. He declined to make the tax returns public, as requested by committee member Claiborne Pell (D R.I.) and Common Cause, but said the committee could do so if it wished.

Chairman Cannon opened the hearing with a pledge not to hold Ford's nomination "hostage" to domestic political warfare over the Watergate tapes and related issues. He said the committee should not consider Ford's voting record—even though members might disagree with it—since Congress should not deny the President the right to choose a man "whose philosophy and politics are virtually identical to his own." What it should consider, Cannon said, were Ford's views of the presidency itself and what he would do if he were president.

Ford, in his opening statement, said his public life was "an open book—carefully reread every two years by my constituents." Since his nomination Oct. 12 his private life had been opened as well, he said. He pledged to follow the late President Eisenhower's "simple rule for people in public office...do what's best for America."

His strongest point as Vice President, he said, would be his ability to serve as "a ready conciliator and calm communicator between the White House and Capitol Hill, between the re-election mandate of the Republican President and the equally emphatic mandate of the Democratic 93rd Congress."

His 25 years of experience in Congress, including nine as minority leader, and his 25-year friendship with President Nixon would help him bridge the gap, Ford said. He called that "the greatest single need of our country today," since many people "are beginning to worry about our national government becoming seriously weakened by partisan division."

Ford said his announced decision not to seek the presidency in 1976 if he was confirmed as vice president should help in that respect. "Nobody could accuse me of seeking personal political aggrandizement," he said.

Ford characterized his own political philosophy as "moderate in domestic affairs, conservative in fiscal affairs, and dyed-in-the-wool internationalist in foreign affairs." He said he considered national security the nation's top spending priority.

While Ford apparently made a favorable impression on the committee in his first round of questioning, as committee member Robert C. Byrd (D W.Va.), Senate majority whip, indicated to newsmen, he obviously did not satisfy some of them with his answers to questions regarding the sticky issues of executive privilege, impoundment and appointing a new Watergate prosecutor.

Executive Privilege. "I don't think any president has unlimited authority in the area of executive privilege," Ford said. "On the other hand, I don't think Congress, or the public generally, has any right to all personal and confidential conversations and documents of the president.... We just have to take each case as it comes and do what is in the best interest of the country."

Ford agreed with Byrd that concealment of information where criminal behavior is involved would be obstruction of justice. "Where you have serious allegations of criminal behavior," Ford said, "where documents have an impact on the guilt or innocence of an individual, they should be made available."

National Security. On non-national security matters, he said, "there should be cooperation" in making information available to Congress or the courts. However, he defended the President's right to withhold information where national security is involved.

Watergate Prosecutor. Ford said he recognized the "constitutional and legal problems involved" in President Nixon's original refusal to turn over Watergate tapes to the special prosecutor on court orders. However, he said for political reasons he urged Nixon to do so, and was pleased Nixon eventually agreed.

He also stuck to the administration position that a new special prosecutor should be appointed by the attorney general, not by Congress or the courts, and said Nixon had agreed not to fire the prosecutor without the concurrence of a majority of an eight-member congressional group set up for the purpose.

"You can't prevent by law the dismissal of a person appointed by the President," Ford contended. He said he hoped the new Nixon proposal would satisfy demands for guarantees of independence.

Impoundment. Ford also defended a president's right to impound funds appropriated by Congress for programs. "A president shouldn't have to spend every dime Congress makes available for a program," Ford contended. "If we forced the president to do that, you'd have to have a tax increase of astronomical proportions." He said all presidents he had served with had impounded funds. "Impoundment could be the only way a president could get a program straightened out," he said.

If he were president and faced with a program he didn't agree with, Ford said "I hope my good judgment would tell me I should carry out the law" and appoint as administrator a person who would carry out at least the intent of the legislation.

Impeachment. In answer to a question by Mark O. Hatfield (R Ore.), Ford said he did not think Nixon's impoundment policies were grounds for impeachment, or that there were any other grounds for impeaching the President. However, he said the House Judiciary Committee's current inquiry into impeachment should continue, "to clear the air."

NOV. 5, 7

The only source of major allegations against Ford— former Washington lobbyist and author Robert N. Winter-Berger—testified under oath in closed session Nov. 7. After his appearance Committee Chairman Howard W. Cannon (D Nev.) said the committee did not consider Winter-Berger a credible witness and might refer his testimony to the Justice Department for investigation on perjury charges.

Virtually every committee member praised Ford's cooperation and candor in answering questions. Ten members of the House of Representatives testified Nov. 5 on his behalf, and the committee appeared ready to act favorably, perhaps unanimously, on the nomination. Cannon said he would be "very surprised if we find any roadblocks" to Ford's nomination.

The questions Nov. 5 dealt mainly with how Ford would act if he were president. The committee sought to ascertain Ford's views on foreign affairs, the energy crisis, the Supreme Court, busing, the press, selecting advisers, and his understanding of the characteristics of presidential leadership.

Foreign Affairs. Ford approved U.S. initiatives toward detente with China and Russia, and said he would favor moving closer to the Arab states, Cuba and Sweden if areas of dialogue were found.

Ford emphasized his strong support of Israel and of Nixon's $2.2-billion request for aid to Israel. However, he said he did not think the United States should "guarantee" Israel's borders.

Watergate. Ford said he did not think a president should try to prevent or obstruct an investigation into the executive branch, and said he thought Nixon should turn over all tapes and documents necessary to clear up the question of his involvement in the Watergate scandals, to help "save his presidency." Ford personally believed the President was innocent, he reiterated.

If the president resigned, could the vice president halt or prevent an investigation into the president's affairs, Ford was asked. "I don't think the public would stand for it," he replied. Ford also said he understood why former Attorney General Elliot L. Richardson resigned rather than fire Special Watergate Prosecutor Archibald Cox on Nixon's demand. Ford said if he were in Richardson's position he probably would have done the same.

Energy Crisis. Ford said it was "almost incomprehensible" to him why the United States was so "negligent" for so long about developing cleaner coal-burning capability. He urged greater spending for research into development of domestic fuel resources to help avoid dependence on foreign oil.

Presidential Advisers. Ford said he would seek "strong input" from members of the House and Senate if he were president and needed advice. "There is a great reservoir of knowledge and good judgment there," he said. As for picking staff advisers, Ford said "to my knowledge, no person I've ever employed has made any mistakes; I've never had to fire anyone." With evidence of illegal or unethical conduct, he would fire any staff member, he said.

The Courts. "Even though I have strong differences of opinion with some members of the Supreme Court and other federal courts," Ford said he opposed proposals to require periodic reappointment or reconfirmation of judges. That would "undercut the independence of the judiciary," Ford said. "I think that independence is important even though I don't always agree with them."

Busing. "If the federal courts persist in trying to have forced busing to achieve racial balance in the public schools and there is no other way we could remedy that," Ford said he would favor a constitutional amendment prohibiting busing. However, he said he felt the courts were beginning to recognize that busing is not the answer to improved education. He preferred compensatory education for the disadvantaged instead, Ford said. "Forced busing has caused more trouble and more tension where it has happened than almost anything else in our society."

Presidential Qualities. A president "has to be a person of great truth, and the American people have to believe that he's truthful," Ford said. "...A man of thought, not impetuous. People have to have faith that he's thoughtful and won't shoot from the hip. He has to live his life by the standards, moral and ethical, by which most people live their lives." It is difficult for a president to appear humble; he has to appear to be forceful and strong, Ford said. But he said it is not a sign of weakness to acknowledge mistakes, and a president should be willing to do so.

The Media. "I can't imagine me going out and attacking the press" as former Vice President Spiro T. Agnew did, Ford said. He said he had good relations with the press and did not share what Cannon called "Nixon's blanket condemnation of the media." He agreed the media were the "most significant contributors" in exposing the Watergate scandal.

Winter-Berger Allegations. The Rules Committee members questioned Ford almost apologetically about what one called the "only diversion" in otherwise "constructive" hearings: the allegations of Robert Winter-Berger. They interrogated Winter-Berger for an entire day behind closed doors.

Winter-Berger claimed in a 1972 book, *The Washington Payoff*, and in a sworn affidavit that Ford granted favors in return for campaign contributions, "laundered" campaign contributions, accepted $15,000 in cash from Winter-Berger, and was treated "for at least a year" by a New York psychotherapist, Dr. Arnold Hutschnecker, for irritability, nervousness and depression resulting from the pressures of his job as House minority leader.

Although Winter-Berger told newsmen he stood behind his charges, Cannon said he offered no documentation to prove any of them. He said Winter-Berger could not have "loaned" Ford $15,000 from his personal income between 1966 and 1969, one of the committee's principal concerns, because Winter-Berger's subpoenaed tax returns showed he listed gross income of only $14,076, $7,615, $1,643 and $4,912 for those years. Confronted with the returns, Cannon said, Winter-Berger changed his story and said 90 per cent of the $15,000 paid to Ford was "borrowed" from another lobbyist, the late Nathan Voloshen.

Ford, in his testimony, pointed out that Winter-Berger himself said in his book that he "never knew Ford to accept cash from anybody." Ford also produced records to show that Ford's insurance paid most of his wife's medical bills between 1966 and 1969, which Winter-Berger had said caused Ford's need for money.

Ford said he always did what any congressman does in assisting constituents and friends, but denied that he ever accepted payments for favors. He said he knew of only one Winter-Berger "client" he helped, a well-known Dutch doctor seeking immigrant status. Ford said records showed Winter-Berger made only one $500 contribution to any of his campaigns. Ford also denied he covered up campaign contributions or violated any campaign finance laws.

As for Dr. Hutschnecker, Ford testified he dropped in at the psychotherapist's office once for a 15-minute social chat, at Winter-Berger's insistence, and the doctor may have dropped in at Ford's office once. He denied he ever needed or received psychiatric treatment, since he is "disgustingly sane" and his "mental attitude gets better under pressure."

Hutschnecker also denied he ever treated Ford, and called Winter-Berger's charges "lies" or "fantasies." Winter-Berger also said Hutschnecker had treated President Nixon for several years. The friend who introduced Ford to Winter-Berger, Alice Boter Weston Schowalter, denied she was paid $1,000 to do so.

NOV. 14

The committee Nov. 14 heard five witnesses. Three, for differing reasons, urged that Ford not be confirmed, one supported him, and one cited his "narrow-gauge approach" to civil rights.

Rauh. Joseph L. Rauh, Jr., national vice chairman of Americans for Democratic Action (ADA), made the strongest attack of the hearings on Ford's record and character. He urged Congress to reject Ford and let Nixon nominate a better candidate.

Rauh said Ford's record on civil rights was as bad as the records of Clement F. Haynsworth Jr. and G. Harrold Carswell, Nixon nominees to the Supreme Court who were rejected by the Senate. Indeed, Rauh said, Ford "compares unfavorably...when one considers his northern surroundings."

In addition, Rauh charged, Ford's overall voting record was "much worse than the Nixon administration record generally, not to mention his total lack of experience in foreign affairs, his attack on the judiciary (in his impeachment effort against Supreme Court Justice William O. Douglas), and his pre-judgment (in Nixon's favor) of the Watergate scandal."

Rauh called Ford "a divisive influence who has fought civil rights legislation at every turn." He said Ford was a "final passage man" in civil rights and social legislation—consistently seeking to gut or cripple bills in early stages, then voting for them in final form after passage became certain.

Mitchell. Clarence Mitchell, director of the Washington bureau of the National Association for the Advancement of Colored People, made the same assessment. In addition, he said, Ford had "associated himself with groups in Michigan and across the country who want to turn back the clock on civil rights."

The two black witnesses, Mitchell and Maurice Dawkins, and two Republican committee members, Mark O. Hatfield (Ore.) and Hugh Scott (Pa.), expressed hope Ford would "grow" in his views on civil rights if he became vice president or president, as they said President Lyndon B. Johnson did.

Abzug. Rep. Abzug called for a special election for vice president, and George Washington University law professor John F. Banzhaf III said Ford should not be confirmed until "the suspicious and highly questionable circumstances surrounding (former Vice President) Spiro T. Agnew's forced resignation" were investigated.

Dawkins, speaking for Opportunities Industrialization Centers (OIC), a manpower development organization, endorsed Ford for his support of OIC and other "good work."

Senate Committee Report

The nine-member Rules and Administration Committee after three days of public hearings, nine closed sessions and what it called the most exhaustive FBI investigation in U.S. history of a candidate for public office, concluded unanimously Nov. 20 that it "found no bar or impediment which would disqualify" Ford for the office of vice president. The committee's report (Exec Rept 93-26) was issued Nov. 23.

Not all members agreed with Ford's voting record, political philosophy or public actions in his 25 years in the House. Nor did they necessarily agree he was the best Republican Nixon could have chosen, they noted in the report. But after exploring Ford's philosophy, character, personal and financial integrity, they found that "in these critical areas he fully met reasonable tests."

The committee considered its job "no less important than the selection of a potential president," said Chairman Howard W. Cannon (D Nev.), and members, taking into account public calls for Nixon's impeachment or resignation, did question Ford as if he were a nominee for president rather than vice president.

Areas of Concern. In addition to Ford's views on foreign and domestic policy, executive privilege, impoundment of congressionally appropriated funds, the Watergate affair and other controversial topics, the committee sought information in four principal areas of concern: Ford's personal finances, charges of irregularities in financing his re-election campaigns in 1970 and 1972, allegations of influence-peddling, and a report that Ford had been treated by a psychotherapist because the pressures of his job as House minority leader had allegedly caused him to become nervous, irritable and depressed.

Committee Findings. No violations of law or irregularities were found by the FBI or the committee in
(Continued on p. 46)

Demise of Ford's Predecessor as Vice President:

Spiro T. Agnew Oct. 10, 1973, became the second vice president in history to resign. Under investigation for multiple charges of alleged conspiracy, extortion and bribery, Agnew agreed to resign and avoided imprisonment by pleading *nolo contendere* (no contest) to a single charge of federal income tax evasion.

The plea was the result of a month of White House-initiated plea bargaining between the Justice Department and Agnew's attorneys in which the Justice Department agreed to request a lenient sentence in exchange for the Vice President's resignation and plea of no contest to a single charge. A 40-page document outlining other instances of alleged misconduct by Agnew was submitted to the court by the Justice Department without pressing charges.

After disclosure in early August 1973 of a federal investigation into alleged payoffs he had accepted while executive of Baltimore County, governor of Maryland and later as Vice President, Agnew made a three-pronged effort to curb the probe. First, he charged that news leaks about the investigation jeopardized his civil rights and requested Attorney General Elliot L. Richardson to investigate the leak of information to the Justice Department.

Second, citing precedent for congressional investigation of alleged vice presidential misconduct, Agnew unsuccessfully urged the House to take over the probe into his earlier activities. Finally, Agnew's attorneys petitioned the special grand jury in Baltimore to halt the inquiry on the grounds that a vice president could not be indicted while in office.

Two days after Agnew's resignation, President Nixon nominated House Minority Leader Gerald R. Ford (R Mich.) as his successor. The 25th Amendment, ratified in 1967, required that the President nominate a vice presidential successor to take office upon confirmation by both houses of Congress. In the interim, Speaker of the House Carl Albert (D Okla.) stood next in line for the presidency. In the past, the vice presidency had been vacated 16 times, but before Agnew, only one Vice President, John C. Calhoun, had resigned.

Letters of Resignation. As required by law, Agnew's resignation came in a letter to Secretary of State Henry A. Kissinger, delivered Oct. 10. Similar letters were sent to Nixon and congressional leaders. Agnew had informed Nixon of his decision the evening of Oct. 9.

Minutes after the arrival of the letters, Agnew appeared in U.S. District Judge Walter E. Hoffman's Baltimore courtroom, pleaded *nolo contendere* to charges of failing to report $29,500 in 1967 income and was sentenced to three years of unsupervised probation and fined $10,000.

The court action rendered moot the litigation of other issues raised by his case—the constitutional questions of whether a vice president could be indicted while in office and whether newsmen, claiming the protection of the First Amendment, were obliged to divulge their sources.

Plea Bargaining. Agnew's fine and probationary sentence on the tax evasion charge were the result of the complicated plea bargaining process among the White House, the Justice Department and Agnew's attorneys. Under the final agreement, Agnew waived his right to a trial, agreed to resign from office and agreed to accept sentencing on the single tax charge. Judge Hoffman advised Agnew that the plea of *nolo contendere* was the "full equivalent to a plea of guilty."

In return, the Justice Department agreed to drop all but one pending charge against Agnew and to request leniency on the sentencing. Publication of the department's 40-page summary outlining other charges was also part of the final agreement.

At a news conference Oct. 11, Richardson disclosed that the White House had initiated the plea bargaining process. He told reporters that White House Counsel J. Fred Buzhardt Jr. had telephoned him in early September to ask if he would meet with Agnew's attorneys. Richardson described Buzhardt's role in the plea bargaining process as one of "facilitating communications."

The attorney general said that Nixon had been kept "fully informed at all times," and that he had "fully approved each of the major steps" in the Justice Department's action against Agnew. But he added that Nixon had felt "it was not appropriate for him to be informed of the details of the case." Gerald L. Warren, deputy White House press secretary, had said Aug. 14 that Nixon was not being given reports on the case and would not intervene.

Agnew's attorney, Judah Best, Oct. 11 contradicted Richardson's statement that Buzhardt had served merely in "facilitating communications." Best said he had met with Buzhardt in Miami Oct. 5-6 and their meeting was critical to the final agreement between Agnew and the Justice Department.

The New York Times reported Oct. 12 that Agnew had been prepared to resign as early as mid-September, when negotiations first began with the Justice Department. According to sources, Agnew's resignation was delayed because of disagreement over the amount of evidence against him that was to be made public. Other sources cited by the *Times* estimated that the 40-page document submitted to the court contained about 10 per cent of the evidence accumulated against Agnew.

Disclosure of Investigation

On Aug. 1, 1973, U.S. Attorney George Beall informed Agnew's lawyer, Best, that the Vice President was under investigation for alleged violations of conspiracy, extortion and bribery and tax statutes.

The allegations concerned reported kickbacks from private architectural and engineering firms that had been improperly awarded state and federal contracts during Agnew's years as executive of Baltimore County, Maryland governor and later as Vice President. The prosecutor's office asked Agnew to turn over a number of documents, including bank records and income tax returns. Ironically, the investigation had begun in October 1972 as an inquiry into reported kickbacks to Democratic officials in Maryland.

Agnew's Resignation After Criminal Investigation

The story of the Agnew investigation was first made public Aug. 6 by the Vice President as the first printed account to appear in *The Wall Street Journal* was going to press. Informed of the forthcoming article, Agnew released a brief statement saying, "I am innocent of any wrongdoing...and I am equally confident that my innocence will be affirmed."

Agnew disclosed at a nationally televised news conference Aug. 8 that he had heard rumors in February 1973 that investigators had repeatedly turned up his name in that probe. He denied any misconduct on his part. He told reporters he was defending himself, instead of "spending my time looking around to see who's supporting me."

Responding to questions from a packed auditorium of newsmen, Agnew called the charges "damned lies." He said he had "no expectation of being indicted" and that he had given no consideration to leaving the post of vice president, even temporarily. He indicated his willingness to cooperate with the investigators, a move he followed up on Aug. 14, when he turned over subpoenaed records to the authorities.

Richardson's Decision. Responsibility for the Agnew investigation rested with the Justice Department. Attorney General Richardson said Aug. 19 that he would personally decide whether evidence gathered by federal prosecutors in the investigation should be presented to a grand jury. In making that decision, he said, he also bore the responsibility for the "ultimate resolution" of the key constitutional issue of whether a vice president could be indicted for a crime while he was still in office.

On Sept. 28, Agnew's attorneys petitioned the Baltimore federal district court to halt the grand jury investigation on the grounds that a vice president was immune from prosecution while in office. The Justice Department twice filed responses, but the immunity issue was never decided because of Agnew's resignation.

In its first reply, filed Oct. 5, the Justice Department claimed that a vice president could be indicted in office. It said it would wait a "reasonable time" to allow the House to impeach and the Senate to try Agnew if he were impeached. The department argued that while indictment of a president in office would "incapacitate" the government, a vice president's functions were not "indispensable to the orderly operation of government."

The department filed its second reply Oct. 8. It termed "frivolous" Agnew's accusations that prosecutors had deliberately leaked information to the press to undermine his position. Furthermore, the reply charged, Agnew's lawyers were engaging in a "fishing expedition" by an Oct. 5 move subpoenaing newsmen to question them about sources for stories on the investigation.

Appeal to the House

Agnew, apparently deciding not to resign but to fight the charges against him, asked the House Sept. 25 to conduct a full inquiry into allegations that he had accepted bribes and kickbacks from Maryland contractors.

His request was made formally in a meeting with House leaders late in the afternoon. It came just as Richardson ended weeks of rumors with an announcement that on Sept. 27 the Justice Department would begin presenting evidence to a federal grand jury involving Agnew's role in alleged bribery and extortion.

Agnew's move was interpreted as an effort to block the grand jury proceedings. He said he would fight any criminal proceedings against him, contending that it was constitutionally impermissible for criminal prosecution to be begun against a sitting president or vice president. But, Agnew, said, he would cooperate fully if the House, as he asked, undertook a full inquiry into the charges. As precedent, he cited the 1827 investigation by the House which cleared Vice President Calhoun of charges of wrongdoing. The House, said Agnew, was the proper authority to undertake such an investigation because it had constitutionally granted power to investigate charges and decide if they warranted impeachment.

Nixon's role in the decision made by Richardson and Agnew was unclear. He had met with both separately the morning of Sept. 25. That afternoon, after both made their announcements, he issued a statement urging that Agnew be accorded "basic consideration and the presumption of innocence."

House Rejection. At noon Sept. 26, after further leadership meetings during the morning, Albert announced a decision: "The Vice President's letter relates to matters before the courts. In view of that fact, I, as speaker, will not take any action on the matter at this time." "They made a Democratic decision," said House Minority Leader Ford. "I don't think there's anything we can do, since we are in the minority."

Final Negotiations

On Oct. 1, the White House confirmed reports that Buzhardt was involved in a "direct and indirect way" in negotiations between Agnew's lawyers and the Justice Department over plea bargaining.

In court, the Justice Department continued to hit hard at the arguments raised in Agnew's defense. The department contended Oct. 5 that a vice president could be indicted and tried on criminal charges while in office. Government prosecutors Oct. 8 attacked Agnew's claim of a calculated campaign of news leaks and criticized his efforts to subpoena newsmen.

Buzhardt and lawyer Judah Best conferred in Miami Oct. 5-6. They reached a secret final agreement on the terms under which Agnew would resign and accept sentencing on the single charge of income tax evasion. According to Agnew's attorneys, two provisions were crucial to the final agreement: Agnew would be free to deny in court the information contained in the Justice Department's outline of other alleged misconduct, and he would be able to review the evidence compiled against him.

On Oct. 10, Agnew made public his decision to resign, pleaded no contest to the single tax charge and was sentenced by Judge Hoffman.

Swearing-in Comments: 'I Am a Ford, Not a Lincoln'

Following is the text of the remarks made by Gerald R. Ford after he was sworn in as Vice President Dec. 6, 1973:

Together we have made history here today. For the first time we have carried out the command of the 25th Amendment. In exactly eight weeks, we have demonstrated to the world that our great republic stands solid, stands strong upon the bedrock of the Constitution.

I am a Ford, not a Lincoln. My address will never be as eloquent as Mr. Lincoln's. But I will do my very best to equal his brevity and his plain speaking.

I am deeply grateful to you, Mr. President, for the trust and the confidence your nomination implies. As I have throughout my public service under six administrations I will try to set a fine example of my respect for the crushing and lonely burdens which the nation lays upon the president of the United States. Mr. President, you have my support and loyalty.

To the Congress assembled, my former colleagues who have elected me on behalf of our fellow countrymen, I express my heartfelt thanks. As a man of the Congress, let me reaffirm my conviction that the collective wisdom of our two great legislative bodies, while not infallible, will in the end serve the people faithfully and very, very well. I will not forget the people of Michigan who sent me to this chamber or the friends that I have found here.

Mr. Speaker, I understand that the United States Senate intends in a very few minutes to bind me by its rules. For their presiding officer, this amounts practically to a vow of silence. Mr. Speaker, you know how difficult this is going to be for me.

Before I go from this House, which has been my home for a quarter century, I must say I am forever in its debt.

And particularly, Mr. Speaker, thank you for your friendship, which I certainly am not leaving. To you, Mr. Speaker, and to all my friends here, however you voted an hour ago, I say a very fond goodbye. May God bless the House of Representatives and guide you in all the days ahead.

Mr. Chief Justice, may I thank you personally for administering the oath, and thank each of the honorable justices for honoring me with your attendance. I pledge to you, as I did the day I was first admitted to the bar, my dedication to the rule of law and equal justice for all Americans.

For standing by my side as she always has, there are no words to tell you, my dear wife and mother of our four wonderful children, how much their being here means to me.

As I look into the faces that fill this familiar room, and as I imagine those faces in other rooms across the land, I do not see members of the legislative branch or the executive branch or the judicial branch, though I am very much aware of the importance of keeping the separate but coequal branches of our federal government in balance. I do not see senators or representatives, nor do I see Republicans or Democrats, vital as the two-party system is to sustain freedom and responsible government.

At this moment of visible and living unity, I see only Americans. I see Americans who love their country, Americans who work and sacrifice for their country and their children. I see Americans who pray without ceasing for peace among all nations and for harmony at home. I see new generations of concerned and courageous Americans—but the same kind of Americans who met the challenge of December 7th, just 32 years ago.

Mr. Speaker, I like what I see.

Mr. Speaker, I am not discouraged. I am indeed humble to be the 40th Vice President of the United States, but I am proud—very proud—to be one of 200 million Americans. I promise my fellow citizens only this: To uphold the Constitution, to do what is right as God gives me to see the right, and within the limited powers and duties of the vice presidency, to do the very best that I can for America. I will do these things with all the strength and good sense I have, with your help, and through your prayers.

Thank you.

Ford's personal or political financial affairs, the report said. The other allegations against him were denied by Ford and other persons involved, and since no evidence was produced to support the charges, the committee said it could not accept them. Ford's principal accuser, former Washington lobbyist Robert N. Winter-Berger, made contradictory statements under oath and failed to produce documents, as promised, to prove his charges, the committee said. The committee labeled Winter-Berger "not a credible witness" and agreed unanimously to submit his testimony to the Justice Department for possible prosecution for perjury and contempt of Congress.

Ford's Finances. Because Agnew's resignation from the vice presidency resulted from improper financial dealings, the committee delved especially deeply into Ford's finances. His income tax returns were examined and audited, but the committee decided not to make them public since other public officials had not been required to disclose theirs.

Records from Ford's tax accountant showed Ford's gross income had averaged more than $75,000 a year since 1967. His salary as minority leader was $49,500 a year, with the remainder coming mainly from honoraria for speeches and appearances, Ford testified. He listed honoraria of $32,000 in 1967, $30,000 in 1968, $28,000 in 1969, $47,000 in 1970, $22,000 in 1971 and $18,000 in 1972.

Ford's (and Mrs. Ford's) net worth was $256,378 on Sept. 30, the records showed. Of that, $162,000 was in real estate (the family home in Alexandria, Va., a vacation condominium in Vail, Colo., and a two-family rental dwelling in Grand Rapids, Mich.) and $13,570 was from stocks.

The Internal Revenue Service audit of Ford's tax returns turned up one "business expense" deduction which it disallowed: $871.44 for clothing Ford bought for the 1972 Republican national convention, over which he presided. As a result, Ford paid $435.77 in additional tax, without penalty, on Nov. 9.

Allen View. Committee member James B. Allen (D Ala.) said the committee should have taken a more affirmative approach in its report. Rather than simply saying it found no reasons not to approve Ford, Allen said it should have stressed Ford's reputation as "a man of honor and high principle, a man of ability and dedication, a man of noble purpose and unimpeachable integrity."

He called Ford "an excellent choice."

Senate Floor Action

The Senate Nov. 27, by a 92-3 roll-call vote, approved the nomination.

The overwhelming vote for Ford came one week after the Rules and Administration Committee unanimously recommended his confirmation, and six and a half weeks after his nomination Oct. 12 by President Nixon to replace former Vice President Spiro T. Agnew.

The only votes against Ford were cast by three Democrats: Gaylord Nelson (Wis.), Thomas F. Eagleton (Mo.) and William D. Hathaway (Maine). Five senators were absent: George McGovern (D S.D.), Stuart Symington (D Mo.), Paul J. Fannin (R Ariz.), Edward J. Gurney (R Fla.) and James A. McClure (R Idaho). Symington, Fannin and Gurney would have voted for Ford if present, it was announced.

Debate on Ford's nomination Nov. 26 and 27 brought many statements of praise for his honesty, integrity and candor. A number of Democrats stressed that their votes to confirm Ford did not imply endorsement of his political philosophy or voting record. But they felt the President had a right to nominate a man who shared his views, and that Ford had successfully met the tests of character demanded by the office.

Several senators expressed the belief or hope that Ford would grow in stature in the vice presidency and that his views on civil rights, criticized in the hearings, would broaden.

"Frankly, I am astonished to hear myself, a lifelong Democrat, support a Republican for vice president," said Alan Cranston (D Calif.). Cranston said Nov. 26 he had surveyed several hundred persons about Ford and found only five who opposed him, and none who questioned his honesty. Cranston was impressed with the "almost startling consensus of conciliation" developing around Ford, who he said "has come into focus as someone who appears to offer the nation a steadiness and a dependability for which it yearns."

"I doubt if there has ever before been a time when integrity has so surpassed ideology in the judging of a man for so high an office in our land," Cranston said.

Philip A. Hart (D Mich.) said Nov. 27 he disagreed with Ford's voting record but maintained the nominee "would be a steady, decent and believable chief executive. And those attributes, I believe, are what this nation needs most at this particular moment in history."

Robert Taft Jr. (R Ohio): "When questioned (at the committee hearings) about matters such as executive privilege, separation of powers, presidential immunity, the (Watergate) special prosecutor and the missing tapes, Mr. Ford demonstrated a respect for not only the letter of the law but the spirit of the law."

Gaylord Nelson, however, found his philosophical differences with Ford too fundamental to compromise, he said Nov. 27. He cited Ford's record on human and civil rights and the war in Vietnam, and said he did not believe Ford could provide "the kind of inspirational leadership this nation will need should he succeed to the presidency."

Eagleton also questioned Ford's leadership ability.

Hathaway said Nov. 26 his negative vote was not based on Ford's character or qualifications but on his

---

Cramer Presence

Present throughout the House committee hearings, which ended Nov. 26, were Washington attorney and former Rep. William C. Cramer (R Fla. 1955-71) and his two law partners. Democratic Representatives Edwards of California and Conyers of Michigan expressed their concern that Ford, if he became president, might appoint Cramer to a high position in his administration—possibly attorney general, Edwards suggested.

Conyers said Nov. 26 he was "deeply disturbed" about the sort of people Ford might appoint, based on his conservative associations. Cramer was the only one he mentioned by name. Conyers said Cramer had a well-known anti-civil rights record in Congress.

Ford said the lawyers were assisting him without compensation and denied he had made any job commitments. However, Ford said: "I happen to believe he (Cramer) is a very able lawyer and was an extremely competent legislator, and I would have no hesitancy to recommend his appointment to any job in the administration."

---

view that a president undergoing impeachment investigation should not be allowed to appoint a successor, and that the country should not be governed for a prolonged period by an appointed chief executive. If Nixon left office, Ford would be the first non-elected president in U.S. history, and a "dangerous constitutional precedent" would be set, Hathaway said. He urged the Senate to withhold confirmation and pass his bill (S 2678) providing for a special election when both the presidency and the vice presidency were vacant.

House Committee Action

Hearings

The House Judiciary Committee held hearings Nov. 15-26 on the Ford nomination.

NOV. 15-16

Before Ford could give his opening statement, Rep. John Conyers Jr. (D Mich.) objected to proceeding on the nomination. Robert W. Kastenmeier (D Wis.) and Don Edwards (D Calif.) expressed the same view.

"It is totally inappropriate for the Congress to expedite action on a nomination submitted by a President who is the subject of a serious impeachment inquiry and whose credibility has been so irretrievably damaged that even members of his own party are calling on him to resign," Conyers said.

Committee Schedule. It appeared the House committee would have difficulty finishing its hearings by Nov. 21, the deadline set by Rodino. He planned evening sessions if necessary. With 38 members on the committee, 21 Democrats and 17 Republicans, all lawyers, it took hours to complete a single round of questions.

In addition, there were occasional eruptions of the committee infighting which had preceded the opening of the hearings. Conyers and Rep. Jerome R. Waldie

(D Calif.) were incensed that only eight members of the committee had been allowed to read the 1,700-page FBI "raw files" of data collected in the investigation of Ford—especially when Rep. Thomas F. Railsback (R Ill.) read at length laudatory statements made to the FBI in praise of Ford including remarks by Sens. George McGovern (S.D.), Edmund S. Muskie (Maine), United Auto Workers President Leonard Woodcock, and Ford's opponent in his last election.

Rodino ruled out of order a Conyers motion to make the entire FBI file part of the record of the hearings.

Ford Statement. Ford reiterated his beliefs in looking forward rather than backward, in truthfulness and in "friendly compromise." He stated his continued support for President Nixon, but pledged to be his own man and to tell the President when he thought he was wrong. He agreed Nixon was having credibility problems, and said he had advised him to release the Watergate tapes, meet with members of Congress, hold more press conferences and get out among the people to try to restore public confidence.

Ford said he thought his 25 years of service in Congress were "fine training" for the presidency, if he should succeed to that office; Presidents Johnson, Kennedy and Truman came from Congress and "will go down in history as better-than-good presidents. I would think my odds might be the same," Ford said. He said his background in foreign affairs was at least equal to that of previous vice presidents.

NOV. 19-21

The Senate committee's unanimous vote for Ford came as some Democratic members of the House panel continued to demonstrate their concerns about the nominee, who would be "one heartbeat, or one impeachment, away from the presidency," as Rep. Charles B. Rangel (D N.Y.) put it.

Concerns were expressed about Ford's record on civil rights, civil liberties and social programs, and his overall qualifications for leadership, based on the assumption of some members that Ford would succeed to the presidency because of the impeachment or resignation of President Nixon. Said George E. Danielson (D Calif.): "I'm thinking you're going to be president within a year."

Criteria. Several committee members discussed and questioned witnesses as to just what role the House should play in its first vice presidential confirmation proceedings. During the hearings, the committee explored such questions as:

• Should the House follow confirmation procedures similar to those followed by the Senate for routine executive branch nominations? Or does the 25th Amendment (providing for vice presidential selection) give it a broader mandate and responsibility to participate in the choice, as argued on Nov. 19 by Joseph L. Rauh Jr., national vice chairman of Americans for Democratic Action.

• Does the president have the right to nominate his own man—one of his philosophy and principles? Or does the Congress have the mandate to consider and possibly reject the man because of views and voting it disagrees with, as John Conyers Jr. (D Mich.) asked each witness.

• Should Congress approve Ford simply because he had been a member for 25 years, rose to a position of lead-

---

Rhodes Elected Minority Leader

Rep. John J. Rhodes (Ariz.) was elected without opposition by the House Republican Conference Dec. 7, 1973, to replace Vice President Gerald R. Ford as minority leader of the House.

Rhodes, 57, was left as the unopposed candidate for the job when Minority Whip Leslie C. Arends (Ill.) and Republican Conference Chairman John B. Anderson (Ill.) both decided they would not seek it. Within a few days after his announcement of candidacy Oct. 15, Rhodes' victory became a foregone conclusion.

A conservative, like Ford, Rhodes had served in the House since 1953. He had been on the Appropriations Committee since 1959 and was its second-ranking Republican member in the 93rd Congress. Rhodes had been chairman of the House Republican Policy Committee since 1963.

Previous contests for the Republican leadership job had not been nearly as peaceful. Ford won it in 1965, in a close and bitter content against Rep. Charles A. Halleck (R Ind. 1935-69), who had held the position for six years. Halleck himself had taken over only after a bitter intraparty struggle against Rep. Joseph W. Martin Jr. (R Mass. 1925-57), who had been party leader for more than a generation.

---

ership there, and was generally regarded as an honest, decent human being? Or should it demand special qualities of national leadership and excellence that Michael J. Harrington (D Mass.) said Ford lacked.

• Was President Nixon's right to nominate a potential successor clouded, even negated, as some Democrats contended, because he was under threat of impeachment?

Ford Qualifications. Even Jerome R. Waldie (D Calif.), the only committee member to state in hearings that he would vote against Ford, said he was "terribly impressed" with Ford's honesty and candor, summing up what many members of Congress held up as assets of Ford and of a good vice president.

But "in considering the qualifications of a man who stands a greater likelihood of assuming the presidency than any other vice president in our history, honesty and decency are not enough," contended Harrington, the lead-off witness Nov. 19 against Ford.

He said Ford had not demonstrated the "extraordinary leadership capabilities" needed today. He suggested Nixon made an "in-House" nomination because he figured, apparently correctly, that it would be approved easily by Congress. Harrington said he deplored the "Washington-talking-to-Washington" atmosphere of the Ford hearings. Further, he argued that Ford did not measure up to the expectation of the American people, even allowing for the "conservative mandate" of the 1972 presidential election.

Several committee members said the country should not expect a "Messiah," "a superhuman," a "matinee idol" or a "perfect man." They indicated they thought Ford was about as good a choice as Nixon could have made, and suggested, to his detractors, that he might "grow" in the job.

Civil Rights. Several committee members and witnesses attacked Ford's record. Ford defended himself emphatically, saying, "I'm actually proud of my civil rights voting record, and I'm proud of my personal attitude vis-a-vis minority groups."

Clarence Mitchell of the National Association for the Advancement of Colored People (NAACP) said he could not recall any positive or affirmative action Ford ever took as House minority leader for civil rights. He said Nov. 19 that Ford had worked to gut several key civil rights bills, and described him as "restricted," not "committed," on civil rights.

Civil Liberties. Waldie said one of the main reasons he opposed Ford was that Ford's 1970 attempt to impeach Supreme Court Justice William O. Douglas showed Ford was "insensitive" in civil liberties areas and did not understand or accept the independence of the judiciary. That, Waldie said, "could be the most important weakness of all" in a man who could become president and appoint justices to the high court.

Rep. Edward P. Boland (D Mass.), a friend and colleague of Ford's for 21 years, Nov. 19 testified on his behalf, and the National Lawyers Guild opposed the nomination on grounds the 1972 election was illegal and Nixon therefore had no right to appoint Ford.

Committee Report

The House Judiciary Committee Nov. 29 voted 29-8 to report favorably the nomination.

Before voting, Don Edwards (D Calif.) urged rejection of Ford because of his "dismal" record on civil rights, "inappropriate associates," and lack of "high intelligence, great sensitivity and judgment." He and Jerome R. Waldie (D Calif.) criticized Ford for "improper" activities in his 1970 attempt to impeach Supreme Court Justice William O. Douglas.

Jack Brooks (D Texas) urged support for Ford despite political differences. He said Ford was honest, moral and candid, and "if he does become president, he'll be a heck of a lot better than the one we've got." Republicans Lawrence J. Hogan (Md.) and Tom Railsback (Ill.) also praised Ford.

Edward Hutchinson (Mich.), the committee's ranking Republican member, made the motion to report the nomination with the recommendation that the House confirm Ford. Voting fot it were 12 Democrats and all the committee's 17 Republicans:

Democrats: Rodino (N.J.), Donohue (Mass.), Brooks (Texas), Hungate (Mo.), Eilberg (Pa.), Flowers (Ala.), Mann (S.C.), Sarbanes (Md.), Danielson (Calif.), Thornton (Ark.), Owens (Utah) (by proxy) and Mezvinsky Iowa).

Republicans: Hutchinson, McClory (Ill.), Smith (N.Y.), Sandman (N.J.), Railsback (Ill.), Wiggins (Calif.), Dennis (Ind.), Fish (N.Y.), Mayne (Iowa) (by proxy), Hogan (Md.), Keating (Ohio), Butler (Va.), Cohen (Maine), Lott (Miss.), Froehlich (Wis.), Moorhead (Calif.) and Maraziti (N.J.).

Those voting against Ford were all Democrats: Kastenmeier (Wis.), Edwards (Calif.), Conyers (Mich.), Waldie (Calif.), Drinan (Mass.), Rangel (N.Y.) (by proxy); Jordan (Texas) and Holtzman (N.Y.).

John F. Seiberling (D Ohio) voted present, saying he had "very serious problems" with the Ford nomination, and would reserve judgment on it until the floor vote,

tentatively scheduled for Dec. 6. Joshua Eilberg (D Pa.) voted to report out the nomination but said his vote did not necessarily mean he would vote for Ford on the floor.

Before voting to report the Ford nomination, the committee rejected, 5-33, a motion by Elizabeth Holtzman (D N.Y.) to table the nomination.

Report. The committee filed its report on the nomination Dec. 4 (H Rept 93-695). After reviewing the commitee's investigation, the report concluded: "Finally, not every member of the committee subscribing to this report finds himself in complete agreement with the totality of Mr. Ford's voting record, or even with all aspects of his general philosophy of government. Some, though by no means all, are disturbed with elements of his voting record in the area of civil rights and human rights.

"But looking at the total record, the committee finds Mr. Ford fit and qualified to hold the high office for which he has been nominated pursuant to the Twenty-fifth Amendment."

Each of the eight members who voted against Ford filed dissenting views. Seiberling, who voted present, filed separate views in which he suggested that the proceedings on the Ford nomination had "already brought out sufficient flaws in the 25th Amendment to justify a new search for a better way to handle the problem of presidential succession. Such a search should include consideration as to whether it is necessary even to have a Vice President, since, except as a replacement for the President, it is an unnecessary office."

House Floor Action

The House Dec. 6, by a 387-35 recorded vote, approved the nomination of Ford to be vice president of the United States.

The historic vote completing the confirmation process of the nation's 40th vice president came after five hours of floor debate. It was the first time the House of Representatives had participated in a confirmation proceeding, and the first time a vice president was selected under provisions of the 25th Amendment to the Constitution.

The overwhelming 387-35 vote confirming Ford was foreshadowed by the debate. Republican members lined up at the microphones to announce their support for Ford and ask permission to place lengthier statements in the record. They were joined by many Democrats who praised Ford's honesty and integrity even though they had political differences. Some speakers said they expected Ford to become president and that he could help restore the faith of the people in their government.

Main arguments of the opposition were that Ford lacked the qualities of leadership needed in a president, that he was insensitive to the needs of the poor and the black and to the rule of law, and that no nomination should be considered at all until the question of impeaching President Nixon was settled. All the votes against him were cast by Democrats.

Unexpected Votes. The only surprises punctuating the otherwise predictable debate were the announcements by Judiciary Committee Chairman Peter W. Rodino Jr. (D N.J.) that he would vote against Ford, and by Andrew Young (D Ga.) that he would vote for him. Young was the

(Continued on p. 52)

FORD: NINTH VICE PRESIDENT TO FILL VACANT POST

Gerald R. Ford was the ninth vice president to step up to the presidency because of a vacancy in the nation's highest office. He was the first to succeed to the office because of a presidential resignation.

In the past, unscheduled transitions in the presidency have been almost uniformly sudden. The assassination of President John F. Kennedy in 1963, and the deaths of Presidents Franklin D. Roosevelt in 1945, and Warren G. Harding in 1923 all stunned the nation. So did the deaths of Presidents William Henry Harrison in 1841, Zachary Taylor in 1850 and Abraham Lincoln in 1865.

Only in the case of Presidents William McKinley and James A. Garfield was there a warning that the end was coming. McKinley lived six days after being shot at Buffalo, N.Y., in September 1901 and Garfield survived two months and 17 days following wounds inflicted on him in a Washington, D.C., railroad terminal in July 1881.

But the transition to the Ford presidency was unique in American history. President Nixon's resignation was the result of a long period of increasing pressure. By early August, according to the Gallup Poll, 64 per cent of Americans favored impeachment of the President and 55 per cent favored his removal from office. And Republicans as well as Democrats in Congress were calling for his removal.

LYNDON JOHNSON

One of President Lyndon B. Johnson's first acts as president was to address Congress and urge passage of President Kennedy's stalled legislative program. Reminding Congress that "our most immediate tasks are here on this Hill," Johnson said, "No memorial or eulogy could more eloquently honor President Kennedy's memory than the earliest possible passage of the civil rights bill for which he fought so long."

During 1964, Johnson worked hard at implementing Kennedy's legislative program. His efforts were crowned with success when he signed the Civil Rights Act of 1964 July 2. Earlier, on Feb. 26, he signed legislation providing long range tax reduction, also a part of President Kennedy's program.

But no new president is ever satisfied simply to serve as an extension of his predecessor. To stand as president in his own right and with his own program has been the goal of all presidents. "Accidental presidents" —those who are not elected but succeed to the office— have a more difficult time doing this than those who are elected in their own right. Feeling bound by the policies and loyalties of their predecessors, they must balance the demands of the past against the need to develop an identity of their own.

Thus, in addition to Kennedy's proposals, Johnson added a grand new design of his own, the anti-poverty program. This he made the core of his effort to establish a Johnson presidency as opposed to a Kennedy presidency. Then, in 1965, following his smashing election victory over Sen. Barry M. Goldwater (R) of Arizona, Johnson pushed through a series of major new programs, including a voting rights bill, federal aid to education and medicare.

Staff Changes

As with policies, so with personnel. A man suddenly thrust into the White House by accident inherits a Cabinet and full White House staff. He needs the experience and knowledge of those who have been in charge of day-to-day operations of government. But he also needs to feel comfortable and confident with those working for him. For that purpose, the natural inclination of a new president is to bring in his own men, people he has gotten to know and trust over the years.

Again, a balance has to be struck between the desire to demonstrate continuity and the impetus toward establishing a new presidency. When Johnson took office, he immediately sought to retain as many Kennedy appointees as possible. He feared the country would lose confidence in him if there were a sudden exodus of Kennedy aides. So successful was Johnson in his efforts that no Kennedy man left until Ted Sorensen, special counsel to the president, departed on Feb. 29, 1964. And many top figures stayed on through 1964 and into 1965 and beyond, including national security aide McGeorge Bundy; Walter Heller, chairman of the Council of Economic Advisers; Budget Director Kermit Gordon, and Lawrence O'Brien, special assistant to the President and later postmaster general.

Johnson Cabinet

The Cabinet, too, remained. In fact, only Attorney General Robert F. Kennedy, the late president's brother, left Johnson's Cabinet before January 1965. And four Cabinet officers—Secretary of State Dean Rusk; Secretary of the Interior Stewart L. Udall; Secretary of Labor W. Willard Wirtz, and Secretary of Agriculture Orville L. Freeman—remained at their posts throughout the second Johnson administration as well.

HARRY TRUMAN

President Harry S Truman, who assumed the presidency on Roosevelt's death, became president at one of

Vice Presidential Successions		
President	**Date of Vacancy**	**New President**
William Henry Harrison	April 4, 1841	John Tyler
Zachary Taylor	July 9, 1850	Millard Fillmore
Abraham Lincoln	April 15, 1865	Andrew Johnson
James A. Garfield	Sept. 19, 1881	Chester Alan Arthur
William McKinley	Sept. 14, 1901	Theodore Roosevelt
Warren G. Harding	Aug. 2, 1923	Calvin Coolidge
Franklin D. Roosevelt	April 12, 1945	Harry S Truman
John F. Kennedy	Nov. 22, 1963	Lyndon B. Johnson
Richard M. Nixon	Aug. 9, 1974	Gerald R. Ford

the most difficult moments in American—and indeed, world—history. World War II was drawing to a close, and delicate postwar negotiations with the Soviet Union were ahead.

Within a few weeks, a decision had to be made on whether to use the atomic bomb against Japan, a bomb Truman had never even heard of. And domestically, plans had to be developed to cope with the return of millions of veterans and conversion to a peacetime economy.

Cabinet Departures

Despite his lack of experience, Truman set out early to establish control of his presidency. Within six months, seven of the 10 members of the Roosevelt cabinet had gone. The three that remained Truman eventually dismissed, two of them after bitter quarrels.

On Sept. 6, 1945, Truman presented to Congress a massive domestic program, consisting of 21 points. Generally recognized as in line with Roosevelt's New Deal, Truman's proposals included increased unemployment compensation and minimum wage; machinery to provide for a full employment policy; a permanent fair employment practices commission; aid to housing, and liberal veterans benefits.

However, critics accused Truman of abandoning Roosevelt's foreign policy, especially the close wartime relationship established with the Soviet Union. Truman contended that the Soviets were to blame, and eventually adopted a policy which included the Truman Doctrine of anti-Communist aid to Greece and Turkey; the North Atlantic Treaty Organization, a military alliance aimed to deter feared Soviet aggression in Europe, and the engagement of U.S. forces in Korea.

Henry A. Wallace, who had been Roosevelt's vice president from 1941 to 1945, broke with the Truman administration, mainly on foreign policy issues, and eventually ran against Truman in 1948 as the candidate of the Progressive Party. Truman's upset victory that year established his credentials as president in his own right.

CALVIN COOLIDGE

Calvin Coolidge acceded to the presidency just as the massive scandals of the Harding administration were about to break open. Coolidge, with his solid, conservative Yankee background was the perfect man to cope with the scandals.

He simply dismissed those officials who appeared to be involved, including Attorney General Harry M. Daugherty, appointed two special prosecutors, and let the scandals play themselves out in court. His policy proved a success with the voters. He was elected to a term of his own in 1924 and carried the Republicans to increased majorities in both houses of Congress.

Otherwise, Coolidge was a noncontroversial president who did not have to deal with any great crises or problems.

THEODORE ROOSEVELT

Regular Republicans feared Theodore Roosevelt's assumption of the presidency with the death of McKinley in 1901. Republican leaders in New York had promoted his elevation to the vice presidency to get him out of the state, where he was feared by the machine as being unpredictable and impetuous.

Roosevelt lived up to some, but not all, the fears of Republican organization men. One of his first acts in office

Constitutional Requirements

Upon confirmation as Vice President by the Senate and the House of Representatives in 1973, Gerald R. Ford became the first person to assume that office under the provisions of the 25th Amendment which requires that a vice presidential vacancy must be filled. When Ford became President on Aug. 9, 1974, the 22nd Amendment limited his term of service to no more than six and a half years. Thus Ford could seek nomination and election as President in 1976; but, if successful, he could not seek re-election in 1980.

25th Amendment

On Oct. 12, 1973, President Nixon nominated Ford, House Minority Leader and for 25 years representative to Congress from Grand Rapids, Mich., to succeed former Vice President Spiro T. Agnew. Agnew had resigned Oct. 10, 1973, in the face of charges of income tax evasion. Section 2 of the 25th Amendment provides that "whenever there is a vacancy in the office of the Vice President, the President shall nominate a Vice President who shall take office upon confirmation by majority vote of both houses of Congress."

Prior to ratification of the 25th Amendment Feb. 10, 1967, no procedures had been laid down to govern situations when the vice presidency was not occupied. In the nation's history, that office had been vacated 16 times for a total of 37 years, after the elected Vice President succeeded to the presidency, died, or in the case of Vice President John C. Calhoun in 1832, resigned.

22nd Amendment

Under the 22nd Amendment, ratified by three-fourths of the states' legislatures by Feb. 27, 1951, no President can stand for election more than once if he has served for more than two years of his predecessor's term. Thus, because two and a half years remained in Richard M. Nixon's presidential term when he resigned Aug. 9, 1974, Ford could be elected to the presidency in his own right only once.

The 22nd Amendment was quickly approved and sent to the states March 24, 1947, by the first Republican Congress after President Roosevelt's election to four terms. It stipulates that "No person shall be elected to the office of the President more than twice, and no person who has held the office of President, or acted as President, for more than two years of a term to which some other person was elected President shall be elected to the office of the President more than once."

During floor debate on the amendment, supporters of the measure had claimed it had nothing to do with politics, but rather sought only to incorporate into the Constitution the two-term tradition set by George Washington. Opponents cited Washington, Jefferson and Theodore Roosevelt who had stated that an emergency might make it advisable for a person to accept more than two terms as President.

was to file suit against the Northern Securities Company, the nation's first major antitrust suit.

The move upset the nation's conservatives, who predicted economic reverses for the country. But Roosevelt did not recklessly antagonize those who controlled the party machinery, instead making an effort to unite the party behind him.

By a combination of caution and exploitation of his public popularity, Roosevelt won over most of the Republican leaders and in 1904 became the first "accidental" president to receive the nomination for a full term. Moreover, he proved not to be a wrecker, but a great asset to the Republican Party, bringing it its most smashing presidential victory up to that time.

CHESTER ARTHUR

Garfield's assassination in 1881 brought Chester Alan Arthur to the presidency. Arthur was a close ally of Sen. Roscoe Conkling (R) of New York who at the time of the shooting was engaged in a bitter fight with the administration. Thus, Arthur's assumption of the presidency brought another faction of the Republican Party into power.

Garfield's cabinet, headed by Conkling's arch-enemy, James G. Blaine, was soon out of office. Four of the seven cabinet officers resigned before the end of 1881, and two others followed in early 1882. Only Secretary of War Robert Lincoln, son of President Abraham Lincoln, served for the rest of Arthur's term.

Arthur was never able to firmly establish his control over Republican Party affairs and was defeated for his party's nomination for a full term in 1884 by Blaine.

ANDREW JOHNSON

Perhaps the most disastrous transition was that following Lincoln's assassination. Lincoln had chosen Andrew Johnson as his running mate in 1864 to emphasize the coalition of Republicans and pro-war Democrats supporting the Union during the Civil War.

Johnson, a Democrat, had been the only member of the U.S. Senate from a seceding southern state (Tennessee) to remain loyal to the Union in 1861. Lincoln later made him military governor of Tennessee.

Johnson as president was an anomaly. He was a southerner at a time when the South was out of the union; a Jacksonian Democrat who believed in states' rights, hard money and minimal federal government activity running an administration pursuing a policy of expansion both in the money supply and the role of government; a man who had little regard for the Negro in the midst of a party many of whose members were actively seeking to guarantee the rights of the newly free slaves.

On Lincoln's death in 1865, this outsider without allies or connections in the Republican Party succeeded to the presidency.

Johnson's ideas on what should have been done to reconstruct and readmit the southern states to representation clashed with the wishes of a majority of Congress, overwhelmingly controlled by the Republicans. The resulting conflict led to the first vote of impeachment against a president by the full House. However, Johnson was acquitted by the Senate by a margin of one vote.

Johnson had mixed results with his Cabinet. Three of the seven officers stayed on through his entire ad-ministration. A fourth, Secretary of War Edwin M. Stanton remained almost to the end, but Johnson was engaged much of the time in trying to get rid of him.

TYLER AND FILLMORE

The first two unscheduled presidential successions—John Tyler in 1841 and Millard Fillmore in 1850—resulted in sharp changes of policy. Tyler was selected as Harrison's running mate in 1840 to get southern Democratic votes for the Whig ticket. Tyler was an anti-Jackson Democrat and this was a crucial group in the Whigs' attempt to build a winning coalition.

But Tyler did not favor much of the Whig program, including a protective tariff and national bank. When Harrison died one month after his inauguration in the spring of 1841, Tyler assumed the presidency and promptly began vetoing the Whig program. In protest, all but one of Harrison's cabinet, which Tyler had inherited, resigned in September 1841. A stalemate was reached which lasted throughout the Tyler administration. Neither party was interested in nominating him for a full term in 1844.

In Fillmore's case, his succession to the presidency came at a critical moment in the course of a hard-fought legislative battle. Henry Clay was trying to push a group of measures known collectively as the Compromise of 1850 through Congress, but President Taylor had been opposing the measures. Fillmore at once reversed the presidential position, throwing his support to Clay. As a result, the bills, which had largely to do with whether and to what extent slavery would be allowed in the territories newly acquired from Mexico, passed.

Fillmore replaced Taylor's entire cabinet within two months and two days of assuming office. ∎

(Vice Presidential Confirmation from p. 49)
only black member of the House who supported Ford, whose record on civil rights was attacked during his confirmation hearings.

Young was applauded by the heavily pro-Ford House when he broke with "the colleagues I respect most" to support Ford "as an act of faith and hope. I hope and pray he measures up" and can restore public confidence in government through his personal integrity, Young said.

Rodino, who conducted the House hearings on Ford and voted to report his nomination favorably to the floor, had given no indication he planned to vote against Ford. However, having done his duty as Judiciary Committee chairman, Rodino said the needs of his urban constituents "cry out for executive leadership in the area of human rights and the cause of working people.... I vote, not against Gerald Ford's worth as a man of great integrity, but in dissent with the present administration's indifference to the plight of so many Americans."

Nixon Resignation Considered. Despite several last-minute appeals to the House not to put the nation in the position of having a non-elected president and vice president (if Ford should succeed Nixon during his term and then name his own successor), the House became impatient to vote by late afternoon. Several members, however, protested that the debate and their votes were meaningless since the swearing-in ceremony already had been scheduled and television time set. ∎

APPENDIX

CQ

PUBLIC STATEMENTS OF GERALD R. FORD, 1965-74

The following statements of Gerald R. Ford were made during the years he served as House Minority Leader (1965-73) and as Vice President (1973-74).* For additional detail on Ford's statements and actions as Vice President, see p.61 for his statements on President Nixon and impeachment; p.67 for politics and elections; p.70 for foreign policy; and p.71 for domestic policy.

Amnesty

Press Conference, Washington, D.C. Feb. 6, 1973:

...you don't downgrade the 2,500,000 who served in Vietnam by changing the status of those who decided to leave the country and to violate the law.

Blacks in Politics

National Urban League, San Francisco, California, July 29, 1974:

In my opinion a heavy concentration of blacks in one party is not good for the country. It will not produce good government, it is not good for either political party, nor is it good for the black community. Add to this the current and future trends regarding the shifting of increased responsibilities to manage public affairs to the state and local level and it appears more vital than ever that blacks should be drawn into both political parties.

Campaign Reform and Finance

Washington, D.C., Jan. 19, 1967:

Congress must also move ahead on the President's year-old pledge for a Clean Elections Law. Such a law must be in force before 1968.

This Clean Elections Law should guarantee full and accurate reporting of political contributions and expenditures in support of national candidates and put an end to abuses in campaign finance. Legislation also is needed to encourage an increased flow of small contributions. Republicans are proud that 69 per cent of our contributions in the last Presidential campaign were in sums of less than $100....

An illogical federal law now operates to prevent television and radio stations from granting time without charge to major party candidates without making equal time available to a host of minor party candidates. We unequivocally favor nationally televised debates between future Presidential contenders.

We propose legislation requiring television and radio to provide free and equal treatment to major parties and their spokesmen not only in future campaigns, but also for the presentations of divergent political views throughout the periods between formal campaigning....

---

*A source of public statements by Ford for the years 1965-72 is *Gerald R. Ford, Selected Speeches,* ed. Michael V. Doyle, R. W. Beatty, Ltd., Arlington, Va., 1973.

University of Jacksonville, Jacksonville, Florida, Dec. 16, 1971:

I am opposed to the expenditure of tax dollars for political campaigning in principle. I am just as much opposed to the campaign checkoff provision now as I was when it was timed to the 1972 campaign.

The argument is made that the campaign checkoff provision takes the Presidential election out of the hands of the big private donors. But this ignores what happens when there is a fight over a party's nomination. When that happens private money flows profusely into certain primary campaigns, and the person winning the nomination has been helped to the nomination by his assorted financial backers. Under the campaign checkoff provision, the successful nominee then would go on to try to win the Presidency with a tax-financed campaign—and still would be obligated, if you will, to those who made it possible for him to win the nomination....

House of Representatives, May 16, 1973:

I have always felt that timely disclosure before election day is a better way to insure clean campaigns than the most severe punishment afterward.

In politics as in other forms of competition the successful professionals play by the rules, and the rules should be simple, fair, and reasonable. Our two-party system provides a measure of mutual vigilance which must be preserved no matter what reforms are enacted into law....

As a Republican I reaffirm my faith in my party and recall that Republicans led the fight for election reform legislation throughout the 1960s which culminated in the 1971 act signed by President Nixon....

Communist Powers

Duke University, Feb. 2, 1968:

To those who recognize no such entity as "world Communism" the words I now am about to speak will seem meaningless. The same will be true of those who believe the threat of Communist domination of the world is vastly exaggerated. I personally believe that the Communist powers of the world implacably seek the downfall of the Free World nations—chiefly, the United States....

University of Jacksonville, Jacksonville, Florida, Dec. 16, 1971:

The challenge in foreign affairs is to build a foundation for future peace while repelling efforts both on the Right and on the Left to shunt America off into a new posture of isolationism. We must maintain our position of leadership in the world if the world is to have any chance to live in peace.

A new quality of realism now dominates American foreign policy. We have agreed to accept Mainland China as a sovereign nation, adjusting our policies in Asia to meet changed economic and political conditions there. Following our military withdrawal from Vietnam, we will continue to provide support under the Nixon Doctrine for our non-Communist friends in Asia.

In our relations with the Soviet Union, new realism on both sides has recognized a mutual interest in reducing the risk of nuclear war....

I am convinced the bargaining from strength carried on by the Administration at SALT has earned the respect of the Russians. The prospects for agreement today are related, in my view, to our own decision to proceed with strategic weapons development—including the ABM system—during these talks.

We are turning from an era of confrontation to an era of negotiation. But there is no question in my mind that negotiation will prove fruitful only if we negotiate from a position of strength. This is the lesson which is lost on the neo-isolationists.

We are achieving success in foreign affairs because we are continuing to show the world that we are determined to discharge America's responsibilities.

We did not withdraw troops from Europe in the absence of an agreement for mutual troop withdrawal.

Crime and Justice

Academy of Medicine, Cincinnati, Ohio, Oct. 18, 1966:

Some contend that crime springs mainly from conditions of poverty. If this were true, the U.S. crime rate should be falling in...[President] Johnson's great society. After all, the administration brags about the unemployment rate of less than four per cent—never mentioning, of course, that the Vietnam War is a big factor in the situation.

We have traveled farther and farther down the road toward becoming a complete welfare state—and yet the crime rate continues its frighteningly swift rise. I say that economic security from the cradle to the grave is not the answer to the problem of crime.

Crime breeds and spreads in an atmosphere of lawlessness. It feeds on community apathy and the unwillingness of the individual citizen to become involved in law enforcement and to support it adequately....

Washington, D.C., Jan. 19, 1967:

Wiretapping and electronic eavesdropping worry all Americans who prize their privacy. Properly used, these are essential weapons to those who guard our Nation's security and wage ceaseless war against organized crime.

The Congress, the President and the Courts must promptly spell out the permissible limits of their use.

At all levels of government a massive effort should be made to reduce crime by attacking some of its basic causes: poverty, slums, inadequate education and discrimination. However, our laws and actions should never be based on the theory that a criminal is solely the product of his environment.

Fear of punishment remains an important deterrent to crime.

We call upon the independent Judicial Branch of our Government to uphold the rights of the law-abiding citizen with the same fervor as it upholds the rights of the accused.

Illinois Wesleyan University, Bloomington, Illinois, Feb. 10, 1969:

What is our chief domestic concern? There is none greater than that of the public safety—the concern over violence in the streets and the still-rocketing rise in crime. President Nixon is acting to answer that concern.

Abraham Lincoln preached "reverence for the law" and urged that it become "the political religion of the nation," for he knew, as we do, that without order there can be no progress.

Without order there can only be anarchy, chaos and confusion.

We must attack crime with all the manpower and the weapons and the firmness required to curb it—and we will do so.

We must lay a foundation for order by improving the quality and direction of life in America and the responsiveness of its institutions—and we will do that also....

Having assumed the office of President when the pages of American history were flooded with a swelling tide of crime and violence, Richard Nixon has resolved to cool the violent passions that have engulfed this country and to rollback the rising wave of crime. He has made an excellent start.

Wichita State University, Wichita, Kansas, May 7, 1970:

The Nixon Administration recognizes, as do all of you, that the first civil right of every American—black or white—is the right to protection from crime and violence.

I wish more of our Negro leaders throughout America would recognize that. It is an unfortunate fact that it is primarily the poor blacks who are the victims of violent crime in our country.

Economic Policy

Tulane University, New Orleans, Louisiana, April 19, 1968:

Politically speaking, "fiscal responsibility" is not a very exciting phrase. But it's big with the voter who knows there can be neither social progress nor individual progress in a nation with unsound money.

I'm told that inflation doesn't bother today's young people. They have not lived through the Great Depression. They have not seen the economy go smash. But a leading pollster reports that 60 per cent of Americans generally feel that inflation is a major concern. They know that inflation is a fancy word for "high prices" and that the dollar just doesn't buy much any more....

Press Conference, Washington, D.C., March 6, 1973:

The President has to have some flexibility, and I think it is historically true that Presidents have used that flexibility and they are not, in my judgment, obligated to spend every time that Congress appropriates, because Congress, on many occasions, has acted irresponsibly in the fiscal field and Congress, in many instances, will appropriate money in anticipation of one circumstance and those circumstances change and the President shouldn't spend the money just because it was appropriated.

Press Conference, Washington, D.C., Sept. 6, 1973:

We are getting a sound monetary policy, we are increasing the supply of food, we are, at the same time, trying to hold the lid on through the freeze in [President Nixon's] Phase IV and we are trying desperately to keep the Federal budget in balance.

And the Congress in this area can be cooperative or uncooperative and, if the Congress foists upon the President overly generous appropriation bills and requires him to spend and spend and spend, the Congress will have to bear the blame for inflation.

National Conference for Agricultural Stabilization and Conservation Service, Washington, D.C., Aug. 6, 1974:

When the eagle on the dollar screams, the cry must be heeded by all Americans. Inflation cannot be defeated by recrimination and attack from any segment of our society on any other segment. I refer to both business and labor, and the Executive Department as well as the Congress. Let us seek avenues to unity, roads along which we can move together to meet the common enemy.

There are obviously many views and approaches in dealing with inflation. We need to explore a wide spectrum of ideas. I prefer an open and objective spirit of inquiry in which all views are given consideration. Congressional involvement is essential. So is the concentrated determination of the Executive Department. Working together, an example can be set for the Nation.

Let Washington restrain spending, if others are to follow.

Let Washington show the way to increased production.

Let a real partnership of the people and the Government be organized to protect the dollar.

Washington cannot ask others to show restraint unless Government demonstrates its own commitment. Accordingly, we must veto "budget-busting" legislation. We will need political guts to defer programs that are marginally desirable but not really essential. We cannot afford optional luxuries while striving to beat inflation....

We must prevent such budget overruns from taking place....

It serves no purpose to lecture the harrassed public, especially the low and middle income people who have been the main losers from inflation. We are mindful that some people are suffering more than others. Certain groups—older Americans, persons on fixed incomes, the unemployed—may require special help within budgetary limitations. Their plight must be heeded.

Education

Saint Leo College, Bal Harbour, Florida, March 8, 1974:

American higher education today stands foremost in the world both in terms of scholarship and in terms of the opportunities offered our people. We intend that it should continue to occupy that position.

We must not only make that resolve. We must also innovate and relate to the world in which young people find themselves. Innovation is the key if the nation's colleges are to offer quality higher education to growing numbers of Americans of all ages and from all walks of life.

Let us develop new models of teaching and learning and institutional management. There must be new research, a willingness to experiment with change, a readiness to probe into new areas of scholarship.

Electoral College Reform

Newsletter, Washington, D.C., March 5, 1969:

I have stated in this newsletter that I was sympathetic to the direct election of the President in a manner suggested by the American Bar Association (March 6, 1968). When I first came to Congress there was considerable interest in the...proposal for the proportional plan of electoral reform.

I believe in the inherent vitality of the states. I believe in the ability of the states to make significant and essential contributions to the rehabilitation of our metropolitan areas. And despite the trend in recent years, I firmly believe that local problems can be solved by local officials if they are given the tools....

University of Jacksonville, Jacksonville, Florida, Dec. 16, 1971:

In a political sense, there is one problem that currently underlies all of the others. That problem is making government sufficiently responsive to the people. If we don't make government responsive to the people, we don't make it believable. And we must make government believable if we are to have a functioning democracy....

The other party may come forward with its own ideas but I personally feel the best cures for popular lethargy and voter apathy lie in returning power to the people and restructuring the Federal Government.

I am talking specifically about no-strings sharing of Federal revenue with state and local governments and about an overhaul of Federal cabinet departments.

This is not very sexy stuff, but it's what is needed to close the gap between promise and performance in the relationship between government and the people.

Federal revenue sharing is a continuing financial transfusion that can save our federal system and bring new strength to government at the grassroots level. Money is power, and the idea is to put more of the money where more of the power ought to be—at the local level. The idea is to put the money where the problems are, and in that way to solve them.

Press Conference, Washington, D.C., Sept. 6, 1973:

Education, housing, and manpower are areas where we can hopefully consolidate some of the multitude of categorical grant programs, improve education and housing and manpower at the local level and get rid of this top-heavy, bureaucratic control in Washington.

Conference of Lieutenant Governors, Santa Fe, New Mexico, July 12, 1974:

The Union exists because of the states and for the states. It is from the states that the Union receives and retains its power. It is upon the states that the Union confers its strength and bestows its benefits. This is an historical truth that must be restored to focus. It is a need demonstrated by the excesses of federal problem solving—and problem-creating—of the last few decades....

We have learned some lessons the hard way. This has been especially true of social problems. Answers did not come from the dumping of tax dollars on top of the problem. Nor did we solve problems by mobilizing armies of bureaucrats, commissioned to smother the issue under a deluge of processed paper.

The result of such approaches is too often seen in the inflation of the economy and cost of government. We have not experienced a deflation of the problems and difficulties. But we have learned how to do things better....

The federal government should not expect its state and local counterparts to help it do its work without also helping them to put their own administrative houses in order....

A prime motivation behind general revenue sharing was the fiscal crisis of state governments. The remedy worked....

Ford's Humor
Gridiron Club, Washington, D.C., March 9, 1968:

I sort of sympathize with the Senator from New York. I know there's one big dealer here in town who'd like to send this Ford back to Michigan.

But that would be dirty politics at its Nader.

Right now though, the President better keep his eyes on Gene McCarthy. Gene talks a lot about principal, but he's a typical Democrat alright. His interest rate keeps going higher and higher.

Now that George Wallace, there's a horse of a different color.

In your heart, you know he's white.

If George sneaks off with just a few little ol' electoral votes, we may have to pick the next President in the House of Representatives....

I love the House of Representatives, despite the long, irregular hours.

Sometimes, though, when it's late and I'm tired and hungry—on that long drive home to Alexandria—as I go past 1600 Pennsylvania Avenue, I do seem to hear a little voice saying:

"If you lived here, you'd be home now."

Impeachment
House of Representatives, April 15, 1970; speech on the conduct of Supreme Court Justice William O. Douglas:

I have studied the principal impeachment actions that have been initiated over the years and frankly, there are too few cases to make very good law. About the only thing the authorities can agree upon in recent history, though it was hotly argued up to President Johnson's impeachment and the trial of Judge Swayne, is that an offense need not be indictable to be impeachable. In other words, something less than a criminal act or criminal dereliction of duty may nevertheless be sufficient grounds for impeachment and removal from public office.

What, then, is an impeachable offense? The only honest answer is that an impeachable offense is whatever a majority of the House of Representatives considers to be at a given moment in history; conviction results from whatever offense or offenses two-thirds of the other body considers to be sufficiently serious to require removal of the accused from office. Again, the historical context and political climate are important; there are few fixed principles among the handful of precedents.

Judiciary
Dallas, Texas, Nov. 8, 1965:

In my judgment, today we find an erosion of the power and prestige of the legislative branch, a change of the intended direction of the Judiciary and an awesome build-up of strength and use of this power in the Executive arm....

Let me add a word on the relationship of the Legislative arm vis-a-vis the Judicial branch. It is my judgment that today the Judicial branch is to some unfortunate extent arbitrarily elbowing its way into spheres not intended at the time the Constitution was drafted.

I subscribe to the views of the late Supreme Court Justice Felix Frankfurter who so convincingly espoused the philosophy of "judicial restraint." I believe he also soundly raised an arm of caution to the courts suggesting they might wisely stay out of the "thicket" of political matters relying in such cases on the "ultimate sound judgment of the conscience of the voters." Quite frankly, I favor a strong and firm attitude by our courts in those areas where their "arm" can bring reason, order and respect for law to our system....

Middle East, Israel and Soviet Jews
American-Israel Public Affairs Committee, Washington, D.C., April 24, 1969:

I firmly believe that the fate of Israel is linked to the national security interests of the United States. I therefore cannot conceive of a situation in which the U.S. Administration will sell Israel down the Nile....

I have no illusions about Soviet policy and the attempts by the Kremlin to create a sphere of influence in the Middle East that would undermine vital American security interests and threaten the entire southern flank of NATO. The game being played by the Russians, exploiting Arab hostility against Israel, is transparent.

It is my conviction that American policy will not seek to "impose" a settlement as a result of the present Big Four Conference or outside the context of such talks.

President Nixon has pledged that Israel's vital interests will be preserved and that withdrawal can occur only by consent of the parties directly concerned, based upon a contractual agreement establishing a peace involving recognized, defensible, and just boundaries.

At that time I supported this proposal under which the electoral vote of a state would be distributed among the candidates for President in proportion to the popular vote cast. I believe there is merit in the suggestion that electoral votes be determined on a basis of the popular vote in each congressional district with two electoral votes going to the candidate who received the most statewide votes.

Any one of these proposals is preferable to our present system under which the winner of the most popular votes in each state takes all the electoral votes, and the individual elector may vote contrary to the will of the people who selected him.

Environment, Ecology and Energy

"Earth Day" address at the Civic Auditorium, Grand Rapids, Michigan, April 22, 1970:

We are here as part of a nationwide declaration that America must change its way of living or smother in its own wastes....

The first step is to lay down national water and air quality standards, and then we must enforce those standards fairly and vigorously.

We must lay down precise effluent standards for all polluters of our water—both industrial and municipal.

We must take swift court actions when those water quality standards are violated and we must extend Federal pollution control authority to include all navigable waters.

We must establish stringent national air quality standards, particularly for pollutants that are hazardous to health. And we must crack down on violation of those air quality standards with fines of up to $10,000 a day.

At the same time, we must move as swiftly as possible to greatly reduce air pollution from the internal combustion engine. Whether 1973 or 1975 are early enough goals is open to question.

Grand Rapids, Michigan, January 13, 1972:

The problems and challenges in the management of our land, our water and all of our natural resources will require the very best effort on the part of all of us. We must achieve maximum extension of the life of our resources and a new quality of life for the American people.

This is a time for vision, a time to give new life to our dreams of a place in the sun free from the noise and confusion that confound modern man.

News Release, Washington, D.C., April 11, 1973:

I approve of the Environmental Protection Agency decision to give the auto industry a one-year delay in meeting the 1975 anti-pollution standards.

This is a decision which is in the best interests of the consumer. It would have been most unwise to foist untested and highly expensive catalytic converters on the auto-buying public simply to be able to say we had met the deadline.

Press Conference, Washington, D.C., Sept. 6, 1973:

Now, if we are going to avoid being cold in the winter and excessively hot in the summer, if we are going to save jobs in America by permitting us to grow, we have got to develop a domestic energy program through research and the better utilization of coal, better utilization of our nuclear knowledge, and a wide range of other proposals that will save jobs and keep them here rather than exporting them abroad....

American Gas Association, Washington, D.C., May 17, 1973:

The United States' dramatic growth has been due in part to its tremendous abundance of raw materials. Our recent growth to the status of a major world power has been due, to a large extent, to our huge energy resources.

As long as we can provide our own energy supplies or have secure supplies available at a reasonable price, we can expect growth in our economy. If we become dependent on foreign supplies, we can expect curtailment in our growth, since it will be subject to political forces beyond our control—radical forces.

In recent years our ability to develop energy supplies has been so hampered by government, ecological and tax interests that U.S. supplies of energy are being consumed at a much faster rate than they are being developed....

It is on the issue of energy that we are going to meet our first really difficult test of attempting to accommodate conflicting environmental and economic needs....

Let me now sketch for you in broad outline the course of action I believe the United States should follow to deal with the energy crisis.

1. We should establish a Department of Natural Resources to pull together the fragmented structure of the federal agencies and bureaus now dealing with all natural resources.

2. We should establish and enforce environmental standards for all energy developing and consuming industries, with these standards to be modified when justified. Flexibility seems desirable to meet unexpected problems.

3. We should develop all currently known oil and gas resources to the maximum extent consistent with environmental considerations. We should build the Alaskan oil pipeline and a natural gas line from Alaska through Canada, increase lease sales in the Gulf of Mexico and the Outer Continental Shelf of the U.S. and allow development in California waters,

and allow for the import of materials that can be converted to gas.

4. We should encourage domestic oil and gas exploration and development.

5. We should provide incentives for the domestic development of non-historic sources of energy, producing liquid and gaseous fuels from oil shale, coal and tar sands and developing nuclear stimulation where it can be shown to be advantageous....

The nation and the world need both a clean environment and increased energy. Resolving the conflict between these requirements will not be easy, but it can be done. We face a challenge to our scientific research, our longterm governmental and private planning and our imaginations.

This is an issue which demands the participation of every responsible segment in our society. This includes business and government, working together to find the proper solutions. We know what the problems are. It's time for us to act.

Federalism and Revenue Sharing

Academy of Medicine, Cincinnati, Ohio, Oct. 18, 1966:

What has happened to the division of powers between the National Government and the States? When they laid this cornerstone of our system, the writers of the Constitution sought to preserve the traditional role of local government while assigning to the Federal Government the responsibility for the national welfare.

What do we find today? We find the National League of Cities issuing a guide to federal aid for local communities. Why? Because it's a must for city officials trying to grope their way through the federal jungle in search of manna—federal aid for urban programs. I don't blame the National League of Cities in the least. They're acting in self-defense, so to speak. But the dependence of our cities on the Federal Government, the giant tax collector, is a shocking development in the political life of this nation....

Annual Conference of State Legislative Leaders at Honolulu, Hawaii, Dec. 4, 1968:

...Money alone is not the answer. Local citizens and local groups must assume greater responsibility and become imbued with the desire to solve local problems locally. And local governments must find the experts they need to plan and guide local programs.

Through it all, the central consideration is a change of hands on the purse strings...a shift of decision-making and spending power from Washington to the cities and the states. For that reason I urge that categorical grants-in-aid be consolidated into broad problem area grants and that ultimately a percentage of federal income tax revenue be shared under a rebate and equalization formula with the states and local governmental units.

Rally for Soviet Jewry, New York City, Dec. 13, 1971:

It would now appear to me that the President of the United States has an historic opportunity to serve a compelling humanitarian cause on his forthcoming visit to the Soviet Union. The President will be speaking with the prestige of our great nation. The Russians will be seeking various concessions and compromises from the United States. The time would be ripe for President Nixon to very appropriately raise the issue of Soviet Jewry with the Soviet Government.

When Prime Minister Trudeau of Canada visited Moscow he told the Kremlin how Canadians felt about the oppression of the Russian Jews. Leaders of many other nations have similarly expressed themselves. President Nixon can exert the greatest impact on behalf of Soviet Jewry.

Accordingly, I will recommend very strongly to the President that he consider this line of direct action....

I would make a particular point with the President that he place high on his agenda the liberation from Siberian labor camps of all persons jailed for Jewish activities....

American-Israel Public Affairs Committee, Washington, D.C., May 8, 1973:

The United States must continue to give Israel the backing necessary to maintain the credibility of our friendship. The central aim of our policy in the Middle East must be to prevent events that would cause a breakdown in the emerging structure of world peace.

There is another important matter which concerns both the United States and Israel. That is the fate of Soviet Jewry. This matter has become tightly bound up with the entire subject of U.S.-Soviet relations and, most directly, with possible expansion of U.S.-Soviet trade.

We all know that the Soviets have now suspended their infamous "education tax," which had been imposed on some persons seeking to leave the Soviet Union. This is substantial evidence of progress by negotiation. We are also familiar with the sizable annual increase in Jewish emigration from the Soviet Union to Israel.

It is clear, however, that Senator Jackson is not satisfied with the Soviet suspension of the tax and therefore apparently intends to press his amendment barring most-favored-nation treatment for the Soviet Union.

I fully support Senator Jackson's objectives but I feel we should continue to explore all alternatives to achieve the desired end. We want results. That is the main cause of our anxiety....

I fully support the Jackson Amendment in principle. But my hope is that we can work out a solution which will make possible an expansion of U.S.-Soviet trade, will promote improved relations between the United States and the Soviet Union, will help us realize a second SALT agreement, and will help bring about peace in the Middle East.

We must make it possible for Soviet Jews to emigrate freely to Israel. We must devise a Jackson Amendment solution that will permit affirmative action on trade but at the same time show the Russians that the Congress backs freedom of emigration. We must do everything within our power to alleviate the plight of Soviet Jewry without wrecking the movement toward a Soviet-American improvement of relations.

Morality in Government

National Conference of Christians and Jews, Cleveland, Ohio, June 9, 1974:

The morality of politicians—and of the government itself—reflects the morality of the cross-section of people who go to the polls....

The morality of our Government is directly related to the morality of the individual. I make no brief for any breach of the public trust. Nor do I condone injustice in the name of justice by anyone regardless of revolutionary rhetoric or alleged pursuit of social change.

We are living in an age of sweeping generalizations that would blur the choice of free people. We cannot write off every newspaper and every television network with wild generalizations about media conspiracies. But we can choose which newspaper we read and which network we prefer.

News Media

Annual Dinner of the White House Correspondents Association, Washington, D.C., May 4, 1974:

I do depend heavily on the news media for my information, and I find it usually accurate and workmanlike, considering the pressures of competition and headlines....

Personally I do not put as much emphasis on public relations as I do on fundamental human relations and I don't like to categorize "the press" or "the media" as if they were somehow a different species from other people. I like to consider every person I know on his or her own merits and to treat them as I would hope to be treated if our jobs were reversed. I have had a lot of adversaries in my political life, but no enemies that I can remember.

Right to Privacy

Virginia Bar Association, Hot Springs, Virginia, July 20, 1974:

Constant vigilance is essential to protect the right of privacy. Dangers are subtle. They often appear in the guise of increased benefits from collecting more detailed information about individuals when no adequate protections have been developed to assure accuracy of such information and to avoid its misuse.

The legal profession has a vital role to play in developing the law of privacy, in the courts, and in the Federal and State governing bodies. Let us join to face the challenge by devising new ways to protect individual privacy from encroachment. We must reassure citizens that their private lives shall not become "rolls of public tape" in a computer system.

Our action will generate new faith in our democratic society and make it more respectful of the personal freedoms of all citizens.

Social Welfare

Washington, D.C., Jan. 19, 1967:

As in the past, Republicans now favor an increase in permitted earnings by Social Security recipients. Present earning limitations reflect the depression mentality of the thirties and make no sense for the seventies. Widows' benefits and minimum benefits must be brought into line with today's inflated living costs. Those still uncovered should, as soon as possible, be blanketed into the Social Security system at least by age 72.

Our older citizens must be protected from the extortions of Great Society inflation. They can't wait while we debate.

Congress should enact, retroactive to January 1, an 8 per cent increase in Social Security benefits. These increased benefits can be achieved without any tax increase.

About 1/3 of the nation's poor are elderly citizens. Their situation is tragic and desperate. The Poverty War has passed them by....

Republicans will continue to press for total revamping and redirection of the Poverty War. We want an Opportunity Crusade that will enlist private enterprise and the states as effective partners of the federal government in this fight. We would give the children of poverty the very highest priority they deserve. As Republicans have urged for two years, Head Start requires follow-through in the early grades.

We propose a new Industry Youth Corps to provide private, productive employment and training on the job.

We propose the Republican Human Investment Act to induce employers to expand job opportunities for the unskilled.

Sesquicentennial Alumni Celebration, The University of Michigan, March 2, 1967:

Proposals for increased federal payroll and income taxes are contributing to what I call the disincentive sickness in America. They also help create an imbalance in our economy that results when taxation takes far too large a portion of our gross national product.

In my Republican State of the Union Message last January 19, I called for a "New Direction" in federal policy-making.

This "New Direction" is synonymous with a new federal philosophy, a new approach to solving many of this Nation's domestic problems. The key is sharing of federal income tax revenue with the states and cities.

Other facets are tax credits to industry to promote massive attacks on air and water pollution and structural unemployment, the latter through large scale on-the-job training.

Still other embryo programs include the possible harnessing of industrial know-how for an attack on assorted urban ills, the promotion of a kind of "cities industry" employing problem-solving techniques similar to those in the space industry. The possibilities are almost endless....

Wichita State University, Wichita, Kansas, May 7, 1970:

Workfare instead of Welfare. This is the way of dignity and decency. This is the American way. A hand up instead of a handout. That's the only way to bridge the gap between the haves and have-nots in America....

University of Jacksonville, Jacksonville, Florida, Dec. 16, 1971:

We must reform our antiquated and demeaning welfare system. The present system is a scandal. It just isn't working. Nobody is for a system that makes it more attractive to be on welfare than to work.

The answer, I think, is the Administration's new Family Assistance Plan—a plan tied to the work ethic, a plan that encourages families to stay together, a plan that would put a floor under the income of every family in America. It is the key to taking people off welfare rolls and putting them on payrolls. It is the means to a life of dignity for low-income Americans....

There is still another key problem where initiative must be taken on the Federal level. That is the problem of health care....

One of the major parties would meet the challenge by putting the Federal Government in charge of the entire health delivery system and underwriting all health care through the Federal Treasury. My party would expand the government role of financing care for the helpless and needy while improving basic health insurance coverage for all others. Employers would pay the bulk of the health insurance premiums for the working population. Catastrophic illnesses would be covered up to $50,000 for each family member. The plan also would stress preventive medicine—keeping people healthy instead of sending them into hospitals with minor ailments and thus escalating the nation's health care bill.

My party believes the health care problem can best be met by improving the present system, not by scrapping it and erecting a Federal bureaucratic structure in its place.

Republican Party

University of Florida, Gainesville, Florida, Nov. 3, 1966:

The minority [Republican] party has an obligation to its supporting electorate and the entire nation to provide a system of checks and balances as intended in the Constitution, the blueprint of our Republic.

The minority party has an obligation to rebuild its strength so that it may again provide a healthy balance in the American political system.

Looking at the current situation purely as a student of government, I call for new strength for the minority so that it may not only serve as a counterweight but also initiate positive and constructive legislative proposals. That way lies a healthy government.

Washington, D.C., Jan. 19, 1967:

Never forget, the Republican Party came into being to make real the belief that all men are created equal and endowed by their Creator with inalienable rights....

Republicans have faith in the constitutional concept of Federalism, which requires strong and vigorous state as well as national action on a variety of problems. Yet, seen through the Democrats' rear-view mirror of the Thirties, everything can be cured by Federal dictation and Federal funds, doled out through grants-in-aid which keep Washington as the manipulator of all strings....

Vietnam

Yale Law School, New Haven, Connecticut, April 30, 1965:

During the recent Easter weekend demonstrations in Washington, some placards read: "Why Die for Viet-Nam?"

How many of us remember the similar question raised by irresponsible voices in Chamberlain's Britain a little over a quarter century ago: "Why Die for the Sudetanland?" and "Why Die for Danzig?"

We know now—and many of us did then—that these pacifist voices were serving the purposes of Nazi aggression. The placard-bearers cried for peace—while the seeds for Buchenwald and Belsen were taking root.

Today, our so-called "teach-ins" and "peace" demonstrations cry for peace-at-any-price—while the seeds of Communist atrocity take root. And yet the appeasers speak of morality.

National Press Club, Washington, D.C., July 21, 1965:

Our lesson in Cuba ought to guide us during the third great crisis of this decade—in Viet Nam. In Cuba, our early vacillation encouraged the Communists to bolder and bolder aggression.

We cannot—we dare not—lead them to repeat that mistake in Viet Nam.

The Communist leaders in Moscow, Peking and Hanoi must fully understand that the United States considers the freedom of South Viet Nam vital to our interests. And they must know that we are not bluffing in our determination to defend those interests.

Mao has said that America will soon tire of the war in Viet Nam. It is President Johnson's grave responsibility to convince Mao and his Communist allies otherwise.

Our power is known to the enemy. The enemy must be convinced of the fact that we will use that power to meet the threat of aggression.

Toward this end I recommended a short time ago that we intensify our air strikes against significant military targets in North Viet Nam. Predictably, I was denounced by armchair theorists.

Watergate

Press Conference, Washington, D.C., May 23, 1973:

I believe the President had no knowledge whatsoever of the Watergate affair; he had no personal knowledge of any alleged coverup, and I believe the American people believe that.

And in the President's statement [May 22, 1973], if you have read it, as I think all of you have and some of us have, he was trying to separate the Watergate aspects and, on the other hand, separate them from the national security aspects of the last year or so.

It is my judgment that the President was trying to get the CIA out of the Watergate affair and not in it. And furthermore, as far as the governing of the country is concerned, what Senator Scott said is absolutely true. It is my judgment that the American people are behind the President.

Women

Convention of the National Federation of Republican Women, Washington, D.C., Sept. 27, 1969:

I call you leaders of the world because I have long felt that it is really the women who are running the show. Maybe it's a behind-the-scenes sort of operation in many cases, but there's no question that the women of the world...and particularly women in America...wield tremendous power.

It could be you don't quite know just how powerful you are, and that's a lucky circumstance for us men....

A revolution has taken place among American women, now that they have finished stepping down from their pedestals—for better or for worse....

This is one aspect of the women's revolution I thoroughly agree with—giving women the place they deserve in American government and in the political sphere.

Our whole society today calls for women to play a significant role in nearly every way—not just as wives and mothers but intellectually and politically.

VICE PRESIDENT FORD ON NIXON AND IMPEACHMENT

October 1973

12—Nixon names Ford as his nominee for vice president in White House ceremony. He is the first vice president to be nominated under procedures outlined in the 25th Amendment.

17—*The New York Times* quotes Ford's feeling that Nixon ought to release tapes requested by Special Watergate Prosecutor Archibald Cox. Ford qualifies his stand by adding, "But I also recognize that serious legal and constitutional issues are involved." He declines to elaborate.

19—Ford announces he is "very encouraged by a White House offer to compromise with Cox on the tapes impasse. The compromise is to involve preparation of transcripts to be verified by Sen. John Stennis (D Miss.) listening to actual tapes. "I think it's an indication that constructive progress is being made," Ford says.

20—Supporting Nixon on the firing of Cox, Ford says the President had "no other choice, after Mr. Cox—who was, after all, a subordinate—refused to accept the compromise solution to the tapes issue." Ford again describes the compromise as "fair and reasonable," but adds he is "deeply sorry" to see Elliot Richardson resign as attorney general.

27—Ford comments on Nixon statement at a press conference that the news media is "vicious, distorted." "I suspect that the President, on second thought, probably wished he hadn't said it," he says. Ford insists he is not being criticial of the President, saying, "We all make little slips and I'm as guilty as anyone else. We all do that and I'm not critical of it."

November

1—Testifying at his confirmation hearings before the Senate Rules Committee, Ford announces he will attempt to be the "peacemaker and calm communicator between the White House and Capitol Hill." He insists that he supports Nixon: "After a play is called, you shouldn't tackle your own quarterback." But he admits that if he had been president, he would have released the tapes several weeks earlier than Nixon. He also thinks the White House should have told the Senate and the courts about "missing tapes" much earlier.

In discussing executive privilege, Ford says, "I don't think a President has unlimited authority in the area of executive privilege. On the other hand, I don't think Congress has unlimited rights to presidential documents." He also adds that in cases where allegations of criminality against an individual would be affected by releasing certain documents, then "bearing in mind the best interest of the country...they should be made available."

He testifies further than "any person, including the president," should obey a Supreme Court order.

5—Again before the Senate Rules Committee, Ford says he is convinced Nixon is "completely innocent" of involvement in the Watergate burglary and cover-up, "but the public wants the President to prove that, through documents and so forth...Whatever doubts there are must be cleared up."

15—At his confirmation hearings before the House Judiciary Committee, Ford states his continued support for Nixon, but pledges to be his own man and tell the President when he thinks he's wrong: "My views are similar to those of the President, but not necessarily identical."

27—The Senate votes 92-3 to approve Ford as Vice President. He states he has mixed feelings: "I am eager and anxious to get in and do a new job, but at the same time I can't help but have regrets over leaving the House and all the wonderful men and women I served with after these 25 years."

December

6—The House votes 387-35 to confirm Ford, and he is sworn in as Vice President, saying "Mr. President, you have my support and my loyalty...." *The New York Times* quotes Ford's remark to a friend, "What I have to watch out for is not to become Nixon's apologist. That won't help either of us."

7—In his first news conference since taking office, Ford says the President has no intention of resigning and, "I see no evidence whatsoever that would justify a favorable vote in the House on impeachment." He further predicts Nixon will be exonerated when all the facts are known.

Ford believes if Nixon continues to solve problems in the Middle East, "there will be a groundswell of support. The American people are far more interested in peace than in a matter like Watergate." In addition, Ford suggests the President could restore confidence in his leadership by taking more trips, holding more news conferences, and disclosing fully all materials sought by the courts and Congress.

9—Appearing on ABC's "Issues and Answers," Ford states that Nixon's recent release of his financial records should satisfy "any reasonable member of Congress" as well as the American people.

He refines his definition of impeachment to the "clear-cut and very clean" Constitutional grounds of treason, bribery, and other high crimes and misdemeanors. (While spearheading the impeachment attempt against Supreme Court Justice William O. Douglas in 1970, Ford had said an impeachable offense was anything a majority of the House decided.)

20—Ford terms the playing of a subpoenaed White House tape at a cocktail party a "gross impropriety." Asked whether this might cause Nixon to withhold tapes in the future, Ford answers, "Well, he ought to have second thoughts."

January 1974

6—Ford appears on NBC's "Meet The Press" and finds the Senate Watergate Committee's demand for 600 tapes and documents to be "far too broad...too much of a fishing expedition." He adds, however, that if the committee would cut back its demands, "then I think there may be—and I underline 'may be'—an area of compromise."

8—Ford is encouraged that a "head-to-head confrontation" with the Senate Watergate Committee might be avoided, as the committee has indicated it might settle for the five tapes it subpoenaed in July 1973.

15—In a speech given to the American Farm Bureau Federation in Atlantic City, Ford accuses groups such as the AFL-CIO, Americans for Democratic Action (ADA) and other "powerful pressure organizations" of waging "an all-out attack against the President." "Their aim is total victory for themselves and the total defeat not only of President Nixon, but of the policies for which he stands," Ford says. "If they can crush the President and his philosophy, they are convinced that they can then dominate the Congress and, through it, the nation."

16—Ford insists again in a speech in Washington that "a massive effort to crush the President" exists. Still he warns against "premature judgment" of the Jan. 15 disclosure that an 18½ minute gap in one of the White House tapes was caused by deliberate erasure. "Even if you take the worst side (of the erasure disclosure) it doesn't justify impeachment."

17—Ford returns home to Grand Rapids, Mich., admitting that the Atlantic City "attack" speech was based on a draft prepared by the White House because he didn't have his own speechwriter yet. He claims to have changed at least a third of the text.

22—The White House has information [already seen by Senate Minority Leader Hugh Scott (R Pa.)] that will "exonerate the President and totally undercut the testimony of John Dean," Ford announces. It is his understanding that Special Prosecutor Leon Jaworski has the information, but Ford has not had time to read it.... "There's some question in my mind whether I should see it. It's an open question with me."

25—In speeches in Columbus, Ohio, and Johnstown, Pa., Ford does not mention Nixon's name in the prepared texts. In questions afterward, he says he has decided not to look at the information which Senate Minority Leader Scott claims will exonerate the President. "The President offered me the opportunity to see the evidence," Ford explains, "and I said, 'Well, I'd like to think about it. I'll take your word for it and Sen. Scott's word for it.' Those are two pretty good people to trust." He claims another reason for not looking is that all his "good friends" in the press will ask for details, "and I don't want to be in the position of disclosing such evidence."

Ford also declares "at the present time I plan no lobbying effort on the impeachment issue."

26—Ford praises Nixon's foreign policy at a convention of the B'nai B'rith Anti-Defamation League, saying there is no "credibility gap" there. "The fact is that President Nixon's Middle East policy is a study of credibility, integrity, and consistency."

February

3—Ford is interviewed on CBS's "Face the Nation," and claims that the administration has supplied more tapes to the special prosecutor than he asked for. (Jaworski, appearing on another program the same day, terms Ford's statement "incorrect.")

Ford is in favor of broad subpoena powers for the House Judicary Committee in its impeachment inquiry, but isn't sure whether a subpoena could force the President to testify. He rules out any "fishing expeditions" for presidential papers.

Questioned whether impeachment would "incapacitate" the President and force him to step down, via the 25th Amendment, Ford answers: "I don't think it's ever going to get that far, but even speculating, I don't think a President ought to remove himself from office until he has actually been convicted by the U.S. Senate."

14—Ford embarks on a Midwest speaking tour, and in one speech announces, "Let me say a word about a great American—the President of the United States...a man of integrity, ability, dedication, and great intelligence." When historians review the record, Ford says, they will see "Mr. Nixon has done more for America than any President in our lifetime."

22—At a luncheon sponsored by the National Citizens' Committee for Fairness to the Presidency, Secretary of Agriculture Earl Butz and Sen. Strom Thurmond (R S.C.) both praise the President lavishly. Ford also gives support to Nixon, but adds he wants to "broaden the subject of fairness to the Presidency and to appeal to you and to all our fellow countrymen for fairness to the institutions of government under which we live here in America... Do we not also need fairness to Congress? Do we not also need fairness to the courts—as we expect fairness from the courts?"

25—Ford returns to Washington after speaking in Atlantic City and also watching the President's televised press conference, in which Nixon said he would not resign for the good of the Republican party. Asked by reporters what he thought of the President's performance, Ford replies: "I think he did well in some areas, but I thought he did poorly in others." The *Times* states this is the first instance of open criticism of Nixon since Ford took office in December.

March

2—Ford is questioned in Phoenix, Ariz., about who should properly consider Nixon's possible Watergate involvement. He answers, "Oh, of course, that's what the Constitution provides, that the House of Representatives in the first instance should consider any impeachment charges. Any evidence submitted by anyone, including the grand jury, ought to be put into the mill by the House Committee on the Judiciary." Asked if this evidence should include the secret report of the Watergate grand jury, he continues, "Oh, I think so, good or bad. I would think that's the proper thing. But to speculate about what's in it and the reasons for the action is irresponsible." The *New York Times* lists Ford as being the only top administration official at this time to be in favor of turning over the secret grand jury report to the Judiciary Committee.

8—Speaking about Watergate in a Florida interview, Ford announces, "I know of no more bombshells. I don't think there will be any."

11—Ford seems to temper his unyielding support of the President's innocence when he tells the Harvard College Republican Club, "I don't happen to believe on the basis of the evidence I am familiar with—and I think I'm familiar with most of it—that the President was involved in Watergate *per se* or involved in the coverup, but time will tell."

Still, he insists he won't urge the President to resign: "That would be asking a person to admit guilt when he believes he is innocent."

Ford indicates he's had some preparation for the Presidency. "Many of the responsibilities he (Nixon) has delegated to me have given me an opportunity to see first hand the responsibilities not only of the Vice President, but the President as well."

12—Ford meets with newsmen and says he thinks he would have gone straight to the Attorney General had he been the President and been told about the Watergate cover-up by John Dean. Expressing "grave disappointment" about the effects of Watergate, he fears a White House refusal to comply with the Judiciary Committee subpoena might be a "catalyst" to bring about impeachment.

Regarding resignation, Ford insists, "It would be totally inappropriate for me to ask the President to resign. In the position I am in, I have to be very careful what I say or do as the possibility of impeachment becomes greater than it is now."

15—An audience at the Citadel in Charleston, S.C., hears Ford attack the Judiciary Committee staff as having "too big an influence."

18—Judge John Sirica gives the secret grand jury report on Nixon's possible Watergate involvement to the Judiciary Committee. Ford calls it "probably a right" decision, and repeats that all relevant material should be turned over to the impeachment inquiry.

19—Ford disagrees with Senator James L. Buckley's (Cons-R N.Y.) call for Nixon's resignation.

30—Speaking to Midwest Republican leaders in Chicago, Ford attacks the Committee to Re-elect the President as "an arrogant, elite guard of political adolescents." He assures Republicans "I'm not blaming the President for CREEP. He picked people he thought would do a good job. Unfortunately, they made mistakes." Expressing relief at finally bringing the subject into the open, Ford adds, "I did not discuss it with the President. I spoke as my own man." The White House announces it gave Ford no instructions on the speech and has no comment.

April

1—John Ford, the Vice President's 22-year-old son at Utah State University, is quoted as saying that "of late, I have become disillusioned with [the President]. He has been making a poor defense for himself, making it hard for people who want to believe in him. I'm not so sure my father disagrees with me."

2—Ford comments on his son's remarks and says John is "very upset" and feels he was not quoted fully, as he "supports the policies of the President."

5—Speaking in Denver, Ford says he favors a compromise on the tapes subpoenaed by the Judiciary Committee, "so that the facts could be the determining factor [on an impeachment decision], and not an institutional conflict." He remarks he can't verify whether the Judiciary request is relevant, "but on the assumption that the request is for relevant information, I would hope that the White House would cooperate...and turn over the tapes."

Ford praises Nixon's "good faith and trust" in agreeing to pay $467,000 in back taxes. "It's a tribute to him, not a liability."

9—Ford defends the White House decision to take more time to review tapes and documents and supports a White House judgment of relevancy: "I think any party to a lawsuit has a right to make some determination. Any party to such a matter has some discretion as to what is relevant and what is not relevant." He defends the President—"He has shown a great deal of cooperation in responding in the main to the committee."

13—John Osborne writes an article in *The New Republic* discussing changes Ford would make in the Cabinet should he become President. The article causes some controversy, and former Nixon speechwriter William Safire voices his "dismay and outrage" in a *New York*

Times column. Ford's plan is to keep Secretary of State Henry A. Kissinger, but not Secretary of Defense James R. Schlesinger or Press Secretary Ronald L. Ziegler.

In addition to other changes, he would bring back former presidential adviser Melvin R. Laird and former Secretary of the Treasury George Schultz. Ford says he thought he was talking off the record during his conversation with Osborne, but admits the cabinet changes are "generally my views."

13—In Palm Springs, Calif., Ford describes his role in a White House-Judiciary Committee compromise: "I got involved from both sides...sort of the intermediary, trying to get everybody together. The White House, through me, passed word to the committee and it was agreed that these tapes or the transcripts of them would be delivered as soon as the mechanics were taken care of. Unfortunately, time ran out and the subpoena was issued. I felt this was the very best evidence of the willingness of the White House to cooperate...and the subpoena was unnecessary under the circumstances."

27—At a fund-raiser in Tulsa, Okla., Ford exhorts his audience: "The President is entitled to a fair and impartial hearing. Let us demand that he be accorded every right to present his side of the story and to preserve the office of the Presidency."

May

3—Still claiming he thinks Nixon is innocent of wrongdoing, Ford admits he is "a little disappointed" by the transcripts of conversations released by the White House. Saying this [Nixon] was not the friend he had known for 25 years, Ford says the transcripts contain some "pretty strong language." "The President was in the company of a group different from any that I have known, ever been associated with."

9—Speaking at Eastern Illinois University, in Charleston, Ill., Ford appears to criticize the editing of the transcripts, saying, "While it may be easy to delete characterizations from the printed page, we cannot delete characterizations from people's minds with a wave of the hand." But he adds that it is "unfair to look at just a cold word on a page and extrapolate a meaning from it. You should really be in the room...you cannot condemn or condone cold words on paper." He terms the transcripts "essential in the search for truth." When asked about a possible Ford presidency, he answers, "I will always be ready for any contingency."

10—Ford meets with the President and reports the President told him he was "working too hard." Ford says there was no displeasure shown by the President—"Our rapport was as good as it's ever been, and it's always been very good."

He predicts a majority of the House will not vote for impeachment, and states the "President will not resign and is in excellent shape." Does he still support him as strongly? "I think the answer is yes," Ford says.

11—Speaking in Dallas, Texas, Ford insists he "very strongly disagrees" with Republican leaders who call for resignation, but he can't be critical of them. They "may have a very strong personal feeling this is a better procedure" than impeachment, says Ford, "but I don't think it's the right approach." He reveals that he assured the President that he is not among those "trying to jump off his Ship of State."

18—Ford claims the odds for an impeachment vote in the Judiciary Committee are 50-50, but predicts the President will win in the House by a 4-3 ratio.

21—Judge Sirica orders Nixon to turn tapes over to him that have been requested by Special Prosecutor Jaworski. Ford hopes "there will be some compromise, so as to avoid further litigation."

22—Ford says he still hopes the White House will give additional material to the Judiciary Committee—"the sooner the better." He still supports Nixon saying, "I don't think when all the evidence is in, they've got a case. But let's get it all out there."

23—Ford and Nixon have a meeting, but no word is given of what went on.

24—Ford says the "stonewall attitude" of the White House "isn't necessarily the wisest policy."

26—Ford says in Danbury, Conn., that he warned the President continued White House refusal to turn over more tapes to the Judiciary Committee "could lead to an emotional institutional confrontation, which doesn't relate to an impeachable offense, because I don't think it is. But when you have emotions involved, sometimes the facts are overlooked." Ford admits the two had differences of opinion on the proper approach before their meeting, but "it was laid out quite candidly during the meeting and I haven't backed off from it since.... Obviously he has a somewhat different opinion and I respect it."

27—An article in the *Christian Science Monitor* claims Ford has told friends he is against Nixon's present attitude because he thinks it would be catastrophic for the nation if Nixon were removed from office on procedural, not substantive, charges. Ford thinks his own position as President would then be weakened, because people would be unhappy about the manner in which Nixon left.

28—Ford declines to comment on a *Newsweek* report that Nixon made fun of him to Nelson Rockefeller, supposedly pointing to his chair and laughing, "Can you see Jerry Ford sitting in this chair?"

"I think any comment on that ought to come from the White House," Ford says, adding: "The President and I have had an excellent personal, social, political relationship and I see no change whatsoever, despite what some have speculated. We are firm friends. I admire him." In fact, Ford reports that at that morning's Cabinet meeting, Nixon "was very friendly and very complimentary in several instances."

29—Ford says "I don't think there ought to be any further delivery" of materials to the Judiciary Committee until they "proceed with the 19 tapes they already have, and the transcripts from 20 of the other tapes." He also urges the committee to begin calling witnesses.

31—Ford still objects to the "stonewall" approach of the White House, and thinks it will only harden the attitudes of the people on Capitol Hill. He reiterates that there is no rift between himself and the White House.

June

1—In an interview, Ford denies he is wavering in his support of the President—or "zigging and zagging." He thinks political opponents are saying that to undercut the President. "My own view," Ford says, "is that I think I can support the President when I think he is right. But that doesn't mean I can't indicate publicly that if there is a difference I ought to speak up."

7—Asked in Raleigh, N.C., whether Nixon's being named as an unindicted co-conspirator in the Watergate indictments shook Ford's faith in the President, he replied "none whatsoever." He declares that grand jury action is of "lower consequence" legally and "has less impact" than an indictment. He insists Nixon "has not placed himself above the law" and has the right to use "all appropriate legal methods" his lawyers think proper.

Would he have resigned if named an unindicted co-conspirator? "I would not," he answers.

8—Ford pledges in Logan, Utah, to continue to "head off deadlock," but will also continue to "remain my own man, fly my own course, and speak my own convictions."

10—Ford states he thinks Nixon gained "very slightly" when the ITT and milk fund evidence "sort of fell flat" before the House Judiciary Committee. He predicts the President still holds a 4 to 3 margin against impeachment in the House, and says he still sees no evidence of impeachable offenses, including the controversy over the March 21 "hush money" statement. Ford believes it can be argued the President intended only a customary arrangement to pay Hunt's legal fees, "which is a totally different inference than if he were saying 'take Mr. Hunt something to keep quiet.' "

12—Ford meets with newsmen, attacking the House Judiciary Committee as being "out of control" because of the numerous committee news leaks during the past week. He accuses committee Democrats of having ulterior motives of wanting to impeach the President. He adds that the leaks prove that committee hearings should be made public, and that President Nixon is justified in refusing to turn over subpoenaed tapes and documents.

15—Ford campaigns in New York state, attacking "nameless leakers" who are trying to "undercut" President Nixon and Secretary of State Henry A.Kissinger. Ford asks his audiences, "Are you going to let them do this to the greatest secretary of state...the greatest President for peace in our history?"

17—Ford speaks at the high school graduation in suburban Maryland of Mrs. Ford's chauffeur's son, and tells the graduates: "America in recent months has been shaken by one disillusioning development after another. What these developments have pointed up is the importance of personal integrity and strength of character.

"We have shuddred under the weight of the hammer blows that fall upon a nation when high-placed individuals engage in wrong-doing in the mistaken belief that the end justifies the means. Fortunately, we are finding that our institutions of government are strong—strong enough to withstand all of the tests posed by what is commonly known as Watergate."

19—A *Washington Star-News* article quotes Ford praising the President mainly on foreign affairs to a Republican gathering in Columbus, Ohio. Saying Ford is speaking less about Watergate, the *Star-News* quotes him as stating again he believes Nixon innocent of involvement in the Watergate break-in. In addition, "it's my personal judgment that the preponderance of the evidence clearly indicates that he's innocent of any involvement in the alleged cover-up and we ought to speak out affirmatively about it."

The article also tells of a press briefing staged the previous week by White House communications chief Ken Clawson, in which Ford questions the Watergate grand jury's naming Nixon as an unindicted co-conspirator: "I just respectfully disagree with their judgment."

20—In a speech before the national convention of the United States Jaycees Ford urges a domestic "disengagement" from the controversy over Watergate. He warns against letting "the passions arising from Watergate" be a "copout from the work essential for our continuity and sense of purpose as a great republic." In his view America is in a "domestic impasse which has this nation spinning its wheels." And though he is not against our international successes, "I feel very strongly that the time has come for bold domestic diplomacy to negotiate a return to pride in America." He uses the recent Israeli-Arab peace pacts as a metaphor, saying "despite deep feelings over domestic controversies, [Americans] cannot be less realistic and less ready for mediation and moderation than the Israelis and the Arabs. After all, "If people shooting at each other can disengage, so can people who are shouting at each other."

22—Ford comments in Monterey, Calif., on a possible solution to arguments that the Judiciary Committee's versions of White House conversations differ markedly from the White House versions: "If people are questioning the [White House] transcripts, I'm sure we can find someone, an unbiased third party, to go over the tapes." Asked if he would be the third party, he replies, "I don't think I will. No." To Ford, the main question in the House inquiry is "whether President Nixon was involved in the cover-up. The preponderance of evidence is that he is not."

28—Ford appears on William F. Buckley's interview show "Firing Line" predicting impeachment if the President chooses to ignore a Supreme Court ruling on the subpoenaed tapes. "As of the moment, there aren't enough votes in the House to impeach the President," Ford claims. But if he rejects the Supreme Court, "then it's a totally different ball game...it then becomes an institutional conflict." Ford tells Buckley he thinks the Judidiciary Committee will vote for impeachment, but he doesn't "think there is sufficient evidence" on any of the Watergate charges. The Vice President hopes Nixon will obey the Supreme Court ruling, but agrees with the President's refusal to promise in advance to abide by whatever the Court decides. In addition, Ford says he understands Nixon's reluctance to give more tapes to the Judiciary Committee—"the leakiest committee in the history of the U.S. Congress."

Ford does not comment on a question of presidential pardons for "plumber" type operations, but insists: "Any President under his constitutional authority as commander-in-chief can order certain rather drastic actions, including a break-in." He adds that he doubts that the Ellsberg psychiatrist break-in fits that definition.

July

6—"I think it is assumed any citizen—the President included—would abide by a decision of the Supreme Court," Ford tells a news conference in Dallas, Texas. "But a person involved in litigation does not go out and say publicly what he is going to do," he adds. To Ford impeachment looks less likely since the case against the President "has fallen flat in several areas" in the past few weeks.

7—Back in Washington, Ford claims that his relations with Nixon have grown even better in the past months, though both of them have been traveling: "I think they have improved, broadened and are even on a better basis now than before... We keep in touch." Ford also thinks the mood in Washington is the most favorable toward Nixon that he's seen in a while.

12—At a news conference in New Mexico, Ford talks of evidence released by the Judiciary Committee: "I think the evidence as a whole—the new evidence as well as the old evidence—clearly exonerates the President of any involvement in the break-in, or in any ITT or milk fund impeachable offense.... And I think the preponderance of the evidence—all of it—is in favor of the President and exonerates him of any impeachable offense."

13—Ford meets with Nixon at San Clemente, for the sixth time in a week and says the meeting was "99 and 9-tenths per cent" about the economy and was not about impeachment. Asked later about impeachment, he says "In my judgement, there is a possibility that the House committee will vote a bill of impeachment but I feel just as strongly, if not more strongly, that the House will not vote a bill of impeachment." He describes Judiciary Committee Chairman Rodino as conducting a fair hearing and also says many of the committee members are fair, but "there are some members of the committee who have made up their minds ahead of time...their analysis of the evidence is not as open minded as members of the House as a whole." Asked if Nixon's "stonewall" instruction to his aides in 1973 would be grounds for impeachment, Ford answers "I have grave doubts that just one phrase or sentence is grounds for impeachment because it is only part of the total evidence." He still feels the "preponderance" of the evidence shows Nixon to be innocent. Ford "assumes" Nixon will comply with the Supreme Court ruling.

18—Ford reveals that, at his request, he has listened to some of the Watergate tapes: "I have, I think, read, heard or otherwise absorbed the various material that has been submitted to the Judiciary Committee. There are some differences in the transcripts.... But I've also listened to several of those tapes where there are these alleged discrepancies. If anybody can be 100 per cent certain that their version is any more accurate than any other version, you would have to be a genius."

19—Ford declares he will "not be going out in any arm-twisting, lobbying effort" to prevent an impeachment vote. "If any member asks me for my view, just in case they weren't sure of my sentiments, I'll be glad to tell them." But, he adds, lobbying would be "an insult to most, if not all, members of the House. I never did it when I was a member of the House and when I was minority leader."

"Speaking in Roanoke, Va., Ford states two disagreements. One is with Judiciary Committee counsel John Doar. Ford "respectfully" disagrees with him that sufficient evidence exists to impeach Nixon. The second is with White House Press Secretary Ronald Ziegler that the committee is running a "kangaroo court" to get Nixon. Ford feels Rodino has "done his utmost" to run a fair proceeding, "And I would certainly not call the manner in which that committee has operated a kangaroo court. They've got a great responsibility. I think they've tried very hard to do a good job."

24—In an interview with the *Christian Science Monitor* minutes before the Supreme Court's tape decision, Ford talks of Nixon's possible reaction: "I can't tell you if he will or not,...but if the court rules against the President, it is my belief he ought to comply." If he refuses, Ford thinks "the odds would shift materially in favor of impeachment."

Asked about the White House transcripts, Ford replies, "I don't think the content of the tapes put sainthood on anybody. I think they're not the way I would have hoped the discussions would be carried out in the Oval Office." He explains that his call to Judiciary Committee member Rep.

Larry Hogan (R Md.), who publicly announced July 23 he would vote for impeachment, was to tell him any stand for impeachment was "premature, ill-advised, and ill-timed.... And I still think it was wrong."

25—Ford dramatically defends Nixon in Muncie, Ind., saying "I can say from the bottom of my heart that the President of the United States is innocent...He is right." In addition, Ford declares "It's my judgment that if the President is impeached and convicted, and I don't think he will be, that the impact on the country and on a worldwide basis would be very, very bad." Because of the changes in sentiment, pro and con, over the past few months, Ford is "not sure at this point [impeachment] is a foregone conclusion." In any event, Ford has "absolute confidence" that Nixon has no intention of resigning, even if impeached.

26—Moving on to Chicago, Ford declares Nixon "deserves much better than the treatment he is getting." He refuses to criticize Republicans on the Judiciary Committee who intend to vote impeachment, but attacks those "significant number of Democrats" who would be "overjoyed if and when Mr. Nixon were impeached and convicted." Though he is disappointed that "the margin in the committee is not closer" he finds the anti-impeachment Republicans more convincing. They "reaffirmed my own conviction that the President is innocent of an impeachment offense." Applause greets Ford's remark that when Americans look at the achievements of "a man who has done so much for peace, who has done so much for the country as a whole.... I think they will praise, not condemn our great President."

27—Ford joins Judiciary Committee Republicans in demanding "specificity" in impeachment charges. In Canton, Ohio, for the annual Pro Football Hall of Fame parade, Ford charges "You would think that after spending about $1.5-million under Mr. Doar and Mr. Jenner, they could come up with a page or two of specific charges." To Ford the committee "is not doing in this case what was done in the past in impeachment cases. I think it's a travesty that they are not.... I think the President of the United States deserves as much consideration as a person charged with any illegal act."

27—Speaking to reporters on the lawn of his Alexandria, Va., home, Ford talks about the Judiciary Committee's just-taken 27-11 vote for the first article of impeachment: "The fact that every one of the Democrats on the committee voted for it lends credence that it's a partisan issue, even though some Republicans voted for it." In Ford's view the chances of impeachment by the full House are "pretty close to even." His advice to Nixon is to "do as he has done, indicate as clearly as he can that he is innocent." In fairness to the President, if impeachment proceedings are "expedited...the end result will be in his favor."

29—Once again, in San Francisco, Ford says "In my opinion the evidence produced so far is not sufficient to impeach the President under the Constitution."

30—While traveling in Reno, Nev., and San Diego, Calif., Ford declares, "I have indicated in the past, and I will reiterate now, that I am not going out as I used to when I was minority leader and affirmatively and aggressively try to convince members that they ought to vote this way or that way. I think this is a different session." His plan, "when the opportunity arises, is to discuss with members of Congress, both Republican and Democrat, my views and why I hold them." Ford's speaking schedule alone will keep him out of Washington for much of the month of August. Why is he defending Nixon so strongly? "I've always been a forthcoming, candid in-

dividual. If I have deep convictions, which I do in this one, I feel, based on my convictions, the need to speak out."

August

1—In an interview with the *Christian Science Monitor* Ford declares that his relationsip with Nixon is "excellent, and probably better than it has ever been in our 20-plus years of friendship." He states again he believes Nixon is innocent, but that his tactics for dealing with evidence were wrong. As to the Judiciary Committee, Ford thinks their sessions "generally" have been conducted well. However, he thinks "the leaks that were deliberate, and there were many, were a disgrace, as far as the committee is concerned."

3—Ford says he may "shut up" about impeachment for a while. Insisting "I still believe the President is innocent of any impeachable offense," Ford adds, "Now perhaps there comes a time when it is advisable under the circumstances for me to say, 'I have this viewpoint, I'm not going to say any more.' ...But don't come to any conclusion by my lack of speaking that I've backed off. I have not." Ford says again he doesn't approve of many of the thing that went on in the Nixon White House, "but that's quite different from an impeachable offense." If people want to express disapproval, he is in favor of a censure vote, rather than an impeachment vote, though he thinks "the situation has eroded and the possibility is the vote will be unfavorable...."

5—Ford issues a statement after Nixon's release of transcripts of June 23, 1972, conversations revealing Nixon's participation in the cover-up from late June 1972. In it Ford says, "I have come to the conclusion that the public interest is no longer served by repetition of my previously expressed belief that on the basis of all the evidence known to me and to the American people the President is not guilty of an impeachable offense under the constitutional definition of 'treason, bribery or other high crimes and misdemeanors.' Inasmuch as additional evidence is about to be forthcoming from the President, which he says may be damaging, I intend to respectfully decline to discuss impeachment matters in public...."

6—In the midst of swirling rumors about a possible Presidential resignation, Ford conducts a "business as usual" day. He attends the Cabinet meeting where Nixon says he will not resign.

7—Ford has an interview with the *New York Times* in which he denies any "transition plans" have been made by his staff. Asked whether his morning meeting with General Alexander M. Haig Jr. was concerned with an orderly presidential transition, Ford replies, "I'm not talking about matters of that kind." He also describes talk of possible vice presidents in a Ford administration as "premature." Asked about the President's emotional state, Ford answers "I thought he looked surprisingly well yesterday, considering all the trauma he had gone through." However, his answer to a question whether he felt Nixon had lied to him was "I don't think I ought to answer that."

Later in the day Ford meets with Rep. John J. Rhodes (R Ariz.) and Rep. Albert H. Quie (R Minn.) in Rhodes' office for a prayer meeting. Quie says the sessions have occurred every Wednesday for the past three or four months. When asked if he was praying more these days, Ford replies, "That's for sure."

8—The Vice President calls Nixon's resignation "one of the most difficult and very saddest periods, and one of the very saddest incidents, that I've ever witnessed." ∎

VICE PRESIDENT FORD ON POLITICS AND ELECTIONS

October 1973

13—Ford appears in the House press gallery, the day after he has been named Vice President designate, to say "As emphatically and as strongly as I can, I have no intention of being a candidate for any office, President, Vice President, or anything else, in 1976."

November

1—Testifying at his confirmation hearings before the Senate Rules Committee, Ford repeats that he will not seek the presidency in 1976, so "no one can accuse me of seeking personal aggrandizement...." This will "leave me free to be a peacemaker."

5—The question of how he would run his presidency comes up at the Senate hearings. Ford says if he were president he would seek a bigger role for Congress in formulating foreign policy—"There has to be a two-way street between Congress and the executive branch." Also, as president, he would seek the advice of members of Congress on difficult matters, rather than rely so completely on his White House advisers.

December

7—In his first news conference since being confirmed as Vice President, Ford declares that President Nixon "is not a political liability to any candidate" and that presidential appearances for any congressional candidate "ought to be an asset."

12—Ford meets with reporters and declares his role will be to speak "affirmatively" for the administration, especially on foreign policy. "I'm not going to take any direction," he says. "I will campaign in coordination with the White House, but I'm not going to be told where to go."

Asked about his plans for 1976, Ford again says he will not be running: "I took this job for three years to do the best I could, with no anticipation of trying to get delegates and convince the public I want to be President. I will do none of that and that's positive," he says, slapping the table for emphasis. He describes this position as being "about as close to a Shermanesque statement as you can get." (General William Tecumseh Sherman said in 1884, "I will not accept if nominated and will not serve if elected.")

January 1974

15—Ford speaks in Atlantic City, N.J., attacking groups such as the AFL-CIO and Americans for Democratic Action (ADA), who are promoting impeachment. He asserts that Nixon's critics are a "relatively small group of political activists" who are trying to "stretch out the ordeal, to cripple the President by dragging out the preliminaries to impeachment for as long as they can, and to use the whole affair for maximum political advantage." He predicts that if these activists win, "with the super-welfare-staters in control of Congress, and the White House neutralized as a balancing force, we can expect an avalanche of fresh government intervention in our economy, massive new government spending, higher taxes and a more rampant inflation."

25—Speaking in Johnstown, Pa., Ford supports Harry Fox, the Republican candidate in the special 12th Congressional District election being held Feb. 5 to fill Republican John Saylor's seat. Ford claims "I don't think Republicans are going to have the kind of drop-off in their vote in 1974 that my good friend Barry Goldwater forecast [that Watergate would cost every Republican candidate 10 per cent of the vote in 1974].... If a Republican, a new Republican, can win in this district, I think it's exceedingly significant."

Adding that "I like this kind of campaigning in small towns," he indicates he plans to campaign for other Republicans this year.

29—Ford pledges "total availability" to Republican candidates throughout the nation. He praises Nixon's foreign policy, and says, since the Republican Party has a good story to tell on foreign policy, they should "tell it from the rooftops."

February

2—"The whole country is watching the 12th District," Ford says, three days before the special Pennsylvania election that is won by Democrat John P. Murtha.

14—While on a speaking tour of the Midwest, Ford insists again he has no intention of running for President in 1976—"I will do a better job as Vice President if not suspect as a potential President." However, Rep. Tim Lee Carter (R Ky.) announces to the crowd that he will work for Ford's nomination in 1976. The audience cheers and Ford is seen smiling.

18—"You can't mean that," says Ford when notified in Chattanooga, Tenn., that his old Michigan district has been won by Democrat Richard F. Vander Veen—the first Democratic victory since 1910. Admitting he is "very disappointed by the results," Ford declares he is "sure it's a reflection of the uncertain economic conditions in Michigan particularly, and the country generally." He is "confident that as the economy improves there will be greater support for the Republican candidates."

19—Ford declares, "Well, it's a beating. I'm very upset" about the Vander Veen victory, even going so far as to say he is rather "frightened" by it. He concedes that "to some extent Watergate had an impact," but also blames economic turmoil, heavy spending by the Democrats, low Republican turnout, and "skepticism prevalent about politics today."

20—After meeting with the President, Ford says in Cincinnati that he told Nixon Watergate had affected the outcome of the Michigan special election. "He recognized it," says Ford. "Obviously it had an influence."

22—Ford starts a new "give-'em-hell" approach in Cincinnati, and blames "labor outsiders" for the Michigan election loss, while campaigning for the upcoming March 5 special Congressional election in Ohio's 1st District. "Do you want a bunch of outsiders telling you who to send to Congress?" he asks the crowd. "Hell, no," they answer. "Well, they're moving in here," Ford warns. He admits he had a "real sense of disbelief" when he heard of the Vander Veen victory, and decided "we've got to put a little zip in the campaign." The explanation for his new campaign style: "You have to be on the offensive. It's just like in a football game. If you don't score, you don't win." Though Ford campaigns hard for Republican Willis A. Gradison Jr., the election is won by Democrat Thomas A. Luken.

March

1—At a Republican fund-raiser in Phoenix, Ariz., Ford asks his audience to retain their faith in the party and prevent liberal Democrats from taking over Congress. Continued Republican losses, he says, could mean "the destruction of the two-party system" in America.

4—Ford appears in New York for a fund-raiser on behalf of Republican Sen. Jacob K. Javits' re-election bid. Praising Javits as a politician who is trusted in rural areas, Harlem, and Park Ave., Ford promises to "help and assist" Javits' campaign.

9—Back in New York to address the Women's National Republican Club, Ford urges Republicans to take the offensive in upcoming elections, stress the Nixon policy of "peace and prosperity" and the "failings" of the Democratic Congress. He says the Republicans have a good record on the peace issue, and the American people will support a President who has "achieved" it. He also warns Republicans to shake off their post-Watergate depression, or there will be a Democratic landslide like the "debacle of '36"—the year Democrats won huge congressional majorities in Franklin D. Roosevelt's landslide victory.

23—Ford tells crowds at New Jersey fund-raisers, "I don't like Watergate and you don't like it either," but that the Republicans could be in "deep trouble" because of it. Referring to gloomy predictions that Republicans will lose 50 to 100 seats in Congress, Ford says, "it would be disastrous to our party." He urges Republicans to work hard in their campaigns to convince voters that Watergate was just the work of a few misguided men.

30—Speaking to more than 1,000 cheering Midwest Republican leaders in Chicago, Ford attacks the Committee to Re-Elect the President (CREEP), saying, "The political lesson of Watergate is this: Never again must Americans allow an arrogant, elite guard of political adolescents like CREEP to bypass the regular party organization and dictate the terms of a national election."

Asserting that Nixon might really have done better without it, Ford argues that CREEP failed by not helping enough Republicans get into Congress to ensure the success of Nixon's legislative programs.

"The fatal defect of CREEP," he explains, "was that it made its own rules and thus made its own ruin. It violated the historic concept of the two-party system in America and ran literally roughshod over the seasoned political judgment of the regular Republican Party."

Ford stresses that Republican candidates can run successfully in the fall by stressing the "pluses" of the Nixon administration in foreign policy and "on some domestic ones as well."

The White House had no comment on Ford's speech. He says, "The party needed to speak out about CREEP for a long time. I felt this was a good place to do it."

April

2—Ford says he urged the President to campaign for Republican candidate James Sparling, even though it might turn the April 16 special election in Michigan's 8th Congressional District into a referendum on the President. "But there are always certain gambles in a political cam-

paign," Ford explains. "It's just my feeling the President ought to go and take the risk."

2—Asked if he would accept a draft in 1976, Ford replies, "That's a hard question to answer.... If those circumstances develop, which I don't think will happen, then I've got a hard decision to make." He insists he still has no intention of rounding up delegates, as he doesn't want to "lose my credibility" as an effective Vice President.

9—Speaking in Troy, Mich., on behalf of several Michigan congressmen, Ford says he will not go into James Sparling's 8th District today because he has other commitments. He denies that he is purposely staying out, but some news reports view his absence as a White House desire for a clear-cut test of the President's standing with the people. Sparling will lose the April 16 special election to Democrat J. Robert Traxler.

10—In Detroit, Ford urges Republicans to strengthen their numbers in Congress. Claiming that Democrats have prevented the passage of much of Nixon's legislation, Ford emphasizes, "If the Democrats win 50 seats or 100 seats it will be a one-party House and the quality of legislation will deteriorate."

20—Ford appears on the same platform in San Jose, Calif., with liberal Republican Rep. Paul McCloskey and conservative Rep. John Rousselot and states that both views are needed within the Republican Party.

Taking a hard line, Ford insists, "This year, 1974, not 1976, is the year of decision for the survival of the two-party system in the United States." The issue is not President Nixon, he says, "but whether Republicans can mobilize a return to the ABC's of politics on a personal and precinct level." Ford warns that the Democrats want "to run against the President, although his name is not on the ballot. Our task is difficult. Democrats are seeking maximum exploitation on a national basis of what may be the greatest controversy ever generated about a President of the U.S."

"If Republicans allow themselves to become endlessly embroiled in that issue," he says, "we will forfeit elections from coast to coast—elections that should be decided on the individual merit of the candidates and the basic differences between the two parties."

The solution is not to "point fingers and wring hands" but to organize, unify, and mobilize— "to draw a line of resolve, a line that proclaims we will be pushed no further."

Attacking CREEP once again, he declares, "We must never again permit CREEP or any creepy successor organization to spoil the name of the Grand Old Party." Conceding that "adversity has sharpened our resolve," Ford exhorts the party to "be aggressive in selling our wares. The time has come to believe in us, because we have found new faith in ourselves."

27—Speaking in Texas and Oklahoma, Ford again attacks the Democrats for their "endless exploitation" of Watergate. He sees the Democratic strategy as a continued criticism of Nixon to "turn November into a national referendum on Watergate." Insisting "we cannot let the Watergate issue be turned into a smokescreen," Ford urges Republicans to stand together and "resolve that the Democrats are not going to get away with setting the rules and calling the signals for the November election."

May

26—Ford claims in Danbury, Conn., that this is not the first time dirty tricks have occurred, adding that "there is an effort being made by some, in my judgment, to undo the 1972 election." He admits that most Democrats probably are not involved, "but you've got a few crazies who are undertaking an effort, I think, beyond responsibility."

29—Ford says that public indignation over political corruption should not cause any extreme results. America should not "abdicate the two-party system and abandon our safeguards of freedom inherent in the Constitutional checks and balances.... We must not throw out the baby with the bath water."

31—As Ford travels in New Hampshire, the conservative *Manchester Union-Leader* attacks his integrity and cites his "treacherous" lack of loyalty to the President, adding that "Jerry is a jerk."

June

1—Ford again appears with Rep. McCloskey. Though he doesn't formally endorse him, he is the featured speaker at this event, which gives Nixon foe McCloskey the stamp of being a "real" Republican again. "Pete contributes an input that is needed," Ford remarks. "I urge you to embrace Republicans who are honest, diligent, and hard-working, whether they are on your side of the political spectrum or not. The Republican Party needs this depth." Ford has not cleared his appearance with California Governor Ronald Reagan or the state Republican committee, which results in some ruffled feelings. Ford's staff can only remark, "You must understand the Vice President is a very independent person."

6—In Columbus, Ohio, Ford reiterates, "There is no Republican candidate I know of on the ballot who has anything whatsoever to do with Watergate." On the 1974 elections, he comments: "If the Republican Party takes a disastrous defeat in '74, '76 may be irrelevant. If the Republican Party stands up and can be strong in 1974, it can prevail in 1976. 1974 is the crucial test."

15—Ford campaigns across New York state, warning Republicans they have to keep the Democrats from getting a "veto-proof" Congress. If the Democrats gain 50 seats in the House and seven or eight in the Senate, he says, "not only would the most liberal elements of the Democratic Party be in control of the legislative branch, they would also be in a position to dominate the executive."

22—Ford repeats in California that he won't be a candidate for office in 1976, but admits "I'm ready for whatever contingency takes place. I don't anticipate it, I don't seek it, but if you have worked as hard as I have at doing the jobs I have done, I don't have any lack of confidence."

July

17—A *Washington Star-News* article reports that the Republican National Committee will cut their share of the expenses on Ford's cross-country campaign trips. In the past, the Republican Party paid the entire amount of any trip that included a political appearance. However, it was decided this meant the party was paying more than its share and in the future will pay only for the part of each trip that deals directly with politics.

19—Ford campaigns in Roanoke, Va., for Rep. M. Caldwell Butler, an undecided Republican member of the Judiciary Committee, and announces he is not going to lobby against impeachment. At the same time the Vice President promises he will continue to campaign for Republican House members, regardless of how they vote on the impeachment issue: "There are other important issues that would have to be in the formula and if I think on the broad spectrum he deserves whatever help I can give, I'll come back."

25—Ford tells a Muncie, Ind., crowd "Not all, but a substantial amount, of the effort against the President is an attempt to try to undue the election results of 1972, and don't forget it."

30—Ford defends his travels around the country, saying he feels "a very definite obligation to the Republican party and its candidates.... I'm concerned about the President's impeachment, but I'm also concerned about the Republican party." Asked whether he would be using his travels around the country to collect political support for the 1976 Presidential nomination, Ford answers "I have no intention of being a candidate for any political office in 1976."

August

1—Ford is asked by the *Christian Science Monitor* if he were ready to take over the presidency now, Ford replies, "I think I'm ready for whatever might happen. And I think the best way to be ready for anything is to do the best job I can as Vice-President.... Everything I have done in public life has been a building block for whatever came along, and I am doing anything and everything I can in the job of Vice President, first, so I can qualify to be a good Vice President, and, secondly, for whatever happens thereafter."

4—A *New York Times* article indicates that Ford is drawing bigger and bigger crowds on his campaign swings around the country. More and more the congressmen for whom he is campaigning refer to him as "the most valuable member of the team" or speak of his "moral leadership" and "towering integrity and virtue."

5—With release of the latest Nixon transcripts, Ford announces he is "bowing out" of the impeachment debate in order to be "a calm communicator and ready conciliator between the executive and legislative branches"—a role he had promised to fulfill when he was nominated as Vice President. "The business of government must go on and the genuine needs of the people must be served. I believe I can make a better contribution to this end by not involving myself daily in the impeachment debate in which I have no constitutional role."

7—In the midst of Nixon resignation rumors, Ford gives an interview to the *New York Times*. Asked if he felt prepared to be President, Ford answers "No question about that. I think I've worked real hard. Aside from all the speeches, I've worked very hard." This is in reference to all the meetings and conferences he has had with Cabinet members. He adds, "I think I know as much, if not more, about the Government than any Vice President," but insists the time hasn't come yet to talk about transitions to the Presidency.

8—Ford's office announces he will not make his campaign trip to the West Coast, as Washington awaits Nixon's predicted resignation speech. ∎

VICE PRESIDENT FORD ON FOREIGN POLICY

November 1973

1—At his confirmation hearings before the Senate Rules Committee, Ford describes himself as a "dyed-in-the-wool internationalist in foreign affairs."

5—Still before the Rules Committee, Ford promises that if he were President he would seek a bigger role for Congress in formulating foreign policy, saying, "There has to be a two-way street between Congress and the Executive Branch."

7—The House once again debates the war powers bill before successfully overriding Nixon's veto. Ford opposes the bill, citing the recent Middle East war to show the need for presidential flexibility: "We are not out of the woods yet. We may be a long ways from being out of the woods. I am very, very concerned that the approval of this legislation over the President's veto could affect the President's capability to move forward from the cease-fire and achieve a permanent peace...."

26—Ford talks of "bridge-building" in the Middle East at the "Dinner for Life" held by the United Jewish Appeal, and affirms his support of Israel. He warns Arab nations not to keep pushing the U.S. indefinitely, clarifying that this is not a threat, "but we've all got to live for a long time."

December

6—The House votes 387-35 to approve Ford's nomination to be vice president, completing congressional action.

9—Ford describes his position on foreign policy to *U.S. News and World Report*: "I'm a reformed isolationist who, before World War II, was mistaken like a lot of people.... I have become, I think, a very ardent internationalist."

Admitting that he has supported foreign policy aims of Democratic presidents, Ford declares, "It seems to me that if we are to have a national foreign policy, it ought to be bipartisan."

January 1974

8—Stressing the need for world cooperation, Ford tells the Manufacturing Chemists Association, "Close an oil valve in the Middle East and you threaten to shut down a farm tractor in our Middle West. Halt that tractor and some people in the world will hunger for bread."

14—Ford denies any proposed American military intervention in the Middle East, saying, "I know of no responsible American leader who is saying that military force would be utilized to obtain oil from the Middle East. I think that is preposterous. I would strongly oppose it."

26—Speaking at the convention of the Anti-Defamation League of B'nai B'rith, Ford expresses hope that the Arab oil embargo will end shortly and pledges, "We will never again permit any foreign nation to have Uncle Sam over a barrel of oil."

February

24—In New York for the first time since becoming Vice President, Ford receives the 1974 American-Israel Friendship Gold Medal from B'nai Zion and lends his support to the administration's defense budget.

He declares a four-point defense program: the United States must keep sufficient military power and strength; opponents must know of this power; they must also know it will be used when needed; and at that crucial moment the United States must have the will to use her power.

Speaking about the plight of Soviet Jews, Ford says the U.S. looks "with sympathy and great appreciation upon freedom of thought and expression in all societies." However, he adds, "We have always made clear that our search for a stable peace does not mean approval of [the USSR's] domestic system."

March

22—In a Reuters interview, Ford warns European allies that there might be U.S. troop reductions overseas if the allies oppose a mutual troop reduction pact with the Soviet Union. He warns there is a lot of sentiment in the U.S. to bring some overseas troops home.... "I don't like it," he says, "but it is a fact of life."

28—Ford speaks at the South Vietnamese Embassy in Washington in a ceremony honoring Vietnam Veterans' Day, and he expresses a wish that more countries had joined the U.S. and the Republic of Vietnam in the war.

April

14—Ford discusses a number of foreign policy questions in an interview with the *Sunday Times* of London. He says he has always supported the NATO Alliance and doesn't expect the countries involved to always reflect a unanimous position.

When asked about possible American troop withdrawals from Europe, he answers that "unless we work out some sort of agreement with the Soviet Union and its allies on a mutual balanced force reduction, Congress will probably direct that some troops be withdrawn. I personally am against it...."

He suggests instead that "other members of the Alliance make a bigger contribution, either in regard to troop strength or dollar support." He is "disappointed" that "some of the leading advocates [for troop cuts] come from areas which used to represent the bastions of internationalism, members of Congress from eastern states. This is a sort of carryover from the Vietnam problem." He sees a possible solution in the influence of Henry Kissinger in his new position as "probably the most popular Secretary of State." "If Henry made a strong plea," Ford reasons, "I think it could have a sizeable impact on Congress not to reduce troops unilaterally."

He sees detente as leading hopefully to "a lesser [military] burden for everybody." He thinks detente is "helpful rather than harmful" and he is "a little perplexed at some of the criticism by people who, only five years ago, were talking about detente. Now they are probably the most cynical about it."

On the Strategic Arms Limitation Talks (SALT) he thinks "what we do in SALT II will be more important than SALT I...(W)ill we be able to control the multiple independently targeted warheads which we have and the Russians are now acquiring?" He indicates there still is uncertainty within the administration as to what the final U.S. bargaining position should be, and that his own position is not firm.

He favors a larger volume of trade with the Soviet Union and agrees with Kissinger that multi-polar diplomacy is a better approach than the old alliances, because "we live in a totally different world" with new weapons, communications, and transportation.

May

6—In a speech before the Economic Club of New York, Ford asks Congress to pass the Trade Reform Act "so the President may negotiate elimination of barriers to trade." In his view, "these barriers presently cost the U.S. several billion dollars a year in the form of higher consumer prices and the inefficient use of resources. Freer world trade will mean lower consumer prices and more and better jobs here at home."

7—In a press release after the Senate vote to bar further U.S. military aid to Southeast Asia in fiscal 1974, Ford warns that "in the present Watergate climate any votes by the Congress to cripple the defense budget or commitments to our allies make it much more difficult for the President to negotiate for peace." He insists·again that the only way to get a "satisfactory" arms limitation agreement with the Soviet Union is to "maintain the military strength of the U.S., which contributes a principal part of our diplomatic clout."

12—Ford tells a New Orleans crowd that for America to keep peace in the world, "we must maintain that military capability so that others know America is strong not only in capability but in will." "Strength brings peace," he adds, "and military strength continues peace."

June

4—Ford says that due to Secretary of State Kissinger's Middle East peace achievements, "a new era in world history, an era of negotiation and reconciliation, was 'Made in U.S.A.' " He says the United States will continue to aid Israel militarily, and the Soviet Union will continue to aid the Arabs.

14—Ford says he is "absolutely certain" the U.S. would take "strong and effective" action against any nations, including Egypt, who would use U.S. nuclear aid for military instead of peaceful purposes. "If they do, we'll cut them off in seconds," he says.

August

1—In an interview with the *Christian Science Monitor*, Ford states, "As Vice President, I'm concerned about our national security. I am all for the foreign policy which I think this administration has had and I fully support it in all its ramifications. And I would do, under any circumstances now or at some subsequent time, everything I could to see that it is implemented and executed." He adds, "I'm all for SALT. I hope we can get SALT II. But in the meantime I think it is of maximum importance that we keep a fully adequate defense program for the present, and that we keep our research development moving so that five years from now, whoever is president will have adequate military forces, particularly strategic forces, for arms-length negotiations."

5—Ford tells a veterans group in New Orleans that some members of the House will be using a "meat ax" to cut 5 to 10 per cent off the $83.7-billion defense appropriations bill. He also warns that these same people are trying to cut U.S. forces in Europe. Ford thinks this could hurt U.S. influence in foreign affairs. "I don't impugn their motives; I challenge their judgment," Ford says, reminding his audience that being "nice guys" is no substitute for strength when negotiating with the Soviet Union.

VICE PRESIDENT FORD ON DOMESTIC POLICY

October 1973

19—Ford tells the Southeastern Manufactured Housing Institute in Nashville that Nixon will continue to veto bills as long as Congress keeps passing "budget-breaking" legislation. "As Vice President," he promises, "I'd like to help foster the kind of responsible compromise that will make vetoes and impoundment unnecessary." And "despite gloomy scare talks about recession" he thinks America is on the way to reasonably good price stability.

November

1—Vice President-designate Ford describes himself to the Senate Rules Committee investigating his confirmation as a "moderate" on domestic issues and a conservative on fiscal affairs.

5—Ford testifies further before the Rules Committee that it was "almost incomprehensible" to him why the United States was so "negligent" for so long about developing cleaner coal-burning capability. He urges spending more money to find domestic fuel sources and thus avoid depending on foreign sources.

"Even though I have strong differences of opinion with some members of the Supreme Court and other federal courts," Ford says he is opposed to the concept of periodic reappointment or reconfirmation of judges because it would "undercut the independence of the judiciary, and I think that independence is important even though I don't always agree with them."

"Forced busing [to achieve racial balance] has caused more trouble and more tension where it has happened than almost anything else in our society," Ford testifies, and he is opposed to it. He prefers compensatory education for the disadvantaged in place of busing. He warns that "if the federal courts persist in trying to have forced busing to achieve racial balance in the public schools and there is no other way we could remedy that," he would favor a constitutional amendment prohibiting busing. He also admits he was an early critic of federal aid to education, but now finds it acceptable.

Of the media, Ford says, "I can't imagine me going out and attacking the press" as former Vice President Spiro T. Agnew did. He feels he has good relations with the press.

15—Ford defends his civil rights record in testimony at his confirmation hearings before the House Judiciary Committee. "I'm actually proud of my civil rights voting record," he says, "and I'm proud of my personal attitude vis-a-vis minority groups." Adding that every American should have equal treatment, he declares, "I've lived that. I believe that. I insist on that."

Ford tells the committee that if he were President he would insist on careful oversight of the Central Intelligence Agency, so it would not "become an uncontrollable octopus." He also says he is opposed to electronic surveilliance of members of Congress.

December

2—Speaking at a fund-raiser for a Hebrew high school for boys in Brooklyn, Ford favors public support for schools operated by religious groups. He says that, along with Nixon, he is committed to finding a "Constitutional way" to aid parochial schools.

6—Ford is confirmed as vice president by the House on a 387-35 vote, concluding congressional action.

January 1974

9—Ford holds his first White House luncheon since being confirmed Vice President, and his guests are 12 black officials who hold appointive posts in the Nixon administration. "My door will always be open," he tells his guests, and invites them to meet with him "whenever you feel the need." He predicts that "this administration will focus heavily on domestic problems in 1974."

11—Ford meets with non-administration black leaders at his request. Purpose of the meeting is to discuss the effect the energy shortage will have on the economy.

11—In a *Washington Star-News* interview Ford says he thinks passage of the pending budget reform bill is "mandatory" in order to give legislators the right to veto impoundments by the President. He thinks this will "get us off this head-to-head challenge between the President and Congress."

12—Ford declares the "cries of doom" over America's problems "are badly out of tune" with the true American spirit. He tells his audience at the dedication of the $34-million Baptist Medical Center in Little Rock, Ark., that "we must never let ourselves be distracted by the cries of despair."

22—Ford again expresses the administration's opposition to the windfall tax provisions of the emergency energy bill. The administration plan is to tax oil companies so as to encourage reinvestment of extra profits in exploration and the development of new sources of oil.

February

1—Speaking at the winter meeting of the U.S. Conference of Mayors in Washington, Ford announces an administration plan to increase the number of subsidized housing units by 100,000 and to make $2.8-billion available in the fiscal 1975 budget to carry over current community development projects until Congress can pass a new housing bill. City officials had complained that administration housing freezes were ruining their local Model Cities and urban renewal projects.

Departing from his prepared text, Ford talks about strained relations between Congress and the White House: "We've had the exercise over the past several years, particularly in 1973, where there would be a polarization of viewpoints on the part of the administration and on the part of a majority in Congress, and the net result would be no compromise and a veto, and then we had to start all over again...it just doesn't make sense. What I'm really trying to say is, to you who are sophisticated public servants, don't freeze yourself in, and I'll try not to and hope the administration doesn't."

5—Ford tells a conference of the U.S. League of Savings and Loan Associations that the administration will try to make mortgage money easier to get for home buyers. Predicting a "significant reduction" in inflation during the second quarter of 1974, he adds that "up to $6.6-billion in mortgage financing will be made available with federal assistance" to help low-income families.

9—On a hop-and-skip fund-raising tour of Michigan, Ford says, "The country as a whole is not going to have a recession. We are going through a period of economic readjustment based on the energy crisis."

14—Ford uses the football metaphor in describing America's problems at a dinner for the American Cancer Society: "I only wish that I could take the entire United States into the locker room at half-time. It would be an opportunity to say that we have lost yards against the line drives of inflation and the end runs of energy shortages, and that we are not using all our players as well as we might because there is too much unemployment."

He adds, "There would be no excuses about previous coaches and previous seasons. I would simply say that we must look not at the points we have lost but at the points we can gain. We have a winner."

15—Ford charges that public financing of federal election campaigns would be "a very serious mistake." "Once politicians have their campaigns paid for by public taxes, we'll never go back," he says. "I hesitate to take that step.... I personally would oppose it." His aides insist the Vice President always has been against public financing of campaigns but that his views were never publicized before.

Speaking about the energy crisis, Ford says, "There is no ground for a psychological complex of defeat. We have run short of gasoline. But we have not run short of American initiative."

18—Ford tells an engineers meeting in Chattanooga, Tenn., to develop new ingenuity to solve the country's energy problems. He insists he has confidence in the talent of American engineers, but "what we lack is time." He sees the necessity of finding ways to stop energy waste and increase production without sacrificing air and water quality and keeping costs at a minimum.

19—Along with Secretary of State Kissinger, Secretary of Commerce Frederick Dent, and Sen. Alan Bible (D Nev.), Ford is invited to join the Friendship Veterans Fire Engine Association in Alexandria, Va. The Alexandria Human Relations Council had asked the honorees not to attend the ceremony, charging the historic organization discriminated against blacks. (It was founded in 1774, and George Washington was one of the first members.) Ford is the only one of the four to show up and receive his honorary membership, and praises the fire brigade for showing the spirit of "American volunteerism."

Ford says he personally has "no information" proving the association is discriminatory. "I hope in the future blacks will be the recipients of association awards on the basis of merit," he says.

20—Ford announces in Cincinnati that he has met with the President and urged him to use his contingency funds to help ease the "temporary economic problems" of the times.

March

6—Ford appears at the winter session of the National Governors' Conference in support of the administration's proposals to safeguard individual privacy. He says there must be a "stop to the unwarranted invasions of privacy by the federal government and its agencies."

11—Ford tours a manpower training project in a black section of Philadelphia and promises that federal aid will continue to help such community-based programs to train the unemployed. He later tells the Harvard College Republican Club he does not favor legalizing the use of marijuana, and does favor the return of the death penalty in kidnap cases.

21—Nixon revokes the permission of the Agriculture Department to inspect farmers' income tax returns on an individual basis. A White House spokesman announces that the President's action was recommended by Ford as head of the Domestic Council Committee on Privacy.

April

5—Ford tells a health manpower conference that a good chance exists for enactment of comprehensive health insurance.

22—Ford tells the Associated Press he is against "a quickie, quick-fix tax cut" because it would only "add to the fuel of inflation."

The Vice President thinks Congress should legislate wage and price controls, which are due to expire April 30, over certain parts of the economy for the next 12 to 18 months. This "would give flexibility to the President...and give him the opportunity to focus in on some of the areas where we've had our greatest problems." This legislation looks doubtful to Ford, who fears that "without any tools, the administration will have no real weapon to do something affirmatively about wages and prices."

He also adds, as a man from Michigan, that he thinks emission control and safety standards for automobiles are too arbitrary and inflexible. "The intentions were good," he admits, but they forced the auto industry "to go beyond the state of the art" by a fixed date, which resulted in rising costs and higher gas consumption.

26—In his first major speech on economic policy, Ford tells the American Bankers Association he favors using tax incentives "to increase production in industries where shortages exist." (Chairman Wilbur D. Mills of the House Ways and Means Committee is a firm supporter of this approach, but the Nixon administration is not.)

Ford terms inflation "world public enemy No. 1," says it is caused by too many people "dipping into a limited pot" of world resources. He sees controlling inflation as a prime need, but thinks it "will be a long and difficult effort...requiring public support and a willingness to go the hard way." This "hard way" would be reducing consumption of all natural resources, not just those in the energy field.

The Vice President seems to be at odds with the administration about wage-price controls in his prepared text, advocating that "controls should be put on a standby basis, for temporary use only." The administration is against standby authority once the controls expire April 30. However, Ford's staff indicates that in the actual speech Ford changed his stand, calling for temporary continuation of controls only in a few special areas, such as health services and fuels. This is also the administration's position.

May

3—Dedicating a law building in Columbia, S.C., Ford declares, "Our institutions, like many other American institutions today, are under unprecedented attack. Lawyers are accused of crimes. Prosecutors and police are accused of running roughshod over individual rights. And the courts are often charged with aggravating the crime problem through lenient sentences and endless backlogs of cases." As an effort to reduce court dockets, he suggests that no-fault insurance and no-fault divorce laws "deserve serious consideration." Voluntary arbitration in small civil cases also "deserves more scrutiny."

6—Ford speaks to the Economic Club of New York and says once again he is against a tax cut, but in favor of reduced government expenditures to control inflation. "We all have our pet whipping boy when it comes to inflation," Ford states, "but the real culprit today, as it has been, is excessive demand. Double digit inflation is a result of double digit increases in money supply and double digit budget deficits."

His solution is a "free economy system" to increase production and hold back price increases. In addition, American consumers should lower their rate of "wasteful consumption," as they did during the energy crisis. "A conscious effort by all citizens to avoid wasteful use of resources will help control inflation," Ford says, "and it may also improve the quality of our lives."

He pledges that the administration "must and will continue its efforts to reduce, delay, and cut back expenditures at the federal level." The Federal Reserve System must act to have "less lavish increases in the supply of money and credit." He warns, "For awhile this will mean higher interest rates, but only temporarily. As we reduce inflation, interest rates will fall." He suggests also that tax cuts may serve as an incentive to certain industries to build up production.

Ford does not suggest losing ground against environmental gains, but thinks these gains "must be carefully balanced against the need to stop the inflation through increased supply." He warns that the Justice Department must be "alert to fight monopoly power whether in labor or in industry," since monopoly "inevitably reduces supply and creates artificial high prices."

The Vice President asks Congress to pass the Trade Reform Act, "so the President may negotiate elimination of barriers to trade" which result in "higher consumer prices and the inefficient use of resources."

12—Ford addresses a joint session of the Louisiana state legislature and asks members to look at "what is right in America." He states, "I do not come before you today as the Vice President of a nation suffering from the plagues of slavery, pestilence, famine, revolution, or war." "That we have seen problems in our time is without question," he continues, "but more importantly...historians...will record that some great deeds have been done and some great goals have been accomplished."

The Louisiana lawmakers applaud when Ford announces the administration is trying to deregulate natural gas. Louisiana is one of the major producing states of natural gas, and deregulation would mean price rises. Ford says if Michigan and other states want to use natural gas, they should be willing to pay for "this great resource."

26—The government is trying to hold down "skyrocketing" health care costs, Ford tells his audience at the dedication of a new addition to the Mount Sinai Medical Center in New York. He believes a compromise on the various health insurance bills can be reached—one that is "reasonably satisfactory to all"—and he pledges his "utmost" to achieve it. The "common thread," he says, is that "something must be done about catastrophic illness." Declaring that "the integrity of the patient-doctor relationship must be maintained," Ford believes the new plan should continue "our present system, which allows a patient to choose his own physician." He doubts whether any other method would be satisfactory to either patients or doctors. In addition, "to let a vast new federal bureaucracy take over our health-care system would be a burden which would be unbearable in cost. And, to many, unbearable in principle."

June

7—Ford tells the Georgia Bar Association that the Domestic Council Committee on the Right of Privacy, of which he is chairman, is to decide how to balance "the interests of personal privacy with the increasing claims by government and business to gather and use information about our 211 million American people." He adds that "the administration is considering draft legislation that would prohibit snooping and monitoring of communications entering and leaving a citizen's home via cable television." He also urges lawyers to help assure that official records will not become "rolls of public tape in a computer system."

Ford claims the Privacy Committee succeeded recently in stopping a federal computerized information system called FEDNET. It would have given federal agencies a wide information network, and without proper safeguards "could have escalated the fears of people over the collection and dissemination of personal information." He adds that the growth of information systems already has created a "widespread fear that the 1984 depicted by George Orwell is not just a fictional threat."

9—Ford tells the National Conference of Christians and Jews that "our greatest threat comes from no foreign foe but from those at home who seek to impose the power of negative thinking." Specifically, he attacks those who treat members of the Symbionese Liberation Army as martyrs rather than "outlaws." Ford emphasizes "that it is immoral to condemn by individual sin the government but to condone crime by revolutionaries in California." He warns, "Prophets of negativity try to debunk our whole society and all who try to serve it."

17—Speaking to the Grocery Manufacturers of America, Ford admits there is a "deep and pervasive anxiety" about rising food prices. With "a restrained note of optimism" he believes that if wholesalers, retailers, farmers, and the weather keep cooperating, "it is even possible that prices at the check-out counter may begin to come down." He emphasizes again that though the administration cannot stop inflation "immediately without plunging the nation into a depression, we aim to slow it down over a period of time in such a way as to avoid either a depression or a recession."

20—Ford warns in San Diego that in order to avoid an impasse "the time has come for bold domestic diplomacy to negotiate a return to pride in America." "There is too much deadlock here at home—too much acrimony and animosity, frustration and faint-heartedness," he says. He reminds his audience of United States Jaycees that "we must go on living together. We must rebuild our economy, overcome inflation, tap new energy, provide new housing, improve health care, preserve the environment, and otherwise regenerate our lifestyle."

"If people shooting at each other can disengage," he says, "so can people who are shouting at each other."

26—Ford urges support of legislation to give Americans access to information about them contained in computer files. "I believe the individual should be his own policeman," Ford states. "This approach is complicated and

difficult...but is far superior to...a Big Brother agency taking control."

28—Ford warns members of the journalism society, Sigma Delta Chi, that "Washington is about the worst place in America from which to see America." His advice to the Washington correspondents: "I believe it would broaden your perspective to periodically practice your profession outside the capital so that the vast and valuable differences in the way that Americans think and live would become part of your own news judgments."

30—*The New York Times* reports a recent Ford reply after being accused of having rather limited contacts on his travels around America: "I think meeting with eight to ten thousand Jaycees down in San Diego was a pretty good cross-section of Americans. They are, I think, very representative of America."

In his view, "After 13 elections, I can modestly claim a fairly good ear for the so-called voice of the people, and what I hear...is a lot different from what I hear in Washington, D.C., and I like it a lot better...our people are stout of heart and decent in demeanor."

When asked if he would "broaden the base" of his contacts to include more blacks, or Indians, or rural people, Ford answers he has plans to speak to the Urban League and also some labor representatives.

July

11—Ford tells the National Lieutenant Governors' Conference in Santa Fe, N.M., that federal bureaucrats and "a number of trade associations" are conducting a "quiet but sinister effort...to kill general revenue sharing." He thinks the reason is "they want to help recapture the money and authority lost through governmental decentralization." Ford tells his audience, "Americans must never be reduced to computerized robots by a single center of power."

13—Ford meets with Nixon at San Clemente and states their conversation dealt "99 and 9-tenths per cent" with the economy. "A tax cut is the wrong approach. A tax increase is the wrong thing to to at this time," he says after meeting with the President for the sixth time in one week. Ford admits Nixon has no new economic "blueprint" but plans to keep a tight federal budget. To Ford, the stabilized unemployment rate and recent rise in the stock market show the economy is improving.

24—Asked what the American people really want, Ford says "I think they want reassurance that the United States is the great country they really believe in. And I think they realize that in foreign policy we have been spectacularly successful. But they do have some doubts about our capability to handle such problems as inflation; and they want reassurance that we are going to solve these domestic problems in particular.... They believe America is great, but skeptics and cynics and some of our problems lead them to an opposite conclusion."

25—Ford talks to a crowd in Muncie, Ind., about impeachment: "I think that the uncertainty that will result domestically affecting the economy...will be significant.... and I think it could be multiplied if and when impeachment took place."

29—Ford speaks at the 64th annual convention of the National Urban League in San Francisco. The Vice President defends his civil rights record, saying "Although not what you might like it to be, my civil rights record is anything but negative and it is a long, long way from standing in the doorway of a schoolhouse in defiance of a

(Continued on p. 78)

FORD'S ADDRESS TO JOINT SESSION OF CONGRESS

Following is the text of President Ford's nationally televised speech Aug. 12, his first to a joint session of Congress as President.

Mr. Speaker, Mr. President, distinguished guests and dear friends:

My fellow Americans, we have a lot of work to do.

My former colleagues, you and I have a lot of work to do.

Let's get on with it.

I am grateful for your very warm welcome.

I am not here to make an inaugural address. The nation needs action, not words.

Nor will this be a formal report on the State of the Union. God willing, I will have at least three more chances to do that.

It's good to be back in the people's House.

But this cannot be a real homecoming. Under the Constitution, I now belong to the Executive Branch. The Supreme Court has even ruled that I am the Executive Branch, head, heart and hand.

With due respect to the learned justices—and I greatly respect the Judiciary—part of my heart will always be here on Capitol Hill. I know well the co-equal role of the Congress in our constitutional process. I love the House of Representatives. I revere the traditions of the Senate despite my too-short internship there. As President, within the limits of basic principles, my motto towards the Congress is communication, conciliation, compromise and cooperation.

This Congress, will, I am confident, be my working partner as well as my most constructive critic. I am not asking for conformity. I am dedicated to the two-party system, and you know which party is mine.

I do not want a honeymoon with you. I want a good marriage.

I want progress and problem solving which requires my best efforts, and also your best efforts.

I have no need to learn how Congress speaks for the people.

As President, I intend to listen.

But I also intend to listen to the people themselves—all the people—as promised them last Friday. I want to be sure we are all tuned in to the real voice of America.

Unity in Diversity

My administration starts off by seeking unity in diversity. My office door has always been open and that is how it is going to be at the White House. Yes, congressmen will be welcomed—if you don't overdo it.

The first seven words of the Constitution and the most important are these: We the People of the United States. We, the people, ordained and established the Constitution and reserved to themselves all powers not granted to federal and state governments. I respect and will always be conscious of that fundamental rule of freedom.

Only eight months ago, when I last stood here, I told you I was a Ford not a Lincoln. Tonight I say I am still a Ford, but I am not a Model T.

I do have some old-fashioned ideas. I believe in the basic decency and fairness of America. I believe in the integrity and patriotism of the Congress. And while I am aware of the House rule that one never speaks to the galleries, I believe in the First Amendment and the absolute necessity of a free press.

But I also believe that over two centuries since the First Continental Congress was convened, the direction of our nation's movement has been forward. I am here to confess that in my first campaign for president—of my senior class in South High in Grand Rapids, Michigan—I headed the Progressive Party ticket and lost. Maybe that's why I became a Republican.

Now I ask you to join with me in getting this country revved up and moving.

My instinctive judgment is that the state of the Union is excellent. But the state of our economy is not so good.

Everywhere I have been as Vice President, some 118,000 miles into 40 states and through 55 news conferences, the unanimous concern of Americans is inflation. For once all the polls agree. They also suggest that people blame government far more than either management or labor for the high cost of everything.

You who come from 50 states, three territories and the District of Columbia know this better than I. That is why you have created since I left here your new Budget Reform Committee. I welcome it and will work with its members to bring the federal budget into balance by fiscal 1976.

The fact is that for the past 25 years that I served here, the federal budget has been balanced in only six.

Mr. Speaker, I am a little late getting around to it but confession is good for the soul. I have sometimes voted to spend more taxpayers' money for worthy federal projects in Grand Rapids while vigorously opposing wasteful federal boondoggles in Oklahoma.

Against Unwarranted Cuts

Be that as it may, Mr. Speaker, you and I have always stood together against unwarranted cuts in national defense. This is no time to change that nonpartisan policy.

Just as escalating federal spending has been a prime cause of higher prices over many years, it may take some time to stop inflation.

But we must begin now.

For a start, before your Labor Day recess, Congress should reactivate the Cost of Living Council through passage of a clean bill, without reimposing controls, that will let us monitor wages and prices to expose abuses.

The American wage earner and the American housewife are a lot better economists than most economists care to admit.

They know that a government big enough to give you everything you want is a government big enough to take from you everything you have.

If we want to restore confidence in ourselves as working politicians, the first thing we all have to do is learn how to say "no."

The first specific request by the Ford administration is not to Congress but to the voters in the upcoming November elections. It is this: Support your candidates, congressmen and senators, Democrats or Republicans, conservative or liberal, who consistently vote for tough decisions to cut the cost of government, restrain federal spending and bring inflation under control.

I applaud the initiatives the Congress has already taken. The only fault I find with the Joint Economic Committee inflation study authorized last week is that we need its expert findings in six weeks instead of six months.

Economic Summit

A month ago the distinguished majority leader of the Senate asked the White House to convene an economic conference of members of Congress, the President's economic consultants and some of the best economic brains from labor, industry and agriculture.

Later this was perfected by resolution to assemble a domestic summit meeting to devise a bipartisan action plan for stability and growth in the American economy. Neither I nor my staff have much time just now for letter writing. So I will respond in person. I accept your suggestion and I will personally preside.

Furthermore, I propose that this summit meeting be held at an early date and in full view of the American public. They are as anxious to get the right answers as we are.

My first priority is to work with you to bring inflation under control. Inflation is our domestic public enemy No. 1. To restore economic confidence, the government in Washington must provide leadership. It does no good to blame the public for spending too much when the government is spending too much.

I began to put my administration's own economic house in order, starting last Friday.

I instructed my Cabinet officers and counselors and my White House staff to make fiscal restraint their first order of business, and to save every taxpayer's dollar the safety and genuine welfare of the country will permit. Some economic activities will be affected more by monetary and fiscal restraints than other activities. Good government clearly requires that we tend to the economic problems facing our country in a spirit of equity to all of our citizens.

Tonight is no time to threaten you with vetoes. But I do have that last recourse and am a veteran of many a veto fight in this very chamber. Can't we do the job better by reasonable compromise? I hope we can.

Meeting Half Way

Minutes after I took the presidential oath, the joint leadership of Congress told me at the White House they would go more than half way to meet me. This was confirmed in your unanimous concurrent resolution of cooperation for which I am deeply grateful. If for my part I go more than half way to meet the Congress, maybe we will find a much larger area of national agreement.

I bring no legislative shopping list tonight. I will deal with specifics in future messages and talks with you. But here are a few examples of my seriousness.

Last week the Congress passed the elementary and secondary education bill and I found it on my desk. Any reservations I might have about some of its provisions—and I do have—fade in comparsion to the urgent needs of America for quality education. I will sign it in a few days. I must be frank. In implementing its provisions, I will oppose excessive funding during this inflationary crisis.

As Vice President, I studied various proposals for better health care financing. I saw them coming closer together, and urged my friends in the Congress and in the administration to sit down and sweat out a sound compromise. The comprehensive health insurance plan goes a long way towards providing early relief to the people who are sick.

Why don't we write—and I ask this with the greatest spirit of cooperation—a good health bill on the statute books before this Congress adjourns?

The economy of our country is critically dependent on how we interact with the economies of other countries. It is little comfort that our inflation is only part of a worldwide problem, or that American families need less of their paychecks for groceries than most of our foreign friends.

World Trade

As one of the building blocks of peace, we have taken the lead in working toward a more open and equitable world economic system. A new round of international trade negotiations started last September among 105 nations in Tokyo. The others are waiting for the United States Congress to grant the necessary authority to proceed.

With modifications, the trade reform bill passed by the House last year would do that. I understand good progress has been made in the Senate committee. But I am optimistic, as always, that the Senate will pass an acceptable bill quickly as a key part of our joint prosperity campaign.

I am determined to expedite other international economic plans. We will be working together with other nations to find better ways to prevent shortages of food and fuel. We must not let last winter's energy crisis happen again. I will push Project Independence for our own good and the good of others. In that, too, I will need your help.

Successful foreign policy is an extension of the hopes of the whole American people for a world of peace and orderly freedom. So I would say a few words to our distinguished guests from the governments of other nations where, as at home, it is my determination to deal openly with allies and adversaries.

Over the past five and a half years, in Congress and as Vice President, I have fully supported the outstanding foreign policy of President Nixon. This I intend to continue.

Throughout my public service, starting with wartime naval duty under the command of President Franklin D. Roosevelt, I have upheld all our Presidents when they spoke for my country to the world. I believe the Constitution commands this. I know that in this crucial area of international policy I can count on your firm support.

Let there be no doubt or misunderstanding anywhere. There are no opportunities to exploit, should anyone so desire. There will be no change of course no relaxation of vigilance, no abandonment of the helm of our ship of state as the watch changes. We stand by our commitments and will live up to our responsibilities, in our formal alliances, in our friendships and in our improving relations with any potential adversaries.

United and Strong

On this, Americans are united and strong. Under my term of leadership I hope we will become more united. I am certain we will remain strong.

A strong defense is the surest way to peace. Strength makes detente attainable. Weakness invites war, as my generation knows from four bitter experiences.

Just as America's will for peace is second to none, so will America's strength be second to none.

We cannot rely on the forbearance of others to protect this nation. The power and diversity of the armed forces, the resolve of our fellow citizens, the flexibility in our command to navigate international waters that remain troubled—all are essential our security.

I shall continue to insist on civilian control of our superb military establishment. The Constitution plainly requires the President to be the Commander-in-Chief, and I will be.

Our job will not be easy. In promising continuity, I cannot promise simplicity. The problems and challenges of the world remain complex and difficult. But we have set out upon a path of reason and fairness, and we will continue on it.

Administration Guideposts

As guideposts on that path, I can offer the following:

● To our allies of a generation, in the Atlantic community and Japan, I pledge continuity in the loyal collaboration on our many mutual endeavors.

● To our friends and allies in this hemisphere, I pledge continuity in the deepening dialogue to define renewed relationships of equality and justice.

● To our allies and friends in Asia, I pledge a continuity in our support for their security, independence and economic development. In Indochina, we are determined to see the observance of the Paris Agreement on Vietnam and the cease-fire and negotiated settlement in Laos. We hope to see an early compromise settlement in Cambodia.

● To the Soviet Union, I pledge continuity in our commitment to the course of the past three years. To our two peoples, and to all mankind, we owe a continued effort to live, and where possible, to work together in peace; for, in a thermo-nuclear age, there can be no alternative to a positive and peaceful relationship between our nations.

● To the People's Republic of China, whose legendary hospitality I enjoyed, I pledge continuity in our commitment to the principles of the Shanghai communique. The new relationship built on those principles has demonstrated that it serves serious and objective mutual interests and has become an enduring feature on the world scene.

● To the nations of the Middle East, I pledge continuity in our vigorous efforts to advance the process which has brought hopes of peace to that region after 25 long years as a hotbed of war. We shall carry out our promise to promote continuing negotiation among all parties for a complete, just and lasting settlement.

● To all nations, I pledge continuity in seeking a common global goal: a stable international structure of trade and finance which reflects the interdependence of all peoples.

● To the entire international community—to the United Nations, to the world's non-aligned nations, and to all others—I pledge a continuity in our dedication to the humane goals which throughout our history have been so much a part of our contribution to mankind.

So long as the peoples of the world have confidence in our purposes and faith in our word the age-old vision of peace on earth will continue to grow brighter.

I pledge myself unreservedly to that goal. I say to you in words that cannot be improved upon: Let us never negotiate out of fear, but let us never fear to negotiate.

Individual Rights

As Vice President, as the request of the President, I addressed myself to the individual rights of Americans in the area of privacy. There will be no illegal tappings, eavesdropping, buggings or break-ins by my administration. There will be hot pursuit of tough laws to prevent illegal invasions of privacy in both government and private activities.

On the higher plane of public morality there is no need for me to preach tonight. We have thousands of far better preachers and millions of sacred Scriptures to guide us on the path of personal right-living and exemplary official conduct. If we can make effective and earlier use of the moral and ethical wisdom of the centuries in today's complex society, we will prevent more crime and corruption than all the policemen and prosecutors governments can ever deter. This is a job that must begin at home, not in Washington.

I once told you that I am not a saint, and hope never to see the day that I cannot admit having made a mistake. So I will close with another confession.

Frequently along the tortuous road of recent months, from this chamber to the President's house, I protested that I was my own man.

Now I realize that I was wrong.

I am your man, for it was your carefully weighed confirmation that changed my occupation.

I am the people's man, for you acted in their name, and I accepted and began my new and solemn trust with a promise to serve all the people, and to do the best I can for America.

When I say all the people I mean exactly that.

To the limits of my strength and ability, I will be the President of the black, brown, red and white Americans, of old and young, of women's liberations and male chauvinists and all the rest of us in between, of the poor and the rich, of native sons and new refugees, of those who work at lathes or at desks or in mines or in the fields, and of Christians, Jews, Molsems, Buddhists and atheists, if there really are any atheists after what we have all been through.

Fellow-Americans, a final word:

I want to be a good President.

I need your help.

We all need God's sure guidance.

With it, nothing can stop the United States of America. ∎

PRESIDENT NIXON'S RESIGNATION SPEECH

Following is the text of President Nixon's Aug. 8 televised address in which he announced his resignation from office.

Good evening.

This is the 37th time I have spoken to you from this office, where so many decisions have been made that shaped the history of this Nation. Each time I have done so to discuss with you some matter that I believe affected the national interest.

In all the decisions I have made in my public life, I have always tried to do what was best for the Nation. Throughout the long and difficult period of Watergate, I have felt it was my duty to persevere, to make every possible effort to complete the term of office to which you elected me.

In the past few days, however, it has become evident to me that I no longer have a strong enough political base in the Congress to justify continuing that effort. As long as there was a base, I felt strongly that it was necessary to see the constitutional process through to its conclusion, that to do otherwise would be unfaithful to the spirit of that deliberately difficult process, and a dangerously destablizing precedent for the future.

But with the disappearance of that base, I now believe that the constitutional purpose has been served, and there is no longer a need for the process to be prolonged.

I would have preferred to carry through to the finish whatever the personal agony it would have involved, and my family unanimously urged me to do so. But the interests of the Nation must always come before any personal considerations.

From the discussions I have had with Congressional and other leaders, I have concluded that because of the Watergate matter I might not have the support of the Congress that I would consider necessary to back the very difficult decisions and carry out the duties of this office in the way the interests of the Nation would require.

I have never been a quitter. To leave office before my term is completed is abhorrent to every instinct in my body. But as President, I must put the interest of America first. America needs a full-time President and a full-time Congress, particularly at this time with the problems we face at home and abroad.

To continue to fight through the months ahead for my personal vindication would almost totally absorb the time and attention of both the President and the Congress in a period when our entire focus should be on the great issues of peace abroad and prosperity without inflation at home.

Resign at Noon

Therefore, I shall resign the Presidency effective at noon tomorrow. Vice President Ford will be sworn in as President at that hour in this office.

As I recall the high hopes for America with which we began this second term, I feel a great sadness that I will not be here in this office working on your behalf to achieve those hopes in the next 2½ years. But in turning over direction of the Government to Vice President Ford, I know, as I told the Nation when I nominated him for that office ten months ago, that the leadership of America will be in good hands.

In passing this office to the Vice President, I also do so with the profound sense of the weight of responsibility that will fall on his shoulders tomorrow and, therefore, of the understanding, the patience, the cooperation he will need from all Americans.

As he assumes that responsibility, he will deserve the help and the support of all of us. As we look to the future, the first essential is to begin healing the wounds of this Nation; to put the bitterness and the divisions of the recent past behind us and to rediscover those shared ideals that lie at the heart of our strength and unity as a great and as a free people.

By taking this action, I hope that I will have hastened the start of that process of healing which is so desperately needed in America.

I regret deeply any injuries that may have been done in the course of the events that led to this decision. I would say only that if some of my judgments were wrong, and some were wrong, they were made in what I believed at the time to be the best interest of the Nation.

To those who have stood with me during these past difficult months, to my family, my friends, to many others who joined in supporting my cause because they believed it was right, I will be eternally grateful for your support.

And to those who have not felt able to give me your support, let me say I leave with no bitterness toward those who have opposed me, because all of us, in the final analysis, have been concerned with the good of the country however our judgments might differ.

So, let us all now join together in affirming that common commitment and in helping our new President succeed for the benefit of all Americans.

I shall leave this office with regret at not completing my term, but with gratitude for the privilege of serving as your President for the past 5½ years. These years have been a momentous time in the history of our Nation and the world. They have been a time of achievement in which we can all be proud, achievements that represent the shared efforts of the Administration, the Congress and the people.

Challenges Ahead

But the challenges ahead are equally great and they, too, will require the support and the efforts of the Congress and the people working in cooperation with the new Administration.

We have ended America's longest war, but in the work of securing a lasting peace in the world, the goals ahead are even more far-reaching and more difficult. We must complete a structure of peace so that it will be said of this generation, our generation, of Americans, by the people of all nations, not only that we ended one war, but that we prevented future wars.

We have unlocked the doors that for a quarter of a century stood between the United States and the People's Republic of China.

We must now ensure that the one quarter of the world's people who live in the People's Republic of China will be and remain not our enemies but our friends.

In the Middle East, 100 million people in the Arab countries, many of whom have considered us their enemy for nearly 20 years, now look on us as their friends. We must continue to build on that friendship so that peace can settle at last over the Middle East and so that the cradle of civilization will not become its grave.

Together with the Soviet Union we have made the crucial breakthroughs that have begun the process of limiting nuclear arms. But we must set as our goal not just limiting, but reducing and finally destroying these terrible weapons so that they cannot destroy civilization and so that the threat of nuclear war will no longer hang over the world and the people.

We have opened the new relation with the Soviet Union. We must continue to develop and expand that new relationship so that the two strongest nations of the world will live together in cooperation rather than confrontation.

Around the world, in Asia, in Africa, in Latin America, in the Middle East, there are millions of people who live in terrible poverty, even starvation. We must keep as our goal turning away from production for war and expanding production for peace so that people everywhere on this earth can at least look forward in their children's time, if not in our own time, to having the necessities for a decent life.

Here in America, we are fortunate that most of our people have not only the blessings of liberty, but also the means to live full and good and, by the world's standards, even abundant lives. We must press on, however, to a goal of not only more and better jobs, but of full opportunity for every American, and of what we are striving so hard right now to achieve, prosperity without inflation.

For more than a quarter of a century in public life I have shared in the turbulent history of this era. I have fought for what I believed in. I have tried to the best of my ability to discharge those duties and meet those responsibilities that were entrusted to me.

Sometimes I have succeeded and sometimes I have failed, but always I have taken heart from what Theodore Roosevelt once said about the man in the arena, "whose face is marred by dust and sweat and blood, who strives valiantly, who errs and comes short again and again because there is not effort without error and short-coming, but who does actually strive to do the deeds, who knows the great enthusiasms, the great devotions, who spends himself in a worthy cause, who at the best knows in the end the triumphs of high achievements and who at the worst, if he fails, at least fails while daring greatly."

Parting Pledge

I pledge to you tonight that as long as I have a breath of life in my body, I shall continue in that spirit. I shall continue to work for the great causes to which I have been dedicated throughout my years as a Congressman, a Senator, a Vice President and President; the cause of peace not just for America but among all nations, prosperity, justice and opportunity for all of our people.

There is one cause above all to which I have been devoted and to which I shall always be devoted for as long as I live.

When I first took the oath of office as President five and one-half years ago, I made this sacred commitment: "To consecrate my office, my energies and all the wisdom I can summon to the cause of peace among nations."

I have done my very best in all the days since to be true to that pledge. As a result of these efforts, I am confident that the world is a safer place today, not only for the people of America, but for the people of all nations, and that all of our children have a better chance than before of living in peace rather than dying in war.

This, more than anything, is what I hoped to achieve when I sought the Presidency. This, more than anything, is what I hope will be my legacy to you, to our country, as I leave the Presidency.

To have served in this office is to have felt a very personal sense of kinship with each and every American. In leaving it, I do so with this prayer: May God's grace be with you in all the days ahead. ∎

(Ford on Domestic Policy from p. 71)

federal court order in an ateempt to deny black children a quality education." Ford admits that his confirmation as Vice President was opposed by civil rights leaders: "Let me assure you that during my confirmation hearings, minorities very properly put me on notice of their deep concern." But he renews his pledge to be "Vice President of all the people."

August

5—Ford tells the Disabled War Veterans convention, "Unconditional blanket amnesty to anyone who illegally evaded or fled military service is wrong."

6—Because of today's hastily-called Cabinet meeting, Ford is unable to deliver a speech to the National Conference of the Agricultural Stabilization Service, but sends a staff aid to read the speech. In the speech, the Vice President continues the Nixon administration theme of less government spending: "We must veto 'budget-busting' legislation. We cannot afford optional luxuries.... Reduced expenditures mean reduced government borrowing, reduced interest rates and help for the Federal Reserve in its efforts to slow the inflationary expansion of money and credit." He states: "It serves no purpose to lecture the harassed public, especially the low- and middle-income people who have been the main losers from inflation." He thinks that "certain groups—older Americans, persons on fixed incomes, the unemployed—may require special help within budgetary limitations." Other industries may also need help, such as public utilities, housing, and financial institutions.

Ford's main theme is a call to the future: "At home it is apparent that we must strive for a new confidence in our domestic capacity to deal with inflation. We have made economic predictions that turned out to be wrong. We have all made mistakes. But instead of dwelling on the errors of the past, let us unite and cooperate to face the future.... I welcome the involvement of Congress in efforts to deal with inflation. Neither impeachment nor the November election campaign must interfere with immediate bipartisan efforts to bring inflation under control."

8—Speaking shortly after Nixon's resignation speech Ford pledges "my best efforts and cooperation and leadership and dedication to do what's good for America and good for the world." ∎

BIBLIOGRAPHY OF MATERIALS ON GERALD R. FORD

Books

Doyle, Michael V., Ed. *Gerald R. Ford Selected Speeches.* Arlington, Virginia, R.W. Beaty, Ltd., 1973.

LeRoy, L. David. *Gerald Ford: Untold Story.* Arlington, Virginia, R.W. Beaty, Ltd., 1974.

Vestal, Bud. *Jerry Ford, Up Close: an Investigative Biography.* New York, Coward, McCann & Geoghegan, 1974.

Articles

Alsop, Stewart. "Ford and the Poisonous Primaries," *Newsweek,* April 22, 1974, p. 120.

Bennett, R.K. "What Sort of Man is Gerald R. Ford?" *Reader's Digest,* March 1974, p. 73.

Cameron, Juan. "Suppose There's a President Ford in Your Life," *Fortune,* March 1974, p. 102.

"Delicate Balancing Act," *Time,* February 25, 1974, p. 14.

Elder, Shirley. "Gerald Ford: GOP's Good Soldier Wins Cap to His Career," *Washington Star-News,* Dec. 7, 1973, p. A-3.

Fellman, T.B. "Closest Family in Washington," *McCall's,* May 1974, p. 94.

Ford, Gerald R. "Rule of Law," *Vital Speeches,* Dec. 15, 1973, p. 40.

"Ford: Busy Start as Vice-President and Sidestepping '76 Speculation," *U.S. News and World Report,* Dec. 24, 1973, p. 21.

"Ford Blasts CREEP," *Senior Scholastic,* May 2, 1974, p. 18.

"Gerald Ford: the Politics of Loyalty," *Newsweek,* Oct. 22, 1973, p. 37.

"Good Lineman for the Quarterback," *Time,* Oct. 22, 1973, p. 16.

Greider, William. "Ford Philosophy on Power: 'Secrecy is Enemy of Truth,'" *The Washington Post,* Dec. 30, 1973, p. A-3.

Greider, William. "Vice-President Ford Grew in Stature During Hearings," *The Washington Post,* Dec. 7, 1973, p. A-1.

"Historic Moment," *Nation,* Dec. 10, 1973, p. 612.

"The Ideas of Gerald Ford," *Economist,* Jan. 26, 1974, p. 24.

"If It's Ford vs. Kennedy in '76," *U.S. News and World Report,* June 3, 1974, p. 21.

"Interview with Gerald R. Ford, Vice-President of the United States," ABC's Issues and Answers, Dec. 9, 1973.

"Jerry Ford: the Eisenhower of the Seventies," *Atlantic,* August 1974, p. 25.

"Jerry Ford: the Making of the 38th President," *New Times,* June 14, 1974, p. 14.

Lansner, K. "Open Letter to Vice-President Ford," *Newsweek,* Jan. 28, 1974, p. 28.

"Life with a Perfect Father," *Time,* Dec. 17, 1973, p. 15.

Miller, Norman C. "Amiable Caretaker: Nixon's naming of Ford is Seen as Bid to Make Peace with Congress," *Wall Street Journal,* Oct. 15, 1973, p. 1.

"Mr. Ford and Civil Rights," *Crises,* Jan. 1974, p. 7.

"New Veep's Real Mission," *Newsweek,* Dec. 17, 1973, p. 26.

"Nixon/Ford Choice: Public Prefers Ford to Nixon for Rest of Term," *Gallup Opinion Index,* Feb. 1974, p. 23.

"Notes and Comments: Congressman Ford," *New Yorker,* Nov. 12, 1973, p. 39.

Osborne, John. "Ford on Ford," *New Republic,* Dec. 15, 1973, p. 8.

"Republicans Look to Ford as '74 Worries Mount," *U.S. News and World Report,* April 8, 1974, p. 31.

Sehlstedt, Albert. "'I Am Thinking You Are Going to be President Within a Year'" *The Sun,* Dec. 30, 1973, p. K-3.

Sidey, Hugh. "Jerry Ford's Lengthening Shadow," *Time,* April 29, 1974, p. 20.

"A Talk with Gerald Ford," *Dun's,* August 1974, p. 46.

"The Vice-Presidency: from Cigar Store Indian to Crown Prince," *Washington Monthly,* April 1974, p. 41.

"Vice-President Ford: 'Why I Will Not Run in '76,'" *U.S. News and World Report,* Dec. 17, 1973, p. 24.

"Vice-President Views Business Issues," *Nation's Business,* March 1974, p. 54.

White, William S. "Gerald Ford: the Man to Beat in '76," *The Washington Post,* Oct. 20, 1973, p. A-1.

"With Agnew Out, Why Nixon Picked Ford," *U.S. News and World Report,* Oct. 22, 1973, p. 17.

Documents

"The President's Remarks Announcing his Intention to Nominate Gerald R. Ford to be Vice-President with Mr. Ford's Response, Oct. 12, 1973," *Weekly Compilation of Presidential Documents,* Oct. 15, 1973, p. 1244. Washington, D.C. G.P.O., 1973.

U.S. Congress, House Committee on the Judiciary. *Nomination of Gerald R. Ford to be Vice-President of the United States: Hearings Nov. 15-26, 1973,* Washington, D.C., G.P.O., 1973.

U.S. Congress, Senate Committee on Rules and Administration. *Nomination of Gerald R. Ford of Michigan to be Vice-President of the United States: Hearings Nov. 1-14, 1973,* Washington, D.C., G.P.O., 1973.

OTHER CQ PUBLICATIONS

HARD COVER BOOKS

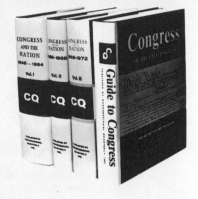

Congress and the Nation

Volume I:	1945-1964	$31.50
Volume II:	1965-1968	$39.50
Volume III:	1969-1972	$39.50

This 4,300 page, three-volume resource brings detail and perspective to the important issues and events in national affairs since World War II, spanning six Presidencies and twenty-eight years. Carefully organized and indexed for reference. Volume I: 1945-1964 (1965) 2,000 pages, 8½" x 11", hard cover; Volume II: 1965-1968 (1969) 1,100 pages, 8½" x 11", hard cover; Volume III: 1969-1972 (1973) 1,200 pages, 8½" x 11", hard cover.

Congressional Quarterly's $39.50
Guide to the Congress of the United States

The definitive reference on Congress—its origins, history and development. Explains how Congress works, its powers, the pressures upon it, and prospects for change. Carefully organized and indexed for reference. September 1971. 984 pages, 8½" x 11", hard cover.

Historic Documents

Volume I: 1972	$27.50
Volume II: 1973	$27.50

Each volume is a collection of significant speeches, court decisions, interviews, reports and treaties. These documents are selected for their current usefulness and lasting reference value. Indexed cumulatively for five years. Volume I: 987 pages, 7" x 10", hard cover; Volume II: 1,000 pages 7" x 10", hard cover.

 PAPERBACKS

Watergate: Chronology of a Crisis

Vol. I	$7.50
Vol. II	$8.50
Set	$15.00

Detailed review of events, issues and personalities beginning with the Watergate break-in and continuing through the May 1974 release of President Nixon's transcripts. Volume I August 1973. 290 pages, 8½" x 11". Volume II June 1974. 435 pages, 8½" x 11".

Impeachment and the U.S. Congress $4.00

Comprehensive treatment of the impeachment issue including constitutional origins, historic precedents and current opinions of Nixon's attorneys vs. the Judiciary Committee's inquiry staff on what constitutes an impeachable offense. March 1974. 60 pages, 8½" x 11".

Current American Government (CQ Guide) $4.00

Updated and published twice each year, in January and August, to serve as an up-to-date handbook on recent significant developments in the legislative, executive and judicial branches of American government. Spring edition (January) and fall edition (August). 144 pages, 8" x 11". Annual subscription for both spring and fall editions is $8.00.

Nixon: The Fifth Year of His Presidency $4.50

Reviews 1973 administration actions on foreign affairs, the budget, nominations and appointments, regulatory agencies. Texts of messages, statements and news conferences. March 1974. 272 pages, 8½" x 11". Also available: *Nixon: The Fourth Year; Nixon: The Third Year; Nixon: The First Year* at $4.50 each.

Energy Crisis In America $4.50

Comprehensive background on the energy crisis that is now a fact of life for millions of Americans. Gasoline prices, Alaska pipeline dispute, strip mining, new energy sources, pollution technology, environmental problems, legislation from 1969-72. March 1973. 93 pages, 8½" x 11".

Dollar Politics, II $4.50

Review of the issues and legislation on campaign spending. August 1974. Approximately 96 pages, 8½" x 11".

The Washington Lobby (second edition) $4.50

The continuing struggle of organized interests to influence government policy, how lobbies work, what they achieve. August 1974. Approximately 128 pages, 8½" x 11".

The Middle East: U.S. Policy, Israel, Oil and the Arabs $4.50

Current and historical background on the problems and issues surrounding America's Middle East policy. Includes a chronology of Middle East developments 1945-1972. April 1974. 100 pages, 8½" x 11".

The Supreme Court Justice and the Law $4.50

Supreme Court history, the federal judiciary (1969-73), a review of the American jury system, court reform and grand juries. Appendix includes Nixon appointees to federal judiciary, complete list of acts of Congress declared unconstitutional and Watergate tapes decisions. January 1974. 124 pages, 8½" x 11".

Congressional Districts In the 1970s $10.00

Complete demographic profiles of all 435 congressional districts based on the 1970 census. Includes maps for each state and largest cities, and background report on political process of redistricting in each state. Statistical data on each district. September 1974. 236 pages, 8½" x 11".

Congressional Roll Call 1973 $8.00

A chronology and analysis of votes in the House and Senate, 93rd Congress, 1st Session. Reports the vote of each Representative and Senator for every roll-call vote taken during 1973. Indexed, March 1974. 320 pages, 8½" x 11", paper. Also available: *Congressional Roll Call 1972, 1971, 1970, 1969* ($8.00 each, set $32.00)

Editorial Research Reports on America's Changing World Role $4.50

Peacetime Defense Spending...Faltering Atlantic Alliance...Vietnam Aftermath...China After Mao...Resurgent Iran...Cuba After 15 Years...Intelligence Community...Trends in U.S.-Soviet Relations. Includes individual Reports mailed to ERR subscribers in 1973-1974. August 1974. 180 pages, 6" x 9".

Editorial Research Reports on the Women's Movement $4.50

The Status of Women...Marriage: Changing Institution...Child Care...Crime of Rape...Women Voters... Women's Consciousness Raising. Includes individual Reports mailed to subscribers in 1969-1973. September 1973. 180 pages, 6" x 9".

Standing order. **Includes future paperback titles which will be mailed upon publication.**